'PAPER-CONTESTATIONS' AND TEXTUAL COMMUNITIES IN ENGLAND, 1640–1675

T0334804

The mass production and dissemination of printed materials were unparalleled in England during the 1640s and 1650s. While theatrical performance traditionally defined literary culture, print steadily gained ground, becoming more prevalent and enabling the formation of various networks of writers, readers, and consumers of books.

In conjunction with an evolving print culture, seventeenth-century England experienced a rise of political instability and religious dissent, the closing of the theatres, and the emergence of a middle class. Elizabeth Sauer examines how this played out in the nation's book and print industry with an emphasis on performative writings, their materiality, reception, and their extra-judicial function. *'Paper-contestations' and Textual Communities in England, 1640–1675* challenges traditional readings of literary history, offers new insights into drama and its transgression of boundaries, and proposes a fresh approach to the politics of consensus and contestation that animated seventeenth-century culture and that distinguishes current scholarly debates about this period.

(Studies in Book and Print Culture)

ELIZABETH SAUER is a professor in the Department of English at Brock University.

'Paper-contestations' and Textual Communities in England, 1640–1675

Elizabeth Sauer

UNIVERSITY OF TORONTO PRESS
Toronto Buffalo London

© University of Toronto Press 2005
Toronto Buffalo London
utorontopress.com

Reprinted in paperback 2022

ISBN 978-0-8020-3884-5 (cloth)
ISBN 978-1-4875-2628-3 (paper)

Cataloguing in Publication information available from Library and
Archives Canada

We wish to acknowledge the land on which the University of Toronto
Press operates. This land is the traditional territory of the Wendat, the
Anishnaabeg, the Haudenosaunee, the Métis, and the Mississaugas of the
Credit First Nation.

This book has been published with the help of a grant from the Federation
for the Humanities and Social Sciences, through the Awards to Scholarly
Publications Program, using funds provided by the Social Sciences and
Humanities Research Council of Canada.

University of Toronto Press acknowledges the financial support of the
Government of Canada, the Canada Council for the Arts, and the Ontario
Arts Council, an agency of the Government of Ontario, for its publishing
activities.

Contents

Acknowledgments

This book is the product of exchanges with various scholars, institutions, and communities – actual, virtual, and textual, beginning with the 1997 Folger Library Institute conference 'Habits of Reading in Early Modern England,' directed by Steven N. Zwicker. The Folger Institute served as the stimulus for this study and two complementary volumes, *Books and Readers in Early Modern England*, edited with Jennifer Andersen (2002) and *Reading Early Modern Women*, edited with Helen Ostovich (2004). My coeditors and our contributors cultivated an intellectual milieu in which *'Paper-contestations' and Textual Communities* was also generated. My research benefited in turn from the many fine critical studies on early modern book and reading history, print and theatre culture, and political history, and from the expert critiques I received on earlier publications and on conference presentations at the Sixth International Milton Symposium, York, UK (1999); the Biennial Renaissance Conference, University of Michigan-Dearborn, Dearborn (2000); 'Playreading in Early Modern England,' organized by Marta Straznicky at the Shakespeare Association of America, Minneapolis (2002); the Symposium on Book History and Print Culture at the Congress of the Social Sciences and Humanities, organized by Leslie Howsam at Dalhousie University, Halifax (2003); and the Victoria University Centre for Reformation and Renaissance Studies, Toronto (2004); and I extend my thanks to the Social Sciences and Humanities Research Council of Canada for generous ongoing funding provided for my research in Canada, the United States, and England, particularly at the British Library and the Library of the Society of Friends. I am also much indebted to the following people: Jill McConkey, editor of the University of Toronto Press, for her valuable support; the two anonymous Press readers for their thoughtful, incisive criticism and guidance; Miriam Skey, copy editor, for her careful attention to the manuscript; and to Michelle Orihel, Lisa M. Smith, Laura Smith, and Barbara MacDonald-Buetter for their precise and diligent editorial work. A Chancellor's Research Chair position I hold helped finance the travel and release time required for this project, and I gratefully acknowledge the efforts of the Office of Research Services and the Vice-President of Research in fostering Brock University's research culture.

Portions of chapter 3 originally appeared in 'Milton and the "Stagework" of Charles I,' *Prose Studies: History, Theory, Criticism* 23.1 (2000): 121–46, and are reprinted here with permission of the Taylor & Francis Group (http://www.tandf.co.uk/journals). Sections of the epilogue to this book are reprinted from 'Milton and Dryden on the Restoration Stage,' in *Fault Lines and Controversies in the Study of Seventeenth-Century English Literature*, edited by Claude J. Summers and Ted-Larry Pebworth, by permission of the University of Missouri Press, copyright © 2002 by the Curators of the University of Missouri.

'PAPER-CONTESTATIONS' AND TEXTUAL COMMUNITIES IN ENGLAND, 1640–1675

Prologue

Press Acts

A good Reader, helps to make a Book; a bad injuries it.
> *King John and Matilda, a Tragedy, As it was Acted ... by her Majesties Servants*
> *as the Cock-pit in Durry-lane. Written by Robert Davenport Gent* (1655)

Truth often getteth hatred, and it is the doom of serious books to be hooted at, by those who have nothing to do but to scrible Pamphlets: Everyone judging according to his capacity or affection. And as Men, so Books are pressed to war.
> *Scutum Regale, The Royal Buckler; or Vox Legis, A Lecture to Traytors:*
> *Who most wickedly murthered Charles the I* (1660)

A history of early modern interpretive communities would open to us the many groups and texts, ideas and beliefs that made up the commonwealth which authority endeavoured to construct as a unified whole. It would render nonsensical the choice we are asked to make between consensus and conflict.
> Kevin Sharpe, *Reading Revolutions* (2000)

I

The mass production and dissemination of printed materials was unparalleled in England during the 1640s and 1650s, thus providing literary scholars and historians with a rich terrain for research on writing and interpretive practices[1] and a unique opportunity to analyse the nation's cultural and political identity. Dramatic, macrohistorical events, including the rise of political instability and religious dissent, the closing of the theatres, and the emergence of a middle class, led, in conjunction with an evolving print culture, to the outbreak of paper wars as well as to the development of various hermeneutic circles and public spheres. Building on scholarship that examines the intersections of mid-seventeenth-century political, religious, and literary cultures,[2] *'Paper-contestations' and Textual Communities* investigates the migration of the theatrical mode into print and the formation of various networks of writers, consumers, and readers of books, who, if not inclined to contest power structures directly, were willing 'to insist that their desires and expectations be heard.'[3] Though not a survey of seventeenth-century interpretive communities, this book presents case studies that animate and punctuate the history of textual production and reception in the revolutionary era.

Scholarly analyses of books, readerships, and the production, circulation, consumption, and appropriations of texts, issues central to bibliographic, literary, and historical research, are burgeoning.[4] Recently, Foucauldian approaches to book history and literary history have been qualified by evidence of the shaping role of culture and the contributions of literature in particular to political and power relationships and community formation. Authorship and textual interpretation ultimately involve negotiations between individual performances and social forms of agency, thus affording opportunities 'both for reinforcing conformity and for improvising disruption.'[5] As Kevin Sharpe recently remarked, a study of interpretive communities consisting of 'the many groups and texts, ideas and beliefs that made up the commonwealth which authority endeavoured to construct as a unified whole' would enable a negotiation between 'consensus and conflict.'[6] This study is partly intended to address the print wars between historians, whose liberal and (anachronistic) Marxist-informed analyses (largely indebted to the work of Christopher Hill) established distinct lines of political division in Stuart England, and revisionists, who exposed continuities underlying English politics (John Morrill, Kevin Sharpe, Conrad Russell, Anthony Fletcher). In their assessments of the politics of consensus in the early modern era, revisionists have tended to deemphasise the role of populist voices of the time and have underplayed the shaping role of culture generally. In conjunction with critics and historians who adopt post-revisionist approaches (i.e., David Norbrook, Peter Lake, David Zaret), I resist the notion of a historical continuum and investigate the interaction between cultural and political representation and between 'paper-contestations' and textual communities.[7]

Linking the multiple strands of this argument are considerations of the self-conscious and strategic uses of the performative text to prompt critical, judicial engagement and to generate interpretive communities, roles traditionally ascribed to the theatre. Martin Butler explained that in the 1630s the theatre was a forum where people gathered and reconstituted awareness of themselves as a society. 'If so,' Nancy Maguire adds, 'the theatre-goers of the Restoration decade had even more need of theatre and an even greater feeling for shared experience'; while London political culture was not consensual, 'London theatrical culture may have been different' in being more homogeneous in its sentiments.[8] But what kinds of possibilities for collective identification or, for that matter, individual and popular protest existed outside or alongside that of theatrical culture, particularly during the theatre closures between 1642 and 1660? In studying the realignment of the dramatic mode as well as the performances of texts, this book takes up the challenge of addressing this question. In doing so, this study is much indebted to the ground-breaking scholarship of Susan Wiseman, Nigel Smith, Dale Randall, and Lois Potter, which shows from a range of perspectives how seventeenth-century literary culture absorbed and appropriated the language of the theatre rather than simply supplanting stage productions. 'Paper-contestations' and Textual Communities differs from these sources by presenting case studies of interrelated theatres of judgement in order to analyse the practices of textual revolt and of collective identification enabled by 'press acts.'[9] Moreover, my emphasis on performative writings and on their materiality, critical reception, and 'afterlife' adds a vital dimension to the histories of reading, theatre culture, political culture, and to the courtroom spectacles of seventeenth-century England.

The implementation of press controls confirmed the affective nature and malleability of print in the public sphere. Until 1637 the prerogative courts of Star Chamber and the High Commission were responsible for censorship in England. After abolishing the Star Chamber in 1641, Parliament, however, wasted little time in introducing its own measures to regulate the press's output. Parliament issued ordinances – acts passed outside of royal consent – in 1643 and 1647, and Acts in 1645 and 1653, after which Oliver Cromwell instituted his Orders of August 1655. The period under investigation in this book is framed by the Star Chamber Decree of 1637 and its Restoration counterpart, *An Act for Preventing the frequent Abuses in Printing Seditious, Treasonable, and Unlicensed Books and Pamphlets; and for the Regulating of Printing and Printing Press* – recently abbreviated to the 1662 *Press Act*.[10] While attending to the meanings of the term 'act' within a judicial and legislative framework, it is necessary to investigate the range of actions and counteractions in which the presses, political officials, authors, readers, and printers participated during the intervening Civil War and Interregnum period.

The issuing of legislation against unauthorized publication coincided with the passing of the 1642 Ordinance against play-acting. The theatre closures led playwrights, actors, and writers off the stage into the marketplace of print where they would produce alternative theatrical modes and discourses for countercultural purposes. Certainly theatrical language had been used in polemical prose before the 1640s to describe politically charged events; and it is true that playlike pieces had already become manifest before 1642 and that they were even performed on occasion. However, pamphleteers now more regularly and self-consciously moved into the space largely vacated by the playwrights and actors. *The Actors Remonstrance* rehearses the complaints of the unemployed players who lament: 'we might be enforced to act our Tragedies.' 'Some of our ablest ordinaire Poets [must] ... get a living by writing contemptible penny-pamphlets'; 'Nay, it is to be feared, that shortly some of them ... will be encited [*sic*] to enter themselves into *Martin Parkers* societie and write ballads.'[11] Moreover, the kind of theatrical language that features prominently in pamphlets printed during this period of heightened political tensions and public consciousness intensified and was used in a new way to incite or engage critical inquiry. Also of importance are the material conditions that transformed literary and political culture, namely the advances in print technologies and in the circulation of print, which invested books with a greater potential to intervene in critical, political, and legal debates. Ultimately, then, the press with its unrefined language, partisan interests, and commercialism displaced the dramatist as spokesperson for the age and became an agent for constituting, evoking, and challenging public opinion.

Despite the measures taken to control stage producers and productions, the dramatic mode did not die in the 1640s and 1650s, but instead reappeared in a variety of experimental forms. The politicizing of theatrical discourse and the work performed by writers on opposite sides of the political divide are of central concern in the early history of the *acting* press.[12] The press in turn activated the responses of would-be playgoers, who assumed new roles as consumers and readers, though remaining conscious of their place in what Sir Walter Raleigh called in *History of the World* a 'stage-play world.'[13] While the comparison of the world to a stage was common to the point of being clichéd in this period when the theatrical heritage was ingrained in the people's imagination, it acquired a new currency in light of controversies and tragedies enacted in the trial literature and on the political and national stages.

As a site where information and persuasion were involved with theatrical modes of presentation, the book as text could claim to be an active part of the public arena by politicizing the reading public, affecting the way that events would be read, and engaging, even making, history. Indeed the life and significance of any particular book does not conclude with its publication. We need to attend, therefore, to the material conditions of a book's circulation as well as to the fields of expectations into which it is written and to the receptivity (or antagonism) of its consumers. The book is in fact less a product than a process, part of an ongoing dialectic – as Ann Hughes says, not a record of events, but events in themselves.[14] The proliferation of printed materials in turn legitimized public opinion, which 'was the center stage for many major events in the midcentury English Revolution, beginning with the Wars between King Charles and Parliament.'[15] Literature itself helped ignite the revolution and was in fact 'at its epicentre,' as Nigel Smith maintains, and as Sharon Achinstein, Steven Zwicker, Susan Wiseman, and others have likewise persuasively demonstrated. Political action included participation in the war of words, which acquired at this time a new potency and combative status: 'as Men, so Books are pressed to war.'[16]

The communities studied here, then, were generated through the various acts of writing and interpretation, which became amenable to political inference during this period of upheaval. The periodical press gave rise to print and political wars on new fronts. Newsbooks or mercuries – weekly publications of daily events with a definite political agenda – are a case in point. The court mercury, *Mercurius Aulicus*, edited by Sir John Berkenhead and Thomas Audley, and Marchamont Nedham's *Mercurius Britanicus* often appropriated each other's language to fuel their battles and both adopted theatre discourses as an important part of their arsenal. The newsbook writers subsumed their personal identities in their public identities, thus lending their newsbooks agency and a social dimension. *Mercurius Britanicus* denigrated the royalists' religion by locating the source and inspiration for their divinity in the works of playwrights, a charge commonly directed at Charles's supporters, and one that John Cook and John Milton would cite in their defamations of the king himself. *Mercurius Britanicus* answers the accusations of *Mercurius Aulicus* against Sir Arthur Haselrig – a zealous parliamentarian whose troops allegedly pillaged the house of an Anglican minister – by insisting that the minister's books, which were cut and torn into pieces, were not biblical and devotional works but '*Shakespeares* Workes' and 'some other Fox ... and not the book of *Martyrs*.' Thereafter *Mercurius Britanicus* reminds readers about the role that the presses perform in the war with the royalists: 'we have Presses here can spell a victory short, or over, as well as you.'[17]

The prospect raised in *Mercurius Britanicus* that print precipitated events which influenced the course of political history is reiterated in the *Fallacies of Mr. William Prynne*. Surmising that the imminent return of the Laudian victim, William Prynne, would be greeted with 'popular Applause,' the anonymous author of the *Fallacies* attempts to deflate Prynne's martyr status by predicting that his 'heroic performance' would constitute 'a prognosticall Prologue to something like our Tragicall Warre.' Of even greater concern is the damage done by Prynne's potent books, which 'are more prevalent than [the] Sermons' by which 'our Preachers indeed have perswaded the people effectually to this pious Warre; but perswasion it selfe seemeth to dwell in the lippes of Mr. *Prynne*.'[18] Thomas May's history of the causes of civil war likewise connects the concepts of a print and political revolution, which serve as the impetus for this investigation: 'those Paper-contestations became a fatall Prologue to that bloudy, and unnaturall War, which afterward ensued'; 'For now the fatal time was come, when those long and tedious Paper-conflicts of Declarations, Petitions and Proclamations, were turned into actuall and bloody Wars, and the Pens seconded by drawn swords.'[19]

In keeping with the cross-disciplinary nature of this subject, I examine a range of heterogeneous literary and polemical texts designed to exhibit the permeability of print as well as the opportunities for collective identification. The genres studied here all have dramatic components and extrajudiciary functions, and include trial accounts; religious tracts; female-authored defences; petitions; newsbooks; closet dramas; political treatises and dialogues; printed speeches; documented speech acts; and other rhetorical writings and performances.[20] These various theatricalized texts offer rich evidence of the print-performance nexus that generated textual communities, critical readerships, and public opinion – the subjects of this book.

II

I told them [the 'Justices servants' (Birch's note)] there was more ways than one, in which a man might be said to call the people together. As for instance, if a man get upon the market-place, and there read a book, or the like, though he do not say to the people, Sirs, come hither and here; yet if they come to him because he reads, he, by his very reading, may be said to call them together; because they would not have been there to hear, if he had not been there to read.

A *Relation of the Imprisonment of Mr. John Bunyan ... 1660,*
in Tho. Birch (London, 1765), 15–16

'Community' refers to a group's 'common character' (*OED community*, sense 2), but in the seventeenth century, the term is associated on the one hand with egalitarian relationships – in opposition to monopolies and hierarchical social and political structures – and, on the other hand, with sites of resistance and subversion.[21] Complicating the matter is the fact that communal relations were constantly in a state of flux, alignments being 'likely to change in such a period, as the overall circumstances and relationships change.' The definition of the community becomes 'peculiarly problematic in periods of accelerated changes when received groupings and ideas come to seem inadequate and anomalous.'[22] Moreover, people occupying diametrically opposed political or religious positions drew on some similar discourses, including those of political participation, resistance, and judicial engagement, as evidenced in the dramatic writings and exchanges of the revolutionaries, royalists, and religious radicals examined throughout this book.

The testimony offered by the dissenter John Bunyan of his dramatic encounter with the authorities in the epigraph to this section marks a confluence of many of the key issues explored in this book, including textual performances and the creation of alternative communities; the interaction of oral and print culture; private and public interpretive practices; and censorship, judgment, and trial. Bunyan's account is excerpted from *A Relation of the Imprisonment of Mr. John Bunyan*, in which the accused is ordered to cease his preaching, which allegedly facilitated the illegal gathering of peoples in ways that resembled the organization of Quaker meetings. Moreover, such assemblies posed the same security risk for the new regime as had the civil disorder of the early 1640s, which prompted the theatre closures and the issuing of the *Ordinance of both Houses for the suppressing of Stage-Playes* (1642).

Textual communities, that is, communities generated through the production of books and various kinds of engagements with them, are imaginatively and materially conceived, constructed, or represented.[23]

The transmission of information was enabled through the circulation of books that were passed among readers, sent by post, or read at public gatherings, as Bunyan's quotation reminds us. Dissenters like Bunyan, in turn, welcomed the printing press because it democratized information by increasing its availability and encouraging self-education and independent thought, as discussed in chapter 5. Unlike drama or the pulpit, which did not require literacy in its audience, books demanded readers, who in turn became catalysts for the development of alternative communities. By examining the ways in which writings not only were read, but also reproduced, circulated, and answered, we can imagine something like a textual community, for lack of a term that parallels the theatrical or musical 'audience.'[24]

The work of historicizing the early modern interpretive community requires a consideration of literacies. The networks examined here all depended on the acknowledgment of communicative, if not written, principles of operation in society and of their effects on both the literate and the illiterate.[25] What does literacy mean in an early modern context, and what kinds of literacy existed in the period? How was information communicated to the illiterate and what was the role of the common people in the information revolution? Research on signatures contained in depositions from southeast English ecclesiastical courts prompted David Cressy's conclusions that writing skills were limited to 30 per cent of the total male population and 10 per cent of the female population by 1640, reaching 45 per cent and 25 per cent respectively by the accession of George I. Observing that levels of reading-literacy were vastly higher than those of signature-literacy,[26] Keith Thomas, Margaret W. Ferguson, and Eve Rachele Sanders, among others, emended Cressy's figures. Not determined by or dependent on verbal literacy alone, the effective communication of information and the construction of informed communities developed through the interaction of oral, manuscript, print, and visual cultures, as this book aims to show by considering the interdependence of images, texts, and different forms of recorded speech, rhetoric, and other oral performances.

Parliament was highly conscious of the power and performance of print to influence public opinion. Meeting originally in November 1640, parliamentarians soon issued a weekly manuscript of their proceedings. The summer of 1641 saw the creation of many presses which printed satirical and news pamphlets on Strafford and Laud, the subject of chapter 2; and in November 1641 the first newsbook appeared, anticipating Parliament's control of the newsbook industry. In 1643 Parliament allowed partisan newsbooks to bypass censorship regulations and energize the war of words. Parliamentary supporters in turn used the press and newsbooks strategically by publishing dramatic and extreme views of their foes and galvanizing public opinion against the king in particular.

News by word of mouth, manuscript, and print facilitated the creation of audiences and readerships, as various literary critics and cultural historians have shown through their studies of 1640s pamphlets, newsbooks, and popular writings generally. Susan Wiseman demonstrated, for example, how periodical news played a formative role in the emerging sense of the citizen as reader and debater of the news, while Alexandra Halasz analysed the influence of the profusion of pamphlets on the marketplace.[27] Literary communities both generated and reflected public opinion. Peter Lake's recent work on early modern English polemical culture effectively illuminates the creation and use of public opinion, particularly by the producers of printed media. Originally public opinion was courted less for its own sake than as an indirect means to which authorities could appeal in order to legitimate or strengthen their positions. Yet the sphere of public participation eventually became available for opponents or critics of the regime, a point highlighted by the above-mentioned scholars, whose approaches complement postrevisionist views on the shaping role of culture. Public views, then, could not simply be coopted by the governing powers for their own ends but could become a formidable force in politics.[28] Moreover, popular consciousness splintered into polarized views, resulting in the emergence of 'a number of inchoate public opinions ... capable of construing authority in a variety of ways.'[29]

In his well-known apology for free speech, John Milton describes the process of re-membering the body of truth and of constructing the temple of God in ways that capture the diversity that marked his distinctive and paradoxical notion of the community. Opposition to the revolutionary acts of community builders impeded God's own work, Milton insisted in his appeal to the parliamentarian court: 'Yet these are the men cry'd out against for schismaticks and sectaries; as if, while the Temple of the Lord was building, some cutting, some squaring the marble, others hewing the cedars, there should be a sort of irrationall men who could not consider there must be many schisms and many dissections made in the quarry and in the timber, ere the house of God can be built.'[30] The labour of advancing the Reformation movement is carried out by sectarians and heretics, and in the *Areopagitica*, by those who oppose Parliament's printing prohibitions and censorship practices, which monopolize knowledge, thus inhibiting the formation of the critically minded collective.

David Aers and Gunther Kress remind us, however, that Milton's designated readership, even in his early period of optimism, constitutes 'the literate minority,' that is, those for whom 'the most important liberty and tyranny centres on the activity of reading.'[31] Certainly this identification restricts membership in the community to the like-minded, and that is equally true of the various circles imagined by Milton's contemporaries and discussed throughout this book. Indeed the rhetoric of inclusiveness in early modern writings can be misleading: in *Areopagitica*, for example, 'implied readers' represent the entire (elect) nation of England; and yet the sophisticated nature of this classically inspired work limits the reading community to the 'middling sort,' that is, to members of a class that enjoyed the social status, if not the mindset, of the author. The readerships are thus distinct from the commoners and the 'vulgar pitch' (*CPW*, 2:539): 'Nor is it to the common people lesse then a reproach; for if we be so jealous over them, as that we dare not trust them with an English pamphlet, what doe we but censure them for a giddy, vitious, and ungrounded people' (*CPW*, 2:536). Moreover, Milton's implied readers are certainly removed from those whose political and religious views and allegiances can, according to Milton, under no circumstances be tolerated, namely royalists and Catholics. Sharon Achinstein accurately observes that in general 'Milton prefers to leave precise details about his reader as a chooser on the plane of the ideal; in this way, he can encompass as large a readership as might exist'; at the same time, she acknowledges that 'Milton's *Areopagitica* may be seen as ... an "unfree" text' ... [that] 'excludes from its potential readership all who are not already broadly in agreement with its puritanical assumptions.'[32] That Milton's ideal readership, though broadly conceived, is selective is only too apparent in his post Civil War period writings. I address the disjunction between his imagined and actual readerships in chapter 3 in reference to *Eikon Basilike* and *Eikonoklastes* and also in the epilogue to this book in a case study focused on Restoration theatre culture and *Samson Agonistes*.

The actual readerships that existed in Milton's England constitute a considerably more variegated group than *Areopagitica* allows. Scholars investigating readerships and interpretive communities should rethink simple divisions between elite and popular readers, categories that do not accurately demarcate a society like that of early modern England.

Developments in print culture at this time ensured, for example, that individuals from the upper classes often shared the beliefs and read the texts that were available to them as well as to those lower on the social scale. In a cultural and material context, the boundaries of the communities which readers inhabited were in a constant a state of flux. Roger Chartier has argued that 'widely distributed texts and books crossed social boundaries and drew readers from very different social and economic levels. Hence the need for the precaution of not predetermining their sociological level by dubbing them 'popular' from the outset.' Also challenging conventional assumptions about early modern readerships, Tessa Watt has shown that the idea of cheap print being 'aimed at and consumed by a definable social group may be a myth'; indeed upper class people also purchased such material. 'The audience presupposed within the cheap print itself,' Watt elaborates, 'appears to be inclusive rather than exclusive.' This audience, she notes, was addressed both as 'readers' and as 'hearers'[33] – a reminder that cheap print conditioned and demanded different kinds of interpretive practices, and that it possessed a performative function.

An example of the motley nature of the actual readerships to which cultural critics and historians have pointed in their various studies is found in the reception history of newsbooks. Among other more established members of society, poets, historians, politicians, lawyers, and merchants read newsbooks. Moreover, readers needed not agree with the political or religious position of the newsbooks authors, who were also known to change allegiances.[34] Sir Samuel Luke, parliamentarian governor of Reading, on whom Samuel Butler's *Hudibras* was supposedly based, was interested in *Mercurius Aulicus*. The royalists Edward Rainbowe and the Lord Keeper of Oxford read *The Moderate Intelligencer*. London correspondents writing to the provinces enclosed newsletters and pamphlets representing very different opinions.[35] The consumption of oppositional writings thus resulted in the interaction of otherwise competing interpretive communities. Perhaps the best example thereof is the mass appeal of *Eikon Basilike*. Deprived of the 'force of Armes,' the king himself resorted to print to wage his war against Parliament, Milton realizes, accurately anticipating the success that Charles's motto, *Vota dabunt quœ Bella negarunt*, and the king's book would have in turning popular sentiment back to royalism (see chapter 3). The considerable impact of and decisively favourable response to *Eikon Basilike* meant that the identities of the book's readers could not immediately be established along predictable political lines. Even parliamentary supporters like Ralph Josselin confessed to being moved by the tragedy: 'I was much troubled with the blacke providence of putting the King to death, my teares were not restrained at the passages about his death.'[36]

The concept of entwined royalist, republican, and radical groups unsettles the rigid classifications of homogenous readerships during the period. 'Men and women live neither by bread nor by party alone,' Derek Hirst states in a pertinent reworking of the biblical adage; while studies of partisan representations have much to teach us, he continues, 'we now know that even in a narrowly defined political life divisions were usually fluid.'[37] Interpretive practices thus contributed to the permeable nature of communities and enabled interactions among different cultural groups. Historians of reading have demonstrated that the study of reading must attend not only to what is read but how it is read or the process of reading, including the appropriation of texts. Chartier's notion of 'appropriation' – the reader's prerogative to make creative use of writings – is the theoretical centrepiece of his approach to the history of reading, which calls for 'a different approach that focuses attention on differentiated and contrasting uses of the same goods, the same texts, and the same ideas.'[38] Under such conditions, cultural practices and cultural experiences – particularly textual production and interpretation – are not strictly socially determined, as revisionist historians have tended to argue, but have a potential to reinforce or resist dominant views. An examination of the multiple ways in which print was deployed for critical, polemical, or judicial purposes illuminates the notion of appropriation, which is enacted in various sites, as outlined in the following section on the 'theatres of judgement.'

III

The sites or theatres of judgment in this book are all trials and spectacles of punishment, the main 'social dramas' in seventeenth-century England.[39] The judicial system at this time underwent some significant changes, including new relationships between judge and jury through the emergence of the ideology of the jury right. This development marked a shift from trials dominated by the self-informing jury to trials based on evidence. From 1641 on, the relationship between the House of Commons and the House of Lords also changed dramatically: the Commons, which previously had no control over prosecution proceedings, assumed a more active role in examining witnesses and weighing evidence in trials before the Lords. Legal proceedings were, however, not restricted to the courtroom, as politicians, legislators, persecutors, and defendants increasingly recognized. Printed speeches, trial accounts, and pamphlets and satires of the period confirmed that judgments were also made by those on the outside. Writers, interpretive communities, and readers thus became coparticipants in the exercise of authority. The wider availability of literary and political texts, news, and judicial documents gave way in turn to intense parliamentary politics, a new wave of petitions,[40] paper-contestations, and communities of 'competing advocates in the court of ... public opinion.'[41] Public relations and political communication now depended not only on the production and distribution of print but also, as I have stressed, on the effective management of its reception.

Correspondingly, readers were accorded an increasingly authoritative role in cultural, religious, and political circles. Among the most commonly used epithets for the reader are 'judge' and 'jury,' which take on an added significance in this period when structures of power are subject to interrogation. Chapter 1, ' "Reader, Here you'l plainly see Judgement Perverted," ' in which these developments are featured, presents the first of various case studies on the formation of textual communities and on the practices of collective identification and judgment that bind community members. Analysed here are the early 1640s anti-monopolist pamphlets designed to heighten awareness of and defend common liberties. The reliance on dialogue as well as on modes of exposition offers evidence of the strategic uses which dramatic conventions served in pamphlet literature. The arguments contesting the patenting and cooption of truth through press regulations are channelled into a printed oratorical performance in *Areopagitica*, the subject of the second half of the chapter, which recontextualizes John Milton's anti-monopolist apology for 'true Liberty,' critical textual engagement, and collectivity.

In chapter 2, 'The Trials of Strafford and Laud in England's "Sad Theater," ' the sites of and occasions for legal inquiry and theatrical and textual performance are the arraignments of Thomas Wentworth, earl of Strafford, and William Laud, archbishop of Canterbury. The 'trial by print' enacted by the politicized dramatic mode in speeches, pamphlets, satires, and prose and verse libels became an integral part of courtroom dramas. The production of extrajudicial popular writings corresponded with Parliament's rise to power and its control of the press's output – a subject that has yet to receive the scholarly attention it merits in the political history of the early 1640s. Beginning with that of Strafford, trials of the 1640s differed from their earlier sensational counterparts in various ways identified in this chapter, including the authoritative role assumed by Parliament and the unprecedented mass distribution of trial literature. The efforts by the officials to publicize the legal process served as 'redressive' procedures[42] that involved the interpretive community in the act of judgment and in turn ignited a competition over the reputations of Charles's chief ministers.

Chapter 2 leads to an examination of the most important political event of the period – Charles I's final performance on the scaffold/stage. The power of the state in managing the theatre of politics and punishment traditionally used to reinforce governmental authority[43] was usurped by the new regime, which deployed the discourse, structures, and expectations of dramatic performances in arraigning and executing the king publicly. Parliament's staging of the trial and beheading of Charles was, however, strategically preempted. The contested site where the social dramas were transferred and in which the king would ultimately be vindicated was the politicized/theatricalized arena of book culture. Having resisted the republicans' 'arbitrary jurisdiction,' Charles in (co)producing *Eikon Basilike* offered his supporters an 'op'n and monumental Court of his own erecting,' as Parliament's celebrated champion writer acknowledged in *Eikonoklastes* (*CPW* 3:341). Works like *Eikon Alethine* and Milton's *Eikonoklastes* helped ignite a war of words and icons by exposing the behind-the-scenes activities of the 'Royal Actor' in an attempt to reclaim the performative for the dissenting writer and reader. Yet these anatomies of *Eikon Basilike* were not successful in the end. The popularity of *Eikon Basilike* also demonstrated the heterogeneity of the book's readerships, thus underscoring the postrevisionist concern with multiple readerly experiences, networks of associations, and diffuse textual histories.

Chapter 4 develops the argument about the transference of the political/theatrical arena to the printed text by investigating the cultural-political work performed by parliamentary-sponsored antiestablishment dramas and then by royalist mock-tragedies and pamphlet dialogues. While Parliament did issue closet dramas and thereby encourage active textual analysis as a form of political intervention and critique, royalists are in fact best known for their use of dramatic modes of expression. Censorship imposed and enforced by Parliament, like that of the Stuart monarchy in the earlier decades, then, was never wholly absolute.[44] Not only did some theatrical performances continue to be staged, but royalists also persisted in composing playtexts, though ones designed only for reading. As political actors, royalists more than parliamentarians have been regarded as working independently rather than collectively. As writers, royalists have as well been identified with the cultivation of civility and a plain style. In this chapter, I present a more nuanced narrative of royalist literary history that examines their shared discourses, the polemical crossfire in which they participated and communicated in the literary/political world during the mid-century. In keeping with the theme of this book and its postrevisionist approach, I examine royalist cultural and textual communities as represented in ballads, political dialogues, closet dramas, and front and end matter added to plays that were staged before but printed after 1642.

The print-performance chemistry found an alternative venue in the culture of dissent as it evolved in spaces outside of state jurisdiction. Community formation was central to the identity of the dissenters, who not only developed actual communities but also produced a vast body of literature designed to enable and defend this work.[45] The creation of specific sectarian textual and speech communities, then, is the subject of chapter 5.[46] I focus in particular on the construction of the spiritual community through the literature of suffering[47] that includes in the context of this book's documented trial accounts. Because Levellers and Friends/Quakers relied especially heavily on the printed word to spread dissenting opinions, their writings are foregrounded. The 'social dramas,'[48] which serve as the forums for and subjects of the literature of suffering, include the arraignments of John Lilburne and of the Quakers James Nayler, George Fox, and Margaret Fell.

Chapter 5 also features speech acts as occasions for resistance and collective responses. Speech act theory analyses the interrelationship between (political) agency and language – whether as speech, writing, or rhetoric. Language thus acquires a performative function and converts 'closed systems of thought' into dialogue.[49] An examination of the documented performances and counterperformances of the Fifth Monarchist Anna Trapnel demonstrates, for example, how Trapnel's self-abnegation and philosophical and legal self-defence are complicated by her response to textual representation, which she denies in reference to the transcribed *The Cry of a Stone* (1654) but affirms in her self-authored *Anna Trapnel's Report and Plea* (1654). Here we must look beyond textual representation in analysing Trapnel's Whitehall performance not captured in *The Cry of a Stone* or in its (selective) public reading during the 1654 courtroom drama, or even in the omissions about which the transcriber or 'relator' of *The Cry of a Stone* confesses. Instead, Trapnel's prophetic utterances, later printed as *The Cry*, point to a speech act in which the fulfilment of the action is enabled by its articulation within a given context. In this case, our attention is directed to the alternative communicative act before a speech community that cannot be reconstructed in the courtroom when her transcribed words are recorded or recited. Her original performance is framed as site- and time-specific; and it is public, formalized, agonistic, and symbolic, in accordance with the characteristics of the trial that Richard Bauman associated with the theatrical drama.[50] Here, in this palimpsest of communicative actions and utterances emerges a new nexus of the oral and literary traditions and a new stage and crucible for the formation of interpretive communities.

The epilogue for this book examines the role of one final political and religious 'dissenter' and prophet in an alternative theatre of judgment. '"Beyond the fifth Act": Milton and Dryden on the Restoration Stage' argues that Milton's religious commitment is channelled through a 'religious commitment to political process,' embodied in his poetry. As posited by the poems, Milton's readership offers evidence of the poet-revolutionary's continued belief in community.[51] Still Milton's major poems produced in the Restoration period appealed primarily to an elite, comprised of Christian readers trained in the classics and distinctly prorepublican. The epics thus perform the cultural and political work of imagining 'an invisible public of like-minded readers.'[52] This readership is ultimately set against the revived theatre community identified in the preface to Milton's closet drama, *Samson Agonistes.*

As a dramatic poem not intended for the stage, *Samson Agonistes* offers an individual, readerly version of the collective experience that the theatre in the ancient republic had produced. As a material object, together with *Paradise Regained* with which it was published, however, *Samson Agonistes* is in commercial competition with a culture Milton cannot contend with. Milton was no more successful in competing with Restoration tragicomedy on the theatrical and political stages than he was with anatomizing *Eikon Basilike.* 'Works – even the greatest works, especially the greatest works – have no stable, universal, fixed meaning. They are invested with plural and mobile significations that are constructed in the encounter between a proposal and a reception,' Chartier observes.[53] The communities of relevance to this book, then, also include the marketplace and the public theatre scene in which Milton's 1671 volume competed with staged and printed Carolean drama. Milton established an antagonistic relationship with early Restoration theatre culture, of which John Dryden was a dominant producer and of which Samuel Pepys was one of the best known and most avid consumers. Curiously, Dryden himself, the foremost literary theorist of the time – who used the print versions of plays largely as his platform – would, in a statement recorded in the front matter to *The Spanish Fryar* (1681), condemn 'all those *Dalilahs* of the Theatre.'[54] This was one of the most crystalline statements about the implications of the print-performance confluence made by the Restoration period's eminent practitioner of both. It demonstrates, moreover, how the theatre community ultimately prevented Dryden from controlling the consumption of his productions, which, like Milton's beforehand, take on new meanings by virtue of their 'appropriation' and reception history.

The realignment of the dramatic mode and the development of textual communities in early modern England have been addressed by scholars in the areas of political history, theatre history, book production, and literary theory, but they have not been analysed in the way I am proposing. My study of the interanimation of performance and print at a time when 'the conquering Sword ... [was] conquered by the Pen'[55] reveals how cultural and political relations develop through dramatic exchanges – those within theatrical works, but also those between writings that answer each other, as well as those among readers, interpretive communities, and the ideological and material contexts in which they are generated. The result is both a new kind of politics and politics of reading: 'From now on the representation and delegation of power find themselves confronted with a new (ideological) power of representation, in the sense that the discursive acts of writing and reading attain to a greater degree of autonomy.'[56] The competition to control the production, distribution, and interpretation of literature demonstrated that authority was now being determined in an arena of debate in which presses acted and writers and readerships performed as never before.

Chapter 1

'Reader, Here you'l plainly see Judgement Perverted'

Among the arenas in this book that serve as sites for political performance and interpretive practices are books and pamphlets, meeting houses, the streets and marketplace, the courtroom, and the scaffold. These forums become alternative theatres and centres of collective activity. The courtroom was a particularly important stage for the performances of 'social dramas.' The major role of the courts was to enforce consensus and maintain order through a system of communal discipline by publicly indicting and punishing those who violated the law. While staged executions presented the most dramatic demonstrations of the contact between the law and popular culture, the law as a whole represented a vital means of transmitting the wishes and aspirations of authority into the popular consciousness.[1] At the same time, the English legal system distinguished itself from its European counterparts through the jury system, which made local laymen not only onlookers but also participants in the revelatory process. While France, Italy, and Germany put decisions about guilt or innocence into the hands of judges, in England the task of the bench was restricted to 'finding law' or to identifying the applicable statutes and precedents. The onus was on the English jury to 'find fact,' that is, to determine and establish the truth and to deliver a verdict.[2] Ordinary people also participated in varying ways in litigation and in administering law, and this engagement in legal processes resulted in the creation of new interpretive communities.

Ideas on the law entered the public sphere through channels other than direct participation: namely, through the literature of the day. In a study of early dramatic works that featured trial accounts, Dorothy Payne Boerner argued that the depiction of law and legal procedures was removed from real life judicial practices. While Renaissance drama functioned as an ideal medium for representing the theatricalized nature of actual trials, the roles performed by some of the key players differed in significant ways from those of their historical counterparts. For example, the part acted by the judge in theatre productions of courtroom scenes was expanded, Boerner explains, to include the double function of judge and prosecutor. But, she continues, 'even more striking than the modification in the role of the judge is the absence of a jury in stage trials. There are almost no juries in the plays, although they were present in many actual courts.'[3] In the alternative dramatic forms that comprised seventeenth-century literary culture, the jury is, as I attempt to demonstrate, cast as the author and the like-minded judicial interpretive community that arraign 'criminals' in print. In the years leading up to the Civil War, literature reinforced the lesson that crime does not pay, with the oft-rehearsed gallows speeches of historical criminals comprising much of the content of the works that were produced.[4]

As people assumed more active roles as interpreters of judicial texts and of the social dramas themselves, they also inevitably influenced legal practices and decisions. It is true that the corresponding identification of writers and readers as judges and juries is a rhetorical device with a long history; but these epithets acquired new meaning at a time when structures of authority were subject to interrogation as never before, when public attention increasingly focused on the processes of gathering evidence rather than on processes of punishment, and when judicial procedures were exposed to public scrutiny, as was the case in seventeenth-century England. Authors themselves gradually recognized that their fate rested in part with their readerships and the circulation of their texts. Popular literature generated audiences hungry for information about current local and national events. As Thomas Cogswell explains, 'A rapidly expanding percentage of the population underwent a crude adult education which left them keen observers of national events and ultimately eager participants in them. In this line of enquiry, the vital question centres on what contemporaries heard and read, which allowed them to translate general predilections into firm ideological positions ... From carefully observing politics, it was only a small step to participating in it,' Cogswell concludes,[5] though, as I suggest throughout this study, critical engagement is in itself a form of participation.

The paper and pamphlet wars that broke out in the early 1640s constitute the first act of this study of the textual communities generated by the realigned dramatic mode. Pamphleteers contributed significantly to the development of public, political discourses and to a culture of debate. They shared the stage with news gatherers, scriveners, and stationers in the 1640s who made and distributed copies of Commons debates designed to direct popular opinion, not infrequently at the request of MPs themselves.[6] The author of *A Presseful of Pamphlets* (1642) complains that the production of such materials is already out of control: stationers 'have a corner in their Venters to breed Conferences, Speeches, Petitions, Declarations.'[7] Critics of the print proliferation in general betray an awareness of the performance of popular writings *as* events in the social dramas of the period.[8] *The Poets Knavery Discovered* – an early response to the controversy over the trial and execution of Thomas Wentworth, earl of Strafford – defends Parliament's order for the 'suppressing of Pamphlets' and claims that 'Since the Earle of *Straffords* death, there have been above three hundred lying Pamphlets printed.'[9] These pamphlets add insult to the executed Strafford, while also reinforcing Laud's guilt. The author, John Bond, identifies various pamphlets modelled on governmental documents and articles that mimic the testimonies presented to Parliament and that are used to build a successful case for the impeachment of other high-ranking Laudian clerics despite the fact that the evidence they offer is fictitious (A3r). Moreover, many of the pamphleteers, according to Bond, were motivated by interests other than the restoration of justice: 'Oh what a lamentable thing it is to suffer the sentence of such penurious, pennilesse wites, who wholly resolve their inke to gall, for a little mercenary gaine' (A4).

For the authors of paper-contestations, the development of print technology corresponded in the mid-seventeenth century with an ideology of common rights and liberties and the emergence of an increasingly litigious climate. Among the popular grievances published at this time were the injustices of monopolizers and patentees. In a dramatically represented judicial account, Mr Spicer, burgess of Warwick, citing his right to speak 'libera mens & libera lingua,' presents a case against patents and monopolies, which he defines as 'a restraint of any thing publick in a City or Common-Wealth to a private use.'[10] Monopolies could be judicial or administrative, as well as being associated with territory conferred by 'letters patent.' Francis Bacon, for instance, recounts the legal case of the Merchant Adventurers of England against the Merchant Adventurers of London 'for *Monopolizing* and exacting upon the Trade';[11] in a lengthy discussion of trade and monopolies, the merchant, Edward Misselden, remarked in the same year (1622) that the complex etymology of 'monopoly' can be summarized in terms of '*Sin-*

gularis Negotiatio, a diverting of *Commerce* from the naturall course and use thereof, into the hands of some few.'[12] Anti-monopolists frequently deployed the language of rights and liberties in denouncing such practices in their paper-contestations. Defining monopolies as 'an Institution, or allowance by the King by his Grant, Commission, or otherwise to any person or persons, bodies politique, or corporate,' Edward Coke, the famous jurist, judges that monopolists seek to deny people 'any freedome, or liberty that they had before ... in their lawfull trade.' Coke observes at the same time that the 'obtaining and procuring' of monopolies 'is much more now punishable,' than was the case in times past, a claim he aims to substantiate by reason and authority.[13]

The focus of this discussion is on the antimonopolist pamphlet literature of the early 1640s designed to heighten critical awareness of and defend community rights and what John Lilburne and his fellow petitioners later described as the equal entitlement to 'the Liberties of the Nation.'[14] The new early modern notion of political liberty, which was based on the ancients, the Bible, and common law, promoted equal justice for the English and offered recourses for fighting abuses by authorities.[15] The advancement of liberties was the impetus for the antimonopolist movement and the corresponding pamphlet wars designed to expose 'Divelish *Projectors*' or in Lilburne's terms, 'unworthy Trade and Liberty-destroying Projectors.'[16] The related literal and figurative cooption of truth through print regulations is the subject of the second half of this chapter. An examination of Milton's denunciation of the patenting of truth follows, establishing a new context for interpreting his famous response to state censorship, *Areopagitica,* which uses the setting of the Athenian court and the defence of liberty of conscience to challenge the licensing of learning. While such Miltonists as Nigel Smith, Sharon Achinstein, and David Norbrook have persuasively situated Milton's tract in relation to historical debates about freedom of expression and the creation of public spheres, and others like Abbe Blum, Stephen Dobranski, and Sabrina Baron have shed light on Milton's contribution to the book trade and his controversial role as censor for the Interregnum government,[17] critics and historians have generally not investigated the relationship of *Areopagitica* to antimonopolist literature and the role of antimonopolist discourse in the protest against censorship. Kevin Dunn and Blair Hoxby are among several exceptions.[18] The former offers a brief consideration of the 'ambivalence about the mercantile' that haunts Milton, while Hoxby goes to the extreme of arguing that the pamphlet's 'only *concept* of liberty was the freedom from monopoly,' and that Milton puts his faith in the marketplace. 'Markets, not methods, lie at the heart of Milton's vision in *Areopagitica*,' Hoxby decides.[19] Though indebted to Hoxby's compelling insights, I will demonstrate that what is at stake in both the antimonopolist pamphlets and Milton's anticensorship treatise is not economic interests as ends in themselves but justice, common rights, and critical readerly engagement. *Areopagitica* defends in particular the divinely mandated right to what Nicholas Fuller identified as a 'living and lawful trade,' which Milton associated with intellectual labour enabled by reading and by printing or what Lawrence Manley characterized as 'the "diffusive" *good* of unrestricted publication.'[20]

The creation and implementation of English patents of monopoly has a long history. Throughout the Tudor and Stuart eras English people were urged to seek opportunities and develop projects, 'ingenuities,' and inventions that would generate profits. Projects went hand in hand with patents and monopolies.[21] These thrived under Elizabeth, though they were hardly immune to abuse and controversy. Elizabeth herself acknowledged that 'many of the poorer sort of her people' had been injured by patents on such items as salt, vinegar, pots, starch, and so on.[22] Thus already by 1601 the Commons sought to overhaul or eliminate the patent system. Protests continued in James's reign, one which was, however, much more scandalous than Elizabeth's and was marked from the start by the famous 1603 lawsuit called the 'case of monopolies' or 'Darcy versus Allen' on the patent for playing-cards. Like James, Charles relied heavily on the promotion of corporations and monopolies and on the sale of charters as sources of revenue that he could attain independent of Parliament. Most lucrative for him were the wine and the tobacco licences and the soap monopoly.[23] His fear of reprisal from Parliament, however, provoked the reform and revoking of many patents, licences, and commissions in the late 1630s. Still monopolies headed the Committee of Grievances's list of abuses of property rights[24] so that when it assembled in 1640, the Long Parliament took up the cause and expelled monopolists from the House of Commons while also cancelling many monopolies.

The introduction of print inaugurated a new culture of critique for the anti-monopolist resistance. In a petition of 1640, 10,000 Londoners voiced their strong opposition to monopolies. Protests repeatedly cited the argument of the violation of divinely granted human liberties by requiring people 'to seek other trades, directly contrary to the law of

God,' as Nicholas Fuller, lawyer of Thomas Allen in the Darcy vs. Allen case, observed, for example.[25] Antimonopolists in turn generated a work ethic and defined labour, and by extension, property, as a God-given duty and right; invoking Deuteronomy, Edward Coke explains that 'a mans trade is accounted his life, because it maintaineth his life; and therefore the Monopolist that taketh away a mans trade, taketh away his life.'[26] More than ever, such violations are inexcusable, Coke warns, reminding his readers of the parliamentary press act designed to preserve the liberties of the nation.[27]

Pamphlets and playlets supplemented, furthered, and corrected the work of the legislators in judging projectors and monopolists. In *The Judges Judgement ... against the Judges* (1641), judges are charged with the collapse of kingship, the confusion of religions, the levying of taxes, and the contamination of the body politic generally. The root of the Commonwealth's disease is the 'extrajudiciall ... doome delivered ... in all Courts, to the subversion of all our fundamentall Lawes, Liberties, and Annihilation, if not Confiscation of our estates.'[28] Thomas Heywood's *Reader, Here you'l plainly see Judgement Perverted By these three; A Priest, A Judge, A Patentee* (1641), the second section of which condemns corrupt judges, includes an indictment of Sir John Finch, who was appointed Lord Keeper Coventry in 1639 at a time when the issue of ship money was debated and denounced by the House of Commons. Judges who gave their blessing to the tax were charged with high treason for their abuse of authority. In 1640 Parliament accused Finch of procuring the tax. While Finch avoided his sentence by fleeing to Holland, other members of the court, Heywood maintains, could not 'evade / Their trial,' and were left to the judgment of 'better Judges,' including the readers of this tract.[29]

The antimonopolists promoted political intervention and legislation designed to protect the rights of trades people. 'Projectors' thus are next in line to receive their sentences in Heywood's tract, representative of the attempt by pamphleteers in general to reclaim the public domain, the res publica, from private monopolies. Patent producers, identified as 'Divelish [sic] *Projectors*, damn'd *Monopolists*,' are accused of taxing everything from food and drink to cloth and tobacco, a true example of what Heywood characterizes and condemns as 'judgement perverted.'[30] Heywood describes the injustices incurred by patents on soap at some length, probably because of the public outcry against the patent and the monopolizing London Company of Soapmakers during this time.[31] *A Short and True Relation concerning the Soap-busines* (1641) outlines the development of the patent and charter in the 1630s by Sir Henry Compton, Sir Richard Weston, and others 'being most part of them Popish Recusants.'[32] The apprentices of the soap trade were not only deprived of their livelihood but also fined and prosecuted by the patentees, the pamphlet states in exposing the truth about the corrupt corporation. Moreover, the quality of the soap declined, and as the author of *A Pack of Patentees* laments: 'It spoyles my skin, if linnen cannot be / Kept cleane and sweet without a *Patentee*, Weel goe like Turkes.'[33]

A Short and True Relation, which concludes with a list of recommendations for restoring the rights of the trades people, links the soap and wine patents: 'And then thinkes one, where sope hath fayl'd without, / Balderdash wines within, will worke no doubt.'[34] Antimonopolist literature on wine patents frequently focused on the recent case involving two lately sentenced projectors, Mr Richard Kilvert and William Abel, alderman of London, who held a patent for French and Spanish wines. *The Copie of a Letter sent from the Roaring Boyes in Elizium; To the two arrant Kings of the Grape, in Limbo* (1641) describes a procession of Bacchic disciples, including playwrights – notably Ben Jonson, as well as (other) corpulent ghosts with scarlet faces and militant soldiers. The company decides to compose a letter of consolation to the recently tried prisoners, Kilvert and Abel. The greetings, pledge of allegiance, and offer of sack from the Bacchic worshippers soon give way to mockery and finally indignation and judgment. A moralistic tone pervades the concluding 'Oration' by Bacchus, who urges the reader to condemn the violators: 'Write me a letter that may fully crush em / And not such ticklying lines as onely brush em, / Can you that are the Poets thinke upon / This sad restraint upon your Helicon, / And not revenge it?'[35] The title page of *The Copie of a Letter*, which bears the oft-reproduced images of Abel and Kilvert, complete with wine barrels and the sign of a bell, foreshadows the doom. The bell sign hangs beside the letter 'A' (A-bell) and now replaces the familiar sign of the ship that hung outside Abel's tavern.

The substitution of the bell for the ship proves ominous in *A Dialogue or accidental discourse Betwixt Mr. Alderman* Abell, *and* Richard *Kilvert* (1641), which adds a dramatic component to the history and sentencing of the two projectors. This playlet opens with Kilvert boasting of his self-professed skills in rhetoric, which enables him to 'intangle Truth,' while Abel declares his greater interest in 'the one Art of getting and accepting' and in cultivating 'that Rhetoricke that makes a ratling pocket.'[36] Kilvert proceeds to recite a formula which he 'eyther read ... in a Pamphlet or heard ... in a Play' that involves the conjugation of the verb 'bribe.'[37] Bribery and extortion have resulted in the legalization of numerous patents, in addition to which Kilvert recommends that of wine, the consequences of which include the impoverishment of vintners generally, according to the pamphlet's narrative voice. But a glimpse into the future reveals a turn of fortune: the printing of the edict on the price of wines leads to the persecution of Abel and Kilvert. Parliament's 26 May 1641 publication, 'Concerning the Prices of Wine, &c.,' outlines the measures taken to criminalize wine patenting.[38] The final scene of A Dialogue or accidental discourse invites the reader to 'imagine they [the projectors] are met' again. Mutual accusation now replaces flattery, and the commotion attracts a crowd, the narrator explains, which serves both as an audience and a jury ready to condemn the projectors, who have been tried in print. Abel and Kilvert's next encounter 'is to bee expected either at the Barre where they are to be arraigned, or the place appointed for their punishment,'[39] a fate now sealed by the parliamentary order.

Once violators were convicted, popular pamphlets frequently staged the criminal's self-confrontation and acts of confession or contrition, which were intended to validate the verdict and serve as a warning for other prospective criminals. The female character in The last Discourse Betwixt Master Abel and Master Richard Kilvert, interrupted at the first by an ancient and angry Gentlewoman (1641; see figure 1) announces that Abel and Kilvert will be discredited by irate wine consumers who will 'make you the examples of their justice before justice herself hath fully censured you.'[40] Hated by all, dispossessed, and tormented by his conscience, Abel acknowledges his guilt, which in turn provokes Kilvert's confession, 'I am even Master Abel in the same pickle my selfe.' An anonymous company of gentlemen – formerly complicit in the projectors' activities – suddenly appears, now resigning itself to an act of judgment, namely, 'inform[ing] the Reader with certainety and truth.' The proceedings are then 'adjourned to a more cleer and a more full relation,' pending the outcome of the projectors' trial.[41]

The patenting and monopolization of goods (and power) are among the crimes committed by two tragic royalist actors in the political arena in the early 1640s. A Description of the Passage of Thomas late Earle of Strafford, over the River of Styx (1641) stages a dialogue between Strafford and Sir William Noy, the former Attorney General who had worked for the implementation of the ship-money tax; 'had I any head in such and such Patents and Monopolies, master Noy, had I any plot at all in the Ship money, and in many more projects that I cou'd name [, they] ...

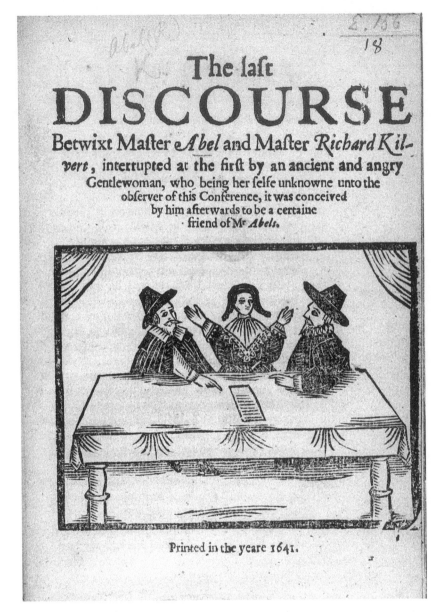

Figure 1. *The last Discourse Betwixt Master* Abel *and Master* Richard Kilvert, *interrupted at the first by an ancient and angry Gentlewoman.* 1641. BL G5549(16). By permission of the British Library.

took their originall all from you.'[42] Having served at Charles's insistence on the Privy Council committees on trade and revenue in February 1635, Laud too is tried in print for his involvement in corrupt business ventures. *England and Irelands sad Theater,* which justifies the executions of the earl of Strafford and Archbishop Laud in 1641 and 1645 respectively (discussed in chapter 2), represents Laud 'in bed' with monopolists. The setting is a dreamscape and a scene of judgment in which historical figures haunt Laud as ghosts, representative of his guilty conscience. The theatre as a whole exposes Laud's corruption and enacts his sentencing. At the foot of the bed on which Laud sleeps is a wolf, with a torch in one paw, a 'patent' in the other; surrounding his waist are tubs, perhaps intended for taxed articles of prime necessity. At the wolf's feet are emblems of Popery – another type of tyranny,[43] which, according to the Reformers, strangled individual liberties.

The assault on monopolies of power corresponded with the anticensorship movement and a call for open communication. 'The granting of patents was the cause of the late King's head being cut off,' Charles II was informed in 1664.[44] In the eighteenth century, the *Boston Gazette* reported that 'the original, true and real Cause' of the Civil War was press censorship and that 'had not *Prynn* lost his *Ears,* K. *Charles* would never have lost his Head.'[45] While certainly a simplification of the multiple and still disputed causes of the civil wars, the connection made here between monopolies and censorship is central for Milton. A number of the historical figures who criticized the abuses of monopolies, including Coke and Bacon, make their way into Milton's anticensorship tract, thus reinforcing the relationship between patents and printing prohibitions.

Until 1637 the prerogative courts of Star Chamber and the High Commission were responsible for press regulation in England. The system for controlling the press that the Crown had established with the cooperation of the Stationers' Company, the King's Printer, and the university presses began to dissolve after the Long Parliament took its seat in 1640. Tempted to assume control over the Crown's apparatus of social control and to acquire the funds that monopolies could provide, Parliament was nevertheless reluctant to grant power to a company of private people who had been accused of being monopolists. Still after successfully repealing church and state censorship through the abolition of the Star Chamber and High Commission, Parliament established a new framework for print regulation.

Since 'writing is more publick then preaching; and more easie to refutation, if need be,'[46] Milton, in imitation of Isocrates, produces *AREOPAGITICA; A SPEECH OF Mr. JOHN MILTON For the Liberty of Unlicenc'd PRINTING* for a readership rather than an audience. The genre of the pamphlet is *boldly* identified on the title page as a 'SPEECH,' beneath which appears Milton's name, as if in judgment of Parliament and the Westminster assembly.[47] At the same time, the title page represents the subject of authorial agency ambiguously insofar as it names Milton as the orator and not as the author or printer of the speech.[48] The received tradition, moreover, casts a judgment on *Areopagitica*: the pamphlet had little impact at the time, not in the least because of its unassuming physical appearance and the lack of distinguishing features on its title page – with the possible exception of the word 'SPEECH' and Milton's name.

The value of the title page for present-day audiences should not be underestimated since it provides insight into the kind of interpretive experience the treatise invites. The identification of the genre of *Areopagitica* as a speech conveys the performative nature of print, which is suggested as well by the resemblance of the typography on the title page to that on title pages of plays.[49] The dialogue Milton establishes with the addressees – the Parliament of England, as the title page indicates – and with the intellectual community and 'judicious friends' enlisted in a defence of critical reading heightens the dramatic quality of this paper-'Protestation.'[50] The action urged by the speech, namely, participation in the material and intellectual work of printing and reading, is predicated on the exercise of 'true Liberty,' a concern registered in the title page's quotation from Euripides, translated for general consumption. The language of the common rights and critical engagement which pervades the treatise in fact lends *Areopagitica* an afterlife that transcends its received tradition as a seventeenth-century work.

The proposition of this unlicensed pamphlet urges a review of the 1643 Licensing Order by demanding that the Commons 'judge over again that Order which ye have ordain'd *to regulate Printing. That no Book, pamphlet, or paper shall be henceforth Printed, unlesse the same be first approv'd and licens't by such*, or at least one of such, as shall be thereto appointed' (*CPW*, 2:490–1). The tract at large is an expression of Milton's liberalism, which promotes the social advantages of readers 'disputing, reasoning, reading, inventing, discoursing ... [about] things not before discourst or writt'n of' (*CPW*, 2:557). Essentially, Milton opposes the monopolization of truth and the prospect that the 'liberty of Printing be reduc't into the power of a few' (*CPW*, 2:570). As patents were denounced, so 'Truth and understanding are not such wares as to be monopoliz'd and traded in by tickets and statutes, and standards. We must not think to make a staple commodity of all the knowledge in the Land, to mark and licence it like our broad cloath, and our wooll packs' (*CPW*, 2:535). The nature of truth is such that it cannot be reduced to a cheap commodity whose manufacture and sale are subject to exclusive control. And the trade in truth, the quotation suggests, cannot be performed or legitimized by means of the papers, documents, regulations, and standards involved in ordinary commercial transactions. 'Ticket' was a term used for placards, price labels, and trade notices, while 'statute' referred to bonds that provided penalties for not paying a debt, for laws regulating or restricting trade, and for legal provisions governing weights and measures called 'standards.' The definition of staple commodity which Milton invokes is a basic article of sale, such as wool, cloth, or leather, for which a person or corporation held a royal monopoly. By emphasizing that knowledge must not be treated like ordinary merchandise, Milton identifies restrictions on publication with those on labouring in the trades or fields.

Having liberated the English from censorship and monarchical tyranny at the start of the Civil War, the new regime itself became oppressive, as judged by antiroyalist, antimonopolist, and anticensorship advocates like Henry Robinson and Levellers including William Walwyn, Richard Overton, and John Lilburne, with whom Milton shared the stage. Indeed throughout this book, Parliament and the Rump are arraigned as often as the royalists, and frequently by parliamentary supporters themselves as well as by religious dissenters. Censors have assumed the roles of Popish monopolists, commodifying and controlling knowledge and language, Milton recognizes. Surely, adds Milton, the Commons itself never intended to be linked with the fraudulent 'old *patentees* and *monopolizers* in the trade of book-selling' (*CPW*, 2:570). In *Mammon's Music*, Blair Hoxby observes that *Areopagitica* 'rests on the assumption that men can be improved by market relations,' and he concludes his examination of the treatise by maintaining that Milton 'puts his faith' not in men but 'in a system of commerce and exchanges' that is 'in the market.'[51] I would argue instead that Milton puts his faith in human reason, liberty of conscience, and the potential of the labourers to advance the Reformation movement. Milton maintains, for example, that the opening of all presses 'was the peoples birthright and priviledge' (*CPW*, 2:541) and that that the nation could 'unite into one generall and brotherly search after Truth' if it 'but forgoe[s] this Prelaticall tradition of crowding free consciences and Christian liberties into canons and precepts of men' (*CPW*, 2:554). The trading and trafficking with truth is conducted by 'the true warfaring Christian' (*CPW*, 2:515) through active debate in a climate of openness.

Milton's discussion of the figurative monopolization of truth is located in the context of a religious culture, in which the 'divine and miraculous invention of printing,' as John Foxe declared, serves as an instrument of Reformation and advances God's glory.[52] The connection between freedom of expression and religious practice sanctions Milton's arraignment of those who coopt truth or who fall prey to the concept of the singular truth: 'our faith and knowledge thrives by exercise, as well as our limbs and complexion. Truth is compar'd in Scripture to a streaming fountain; if her waters flow not in a perpetuall progression, they sick'n into a muddy pool of conformity and tradition. A man may be a heretick in the truth; and if he beleeve things only because his Pastor sayes so, or the Assembly so determins, without knowing other reason, though his belief be true, yet the very truth he holds, becomes his heresie. There is not any burden that som would gladlier post off to another, then the charge and care of their Religion' (*CPW*, 2:543). This famous quotation is certainly an indictment of the spiritually and intellectually inert and of what Henry Burton described in *Truth's Triumph* (1629) as 'the iniquity of the Pontificians, in making a Monopoly of God's grace.'[53] The example in *Areopagitica* that follows, however, specifically implicates those who appoint workers to exercise their religious obligations for them: 'A wealthy man addicted to his pleasure and to his profits, finds Religion to be a traffick so entangl'd, and of so many piddling accounts, that of all mysteries [crafts, trades, privileges] he cannot skill to keep a stock going upon that trade ... What does he therefore, but resolvs to give over toyling, and to find himself out som factor, to whose care and credit he may commit the whole managing of his religious affairs ... So that a man may say his religion is now no more within himself, but is becom a dividuall movable, and goes and comes neer him, according as that good man frequents the house' (*CPW*, 2:544). By refusing to labour in the field of truth, Milton accuses, the authorities commodify their religion, reducing it to a 'dividuall movable' separable from the owner.

Metaphorical and materialist arguments meet as Milton tries licensers for obstructing intellectual and actual labour practices. He compares them to tax collectors, who are guilty of 'tunaging and poundaging,' truth (*CPW*, 2:545), that is, of taxing truth in the same way as customs revenues are extorted from a tax on each large cask or tun of wine and on each pound of other commodities. Print prohibitions impede the course 'toward the true knowledge of what we seem to know' (*CPW*, 2:548) and 'retard[ ] the importation of our richest Marchandize, Truth' (*CPW*, 2:548), possibly alluding to the parable in Matthew 13:45–6: 'The kingdom of heaven is like unto a merchant man, seeking goodly pearls: who, when he had found one pearl of great price, went and sold all that he had, and bought it.' The assembly of the body of Truth is an ongoing process, Milton emphasizes: 'to be still searching what we know not, by what we know, still closing up truth to truth as we find it ... this is the golden rule in *Theology*' (*CPW*, 2:551). The process involves writing and intellectual labour, for which labouring in the fields serves as a metaphor. Such acts are nation-building exercises, which further the Reformation: 'the shop of warre hath not there more anvils and hammers waking, to fashion out the plates and instruments of armed Justice in defence of beleaguer'd Truth, then there be pens and heads there, sitting by their studious lamps, musing, searching, revolving new notions and idea's wherewith to present, as with their homage and their fealty the approaching Reformation: others as fast reading, trying all things, assenting to the force of reason and convincement ... What wants there to such a towardly and pregnant soile, but wise and faithfull labourers, to make a knowing people, a Nation of Prophets, of Sages, and of Worthies' (*CPW*, 2:554). The prophetic voice gives way in the conclusion, which is heavily freighted with antimonopolist discourse and sentiment, to an attack on those who profit from licensing. The Licensing Order, Milton states, represents the interests of fraudulent 'old *patentees* and *monopolizers* in the trade of book-selling ... who doe not therefore labour in an honest profession to which learning is indetted.' Then, claiming no expertise in the '*Sophisms* ... of marchandize' – the logically fallacious, deceptive arguments used in commerce – Milton concludes with a final appeal to the 'liberty of Printing' and the conscience of the Commons to redress their wrongs, an action wherein 'none can participat but greatest and wisest men' (*CPW*, 2:570).

As we have seen in this chapter, central to the antipatent pamphlets and Milton's anti-censorship tract is the defence of labour, liberties, and critical inquiry. Writers and readers emerge as the primary workers in the trade of truth and advance the judicial, divinely mandated labour of 'pens and heads ... sitting by their studious lamps, musing, searching, revolving new notions and idea's wherewith to present, as with their homage and their fealty the approaching Reformation' (*CPW*, 2:554).

Resistance to the free flow of ideas and to intellectual free trade through the prohibitions on printing in particular strangles truth. 'Let her and falsehood grapple; who ever knew Truth put to the wors, in a free and open encounter,' Milton asks (*CPW*, 2:561). Invested with a new sense of liberty and potency, the acting *parliamentary* press thus precipitated events that influenced and corrected injustices. An analysis of the developments in the various intersecting economic, literary, religious, and political cultures of the day requires that we consider not only how literature registers and reenacts events in the public sphere but also how texts intervene in the debates in terms of genre and rhetoric. Further, the antimonopolist, anticensorship literature demonstrates how texts imagine, generate, and court readerships, which were increasingly liberated into critical consciousness, a condition that enabled them (ideally) to recognize the validity of Milton's observation: 'For who knows not that Truth is strong next to the Almighty; she needs no policies, nor stratagems, nor licencings to make her victorious, those are the shifts and the defences that error uses against her power' (*CPW*, 2:562–3).

Chapter 2

The Trials of Strafford and Laud in England's 'Sad Theater'

Laud, Laud, it is thy guilt, thy selfe art hee
Which makes my restlesse ghost disquiet thee
The Ghost of the Deputy to William Laud,
England and Irelands Sad Theater of William Laud (1645)

The courtroom dramas examined in this chapter feature two royalist actors, Thomas Wentworth, earl of Strafford, and William Laud, archbishop of Canterbury, who encounter each other on the political stage (and scaffold) and on the page.[1] Like those discussed in chapter 1, these dramas of justice involve a host of other performers: writers, printers, and readers who arraign the royalists in print and set the stage for the great tragedy of Charles. In terms of the circumstances of the trials, the allegations faced by Strafford, Laud, and Charles, and Parliament's unprecedented authority in arraigning the defendants, these cases differ from such earlier seventeenth-century courtroom dramas as the 1613 Essex nullity suit, the Overbury murder trial involving the earl and countess of Somerset in 1616, and the case against Mervyn Touchet, 2nd earl of Castlehaven, for sodomy in 1631.[2] My primary concern here is with the distinctive role that literary culture and particularly print performed in and outside of the courtroom scenes in the 1640s. Each of these earlier cases certainly generated numerous manuscript and printed accounts, pamphlets, and poems.[3] But on the eve of civil war, the dynamic relationship between literary culture and judicial proceedings was energized and agitated when the vigorous production, circulation, and consumption of literature resulted in cultural and political tensions that undermined even the new regime's efforts at creating an imagined political consensus through the monopolization of print.

This chapter is also intended to offer a fresh approach to the famous trials of Strafford and Laud, particularly as documented in *Cobbett's Complete Collection of State Trials*. The accounts of the two royalists in the *State Trials* are indebted to sources produced over three centuries, including the histories of Thomas May and of Edward Hyde, earl of Clarendon, John Rushworth's *Historical Collections*, William Prynne's *Canterburies Doome*, and Lord Somers' *Tracts*, among others.[4] The trials as carried out in printed speeches, pamphlets, and imaginative literature, however, remain underresearched in scholarship on early 1640s cultural and political history. Disciplinary boundaries have also hampered efforts to examine the subject in all its richness. Historians Terence Kilburn and Anthony Milton, for example, concentrate on printed parliamentary speeches in recreating the scene of Strafford's trial; C.V. Wedgwood, John H. Timmis III, and Conrad Russell characteristically rely on historical and legal documents in manuscript and print. Literary critics Margot Heinemann and Martin Butler foreground pamphlet-plays by pro-parliamentary satirists in their studies of Strafford and Laud, while Robert Wilcher examines an array of genres from news-books to poems in reconstructing the events surrounding Strafford's last days from a proroyalist perspective.[5] The spectacle of judgment, I demonstrate, can best be viewed through the lenses of pro- and antiroyalist political, legal, and literary writings, and the work they perform through their absorption into everyday life, particularly by virtue of their dramatic qualities. The impact of these writings depended on authors' engagements with critically conscious interpretive communities and readers who were commonly cast in quasi-judicial roles. The interaction of literature, writers, and the court of public opinion produced a culture of debate and political dissent and a war of words that fuelled the civil wars. An investigation of the trials exposes in turn more dramatic tensions and ruptures than revisionists, including Russell and Wilcher, have allowed in constructing a unified picture of seventeenth-century history, one that downplays popular opinion and political conflict, as I suggested in the prologue to this book.

I

The trial which most preoccupied Parliament in 1641 was that of the earl of Strafford. Thomas May, who became secretary to Parliament and produced the influential *History of the Parliament of England* (1647), describes the change in dramatis personae on England's political stage: 'These two last Delinquents' (Sir John Finch and Lord Falkland) make their exits by fleeing; 'But now a greater Actor is brought upon the Stage, Thomas [Wentworth] Earle of *Strafford*, Lieutenant of *Ireland*, a man too great to be let escape.' The performance of this 'greater Actor' would in turn change the course of history: 'Many Subjects in *Europe* have played lowder parts upon the Theater of the world, but none left it with greater noise,' May declared in describing the execution of Strafford on the eve of the Civil War.[6]

The arraignment of Strafford and soon thereafter of Laud corresponded with Parliament's rise to power. In recognizing that politics was legitimized when conducted in public, Parliament carried out Strafford's trial in its production of a weekly manuscript of proceedings, as well as in printed speeches, pamphlets, satires, and prose and verse libels. The result was 'an intensely theatrical confrontation of one of Charles I's ministers with some of his most determined critics.'[7] Many London presses in the summer of 1641 assisted in this endeavour by allocating their resources to producing large numbers of small topical pamphlets, notably satires and news pamphlets about Strafford and also Laud, who was likewise tried in print and 'hang'd with Inkie halter.'[8] The competition over the reputations of these historical figures increased awareness of the people's role, if not in making, then in authorizing judgments about the fate of the king's ministers.

Initially the wide circulation of the Commons' nine articles of impeachment, which outlined the charges brought against Strafford during the trial, inflamed public attitudes and stirred up opposition against him. The site of the trial, which began 22 March 1641, was Westminster – 'the most important political theatre in the British Isles'[9] where the court was set up like a theatre and, as Thomas May and John Evelyn both noted, prepared with scaffolds.[10] Coopting dramatic and theatrical modes of expression, the stage managers presented the spectacle before a live audience that included the king.[11] May describes a courtroom stage, featuring burlesqued actors as James's effeminate courtiers are replaced by the feminized court of Charles: 'It seemed a very pleasant object, to see so many Semproniaes (all the chiefe Court-Ladies filling the Galleries at the Tryall) with penne, inke, and paper in their hands, noting the passages, and discoursing upon the grounds of Law and State. They were all of [Strafford's] side; whether moved by pitty, proper to their Sex, or by ambition of being thought able to judge of the parts of the Prisoner.'[12] The courtroom scene is symptomatic of a government and nation in disarray.

The members of Parliament in attendance at the trial also played assigned roles. Their reliance on scripts betrays a concern for performing before an audience beyond the Parliament house; indeed as David Zaret accurately observes, 'coordinating printing plans with legislative strategies had become an art of politics.'[13] Printed parliamentary speeches were among the documents that served as speech acts that shaped events by affecting popular opinion and intensifying opposition to Strafford. *Mr. Maynards Speech Before Both Houses in Parliament* (1641) removes 'the vizard, which my Lord hath put on'[14] by rehearsing the charges from the articles of impeachment which accuse Strafford of conspiring with the Irish and of undermining governmental authority by raising an army to reduce the English to submission. The source of the information about Strafford's 'secret Councell' with the king, during which he divulged his treacherous plot, was contained in notes by Sir Henry Vane which were allegedly found by his eldest son in his father's cabinet.[15] On 5 April another prosecutor, John Glyn, addressed Strafford's complaint that Sir Henry Vane's charges could not be substantiated.[16] Glyn names the English people at large as witnesses to Strafford's alleged crime.[17] In the absence of both evidence and material witnesses, Glyn's reference to the people's authority serves his immediate purpose in prosecuting the defendant; but 1640s pro-Parliamentary trial literature generally betrays a heightened awareness of the extrajudicial role performed by the public to whom the members of the court also pleaded their cases.

At various times during the proceedings, the courtroom drama deviated from the playtext prepared by the trial managers. Print became the embattled site for the contending parties who sought to direct the performance. The parliamentarians failed to anticipate the careful and effective defence of Strafford, whose gallant and courteous manner was recorded by newsletters and even acknowledged by the MPs themselves. In a motion that ultimately did not pass, Sir Simonds D'Ewes proposed that the Commons urge the Lords to cut Strafford's speeches short; indeed he had not followed the script.[18] Strafford's arguments and eloquence ignited a debate over the interpretation of the proceedings; 'the successe of every daies tryall, was the greatest discourse or dispute in all companies,' May admitted.[19] Print fueled the competition. A summary of Strafford's position at the trial was printed in at least seven editions in 1641. *The Earle of Straffords Speech, which he made in his owne Defence* and

The Conclusion of the Earle of Straffords Defence challenge the justness of the charge of treason and the procedures used to indict Strafford, which he claims, have complicated rather than clarified the question of his guilt: 'where Lawes are not cleare or knowne, if there must be a Tryall of wits, I doe most humbly beseech you that the subject and matter may be in somewhat else, then the lives and Honour of Peeres.'[20] Strafford recommends that the Lords burn the 'bloudy and most mysterious Volumes of constructive and Arbitrary Treason' and direct their attention to the letter of the law rather than the 'killing Arts.'[21] The *Conclusion* was answered by various other 1641 speeches, including *Answere to the Earle of Strafford's Oration, Annotations upon the Earle of Straffords Conclusion,* and *In Answer to the Earle of Straffords Conclusion.* The author of the third speech dismisses Strafford's proposal, and calls instead for blood: 'My Lords under favour, your providence may be short, if it reach but to burning of Bookes! a fire of dead leaves will be too weake a fuell for a warning Beacon: A living Author made exemplary will afford a Taller flame.'[22]

Threatened by the prospect that the Lords might vote against them, the Commons replaced the impeachment for treason with an act of attainder, which extinguished the legal rights of the accused. Thus the court would declare Strafford's guilt despite the lack of '*Legal Evidence.*'[23] As the bill made its way through the Commons, justifications for executing Strafford mounted, though the House was not without its critics. Lord George Digby, one of the original managers of the impeachment, challenged Parliament's 'evidence' against Strafford in a controversial speech that contributed to the divisions in the House when the bill was passed on 21 April 1641.[24] Digby gave his printed speech on Strafford to John Moore who made twenty copies. One of these went to George Purslowe who printed 500 more. Digby's would become the only published 'unofficial' speech on the trial of Strafford at a time when the printing of parliamentary speeches was intended, as previously noted, to reinforce the collective view.[25] The printed version of the courtroom speech deepened the ruptures in the case against Strafford. When it was published in a second edition, Parliament ordered Digby's speech to be burnt by the hangman, as Thomason's hand-written note on the title page of *The Lord Digby His last Speech* indicates, and as May reported in explaining Digby's desertion from Parliament.[26] The printed speech triggered many written responses, including *An Answer to the Lord Digbies Speech* (1641), which was, as the extended title indicates, 'printed in regard of the reprinting of that

Speech.' The paper wars erupted alongside the courtroom drama. Another response, *An Aproved Answer to … Digbies Speech … which was first torne in pieces, and afterwards disgracefully burnt by the Hangman* betrays Parliament's fears about the potential of *The Lord Digby His last Speech* to cast doubt on the legitimacy of the case against Strafford. The 'Worthy Gentleman' identified as the author of *An Aproved Answer* to *The Lord Digby His last Speech* worries about the affective power of the printed speech: 'For certainly the strength of it is only great in the kindness (that I say not the weaknesse) of the Reader, stealing away the affection, not convincing the Judgement.'[27] Sir John Coke, who was among those absent when the vote for attainder was taken on 21 April, conveyed his disillusion with Parliament's efforts at enforcing consensus. His recent experience, he explains in a letter to his father, 'shall teach me whilst I live to beware of the public stage and to keep my thoughts at home, for I think I shall never go with any tide.'[28]

The management not only of the public stage of the courtroom but also of the court of public opinion meant that the matter of justice had to be taken to the streets. Under the direction of John Pym, the names of the MPs who had opposed the bill were printed and posted in London and Westminster under the heading of '*Straffordians*, and Enemies to the Commonwealth.'[29] The masses assembled around Westminster Palace,[30] protesting the delay in carrying out the sentence. On 24 April, the Commons received a petition signed by 20,000 Londoners, among them John Lilburne, calling for Strafford's execution. Their fears, May adds, were 'more aggravated, by reason of reports that attempts were made to get the earle out of prison.'[31] Henry Jermyn and Sir John Suckling were among the conspirators, as was the king himself.

The king's role in the drama was particularly controversial. After the House of Lords assented to the bill on 7 May, Charles, with his 'Conscience on the one side, and the Fears of such a Publick Rupture on the other,' acquiesced to signing the 'fatal Bill' three days later.[32] Henry King later reports that Charles complied under duress: '(for so you did enforce / His Hand against His Reason to divorce / Brave *Strafford's* Life) then wring it quite away / By your usurping each Militia.'[33] Strafford himself had given his blessing to the king's act, writing in a letter dated 4 May 1641: 'Now, I understand the minds of men are more incensed against me, notwithstanding your majesty hath declared, that, in your princely opinion, I am not guilty of treason, nor are you satisfied in your conscience to pass the bill … to set your majesties conscience, &c. at liberty, I do most humbly beseech you, for the prevention of such mischief as may happen by your refusal, to pass the bill.'[34] A marginal note in Sir Richard Fanshawe's 'On the Earle of Strafford' describes the moment when the earl heroically though tragically pleads with the king to 'passe the Bill for his death, to quiet the Kingdomes.' Strafford will not 'abide [the] *tryall*,' according to the poet, but will choose to give his blood 'to quench a *Civill Warre*.'[35]

Ironically Charles's reluctant endorsement of the execution, which is rehearsed in countless writings thereafter, haunts the king to the end, becoming a trial of conscience for him and the nation.[36] Strafford remains a skeleton in the king's closet and in *Eikon Basilike*, Charles's closet devotions.[37] Ode II, 'Upon the Earl of Strafford's Death,' in Thomas Stanley's *Psaltorium Carolinum*, portrays a penitent Charles recalling his betrayal of Strafford: 'Thou whose mercies know no bound, / Pardon my compliant sin. / Death in me the guiltless found, / Who his Refuge should have bin.'[38] Milton capitalizes on the episode in *Eikonoklastes*, which features Charles repenting his complicity in Strafford's execution 'with the same words of contrition wherwith *David* repents the murdering of *Uriah*.'[39] Charles's guilt about his acquiescence, Milton claims, plunged him into a 'Sea of innocent blood' (*CPW*, 3:376).[40] Indeed the signing of the bill led to an escalation of tensions climaxing in 'one of the great set-piece dramas of English history' that would serve as a 'curtain-raiser' for the Civil War.[41]

The trial and the execution of Strafford on 12 May 1641, which would become 'the bitterest humiliation of Charles' life,' was a 'high tragedy, unsurpassed for historical and human interest in the political annals of any time or land.'[42] Crowds swarmed to see his death. The management of the final act included the production of a gloss to interpret the lessons offered by the spectacle of punishment and the death speech.[43] Frustratingly for Parliament, however, and in anticipation of Charles's counter-performance on the scaffold, the royalist actor had again deviated from the script. In particular, Strafford failed to provide the confessional, contrite speech that was expected. 'I am very sorry to heare that he was no more penitent, having so many hainous [*sic*] crimes proved against him,' a Scot complains to Strafford's Jesuit defender in *Great Satisfaction concerning the Death of the Earle of Strafford*.[44] Moreover, a controversy erupted over the accuracy of the final printed versions, as suggested by the appearance of *The Earl of Straffords Speech on the Scaffold* (1641) and 'The true Speech, as it was delivered' printed in *The Speech suggested to bee the late Earl of Straffords ... scandalously imputed to him*. Strafford's failed performance – or all-too-effective performance – had to be corrected by a

Tower speech, *The Earle of Strafford, his speech in the Tower*,[45] produced and circulated by Parliament, though attributed to Strafford. William Calley remarked to Richard Harvey that the speech added insult to injury: '[T]he Earl of Strafford should not have made that speech in the Tower which comes forth in print as his is, but, as I formerly said, to put a blemish upon the worth that was conceived to be in him, whom some men may think not thoroughly dead unless they can make it appear there was no way any extraordinary desert in the man why he should longer live.'[46] Then appearing in nine editions in 1641, the composite *Two last Speeches of* Thomas Wentworth intensified the competition over the public image of Strafford by juxtaposing counterstatements in a single document: *His speech in the Tower to the Lords* and the *Earle of Straffords last speech on the Scaffold*, originally printed as *A Protestation against a foolish, ridiculous and scandalous Speech, pretended to be spoken by Thomas Wentworth ... to certaine lords before comming out of the tower* (1641) (see figure 2). The *Two last Speeches* smoothes the transition from the first to the second speech by re-titling *A Protestation* as the *Earle of Straffords last speech on the Scaffold*, and by using the material object of the pamphlet to link the newly printed speeches through complementary and adjacent illustrations, through a brief introduction and contextualization of the scaffold speech, which follows the tower speech, and of course through the use of a catchword. But the differences between Strafford's self-condemnatory and self-vindicating speeches can hardly be glossed over, and the publication of the competing scripts thus contributed another level of debate to the contested site of the scaffold drama.

Strafford's execution in fact released a flood of popular anti-Strafford pamphlets, many of which are identified in J[ohn] B[ond]'s *The Poets Knavery Discovered*.[47] The recent suppression of pamphlets is justified, Bond maintains, in light of the proliferation of anti-Straffordian and anti-Laudian literature. Readers must 'learn how to distinguish betwixt the Lyes, and reall Books' (title page). Bond includes in his pamphlet a list of 'every lying Lybel' printed in 1641, presented for the readers' benefit and Parliament's defence. Imitating the form of a governmental document, *The Poets Knavery Discovered* is identified on the first page as 'An Order from the House of Commons for the suppressing of Pamphlets.' At the same time, Bond proceeds to discredit the authors of fabricated speeches, orders, and proceedings that were attributed to Parliament whose own tarnished reputation he hopes to salvage. 'Since the Earle of *Straffords* death, there have been above three hundred lying Pamphlets printed to ... [Parliament's] credible enumeration,' Bond ched the Marshalls men to make way, then the Sheriffes of London, Officers with their Halberds; after them the Kings Guard, or warders of the Tower: Next came one of his Gentlemen, bare headed, in mourning Habit, the Lord *Strafford* following him clad in blacke cloaath, with divers others in the same habit, which were his attendance; then the Lord Bishop of *Armagh*, and other good Divines; with the Sheriffes of London, and divers honourable parsonages.

When became to the Scaffold, he there shewed himselfe on each side in full view to all people, and made this short speech, with as much alacrity of Spirit, as a morall man cou'd expresse, *viz.*

The

The *Earle* of *Straffords* last speech on the Scaffold, and the manner how he behaved himselfe and spake to the people.

MY Lord Primate of *Ireland*, (and my Lords, and the rest of these Gentlemen) it is a very great comfort for me to have your Lordship by me this day, in regard I have been knowne to you a long time, I should be very glad to obtaine so much silence, as to bee heard a few words; but I doubt I shall not, my Lord. I come hither by the good will and pleasure of Almighty God to pay that last debt I owe unto sin, which is death and by the blessing of that God to rise again through the merits of Christ Jesus to eternall glorie, And hee being desired by the people, hee said, *what is there stee?* and sate downe in chaire: some replyed, The Souldiers kept most stir: *if they said it would be quiet, all the rest would be quiet.* I wish I had been private

B

Figure 2. *The two last Speeches of Thomas Wentworth, late Earle of Strafford.* 12 May 1641. © Copyright The British Museum.

exclaims. As a defender of Parliament and the king, Bond catalogues the paper-contestations against Charles's ministers: 'First, then the Lord Lieutenants *Speech* fabulously fathred upon him in the Tower; but protested against by such eminent Persons as accompanied him some time before his execution; his *Ultimum Vale:* his pittifull *Elegies* fathred upon himselfe; his amorous *Re-greet* to *Clorinda:* his *Ghost*, & suppositions Dialogue betwixt him, and the Lords Grace of *Canterbury'* (A2v). Strafford's and Laud's trial by print at the hands of ruthless libellers, including Richard Overton, he maintains, is relentless and completely unjust: 'Oh what a lamentable thing it is to suffer the sentence of such penurious, pennilesse wits, who wholly resolve their inke to gall, for a little mercenary gaine' (A4). Parliament, however, was unimpressed, and Bond, having modelled his pamphlet on one of Parliament's own printed declarations, lived to regret his act, as suggested in *The Poet's Recantation, having suffered in the Pillory the 2. of Aprill. 1642.*

As the onslaught by the libellers, poets, and satirists continued, the figure of Strafford's ghost emerged to haunt the politically charged literary scene. In *A Description of the Passage ... over the River of Styx*, likely known to Bond (and cited in chapter 1), Strafford encounters another damned soul, Sir William Noy, who prosecuted William Prynne in the Star Chamber, and he unconvincingly professes his indifference to the print assault on himself and his condemned soul mate: 'there is a pretious generation of *Mercury's* above ... Why there are men *Mercury's*, and women *Mercury's*, and boy *Mercury's*; *Mercury's* of all sexes, sorts and sizes; and these are they that carry up and downe their Pasquils, and vent them unto shops ... but let them write even what they will ... and if they bite the dead I care not.'[48] Then at the centre of the woodcut on the title page of *The Great Eclipse of the Sun*, Strafford reappears in order to confront Charles in his own trial of conscience: 'ther's a thing call'd Conscience that doth follow after the King and his Cavaliers, faster then our Armies can doe, it doth bring in a Catalogue of crimes, and will twich the King by the heart and give him shrewd Items, it is worse then *Hamlets* Ghost; for it will haunt him every where, and cry unto him, O King expect revenge for the blood of thy subjects.'[49] Various images from the woodcut in *The Great Eclipse of the Sun* are reproduced in other tracts,[50] thus enabling a ready identification by viewers and readers of the pamphleteers' political allegiances. The frontispiece of *The Earle of Straffords Ghost* features a woodcut of Strafford as a ghost in a shroud holding a torch and terrifying and edifying the 'corrupted soule.' The pamphlet consists of a confessional speech by Strafford who is 'justly tormented' by the scenes of violence in which he originally delighted: 'When the Rebellion in Ireland grew to such a height, that yee supposed no power could hinder your conquest: when yet were either bloody actors, willing spectators, or joyful hearers of the Stories of those horrid massacres ... then were my actions of high esteem, and my Name was famous amongst you' he reminds the 'Romane Catholike Courtiers.' In York, London, and Ireland, 'as in a Theater, the bloody Tragedies I made way for in my life time, are presented to my view,' Strafford laments.[51] The panorama of England's 'sad theater' is one that will torment Laud after his execution.

Opposition to Strafford's arraignment, even among the MPs themselves, is evidenced by the production and distribution of Digby's speech, discussed earlier. Moreover, in the absence of printed royalist speeches in the early 1640s, Strafford's defenders circulated the details of his final hours in an attempt to redeem his image. Proroyalists also turned to more conventional forms of expression to convey their cautious admiration of the noble antihero. In light of the commonplace of the execution as stage play and the interchangeability of the terms 'stage' and 'scaffold,' the most popular representation of Strafford was that of a tragic hero whose final act had a cathartic effect. Sir John Denham's early version of 'On the Earl of Strafford's Tryal and Death,' which is featured in two manuscripts and then later revised for a collection published in the Restoration, commends the command performance of the hero who 'Joyned with an eloquence so greate to make / Us heere with greater passion then he spake.' The conclusion of the brief poem combines praise and antithesis: 'Farewell greate soule, the glory of thy fall / Outeweighes the cause, whom we at once may call / The enimy and martire of the state, / Our nations glory and our nations hate.'[52]

With the passage of time as Strafford's opponents lost interest in trying him in print, portrayals of the earl generally tended to become more idealized. Sir Richard Fanshawe, who served under Strafford in Ireland and was a friend of his son, commends the heroic performance of Strafford in 1647–8: 'Then if 'twill prove no *Comedy*, at least / To make it of all *Tragedies* the best'; '*Times* shall admiring read it [his lifes *last act*], and *this age*, / Though now it *hisse, claps* when he leaves the Stage' (ll. 11–12, 15–16). The language of tragedy became in turn the primary discourse for remembering Charles's scaffold/stage performance in 1649. Andrew Marvell's description of Charles as royal actor on the tragic scaffold in 'An Horatian Ode' may have been influenced by Fanshawe's representation of Strafford.[53]

The royalist tragedy is eventually converted into tragicomedy when the House of Lords and House of Commons passed a bill in 1662 to reverse Strafford's attainder. In response to the change in dramatis personae on England's Restoration stage, royalists reclaimed literary culture for the service of the court. In such a climate, Denham would substitute the concluding lines of 'On the Earl of Strafford's Tryal and Death' with the final verdict on Strafford's performance whose 'last Action all the rest might crown' (l. 30). The printed version of 'On the Earl of Strafford's Tryal and Death' also tries Strafford's prosecutors, who now repent what Denham identified as 'Their Legislative Frenzy' (l. 25). The judicial proceedings thus play out as a trial of conscience for the upstaged producers of Strafford's tragedy.

II

The final episodes in the life of William Laud, archbishop of Canterbury, the next major royalist actor on England's political stage, reenact Strafford's tragedy and likewise foreshadow Charles's. Laud was the king's principal advisor and like Charles believed strongly in the uniformity of worship practices, the value of ceremony, and obedience to political and religious superiors – values which were readily aligned with Catholicism. The radicalized Puritan opposition was particularly incensed when the English government proposed to introduce the new service book into Scotland in 1637. In the same year, the return from exile of William Prynne and the investigation of the Commons into the proceedings against Laud's three best-known victims would (in retrospect) constitute 'a prognosticall Prologue to something like our Tragicall Warre.'[54] Laud himself helped produce his tragedy and that of the nation by enforcing censorship, by mishandling the punishment of the three conspirators, and by leaving a record of his personal trials in the *Diary of William Laud*.[55] These actions set the stage for Laud's impeachment for high treason in 1640 and his imprisonment in the Tower the following year. His trial took place in 1644 and his execution 10 January 1645.

The chief actor in and author of the prologue to Laud's tragedy was the Presbyterian, William Prynne, who was jailed throughout the 1630s for writing 'seditious' pamphlets and for his famous attack on stage plays, *Historiomastix*. In 1637 Prynne was again publicly punished, this time along with Henry Burton and John Bastwick, for vilifying episcopacy in his writings and condemning Laud. The archbishop's justifications for the extreme measures against three Puritans included his remark that their undermining of church authority posed a national threat: 'these Men do but begin with the Church that they might after have freer Access to the State.'[56] In his *Diary*, Laud reports that on 14 June 1637 'J. Bastwick, Dr. of Physic; Hen. Burton, Batch of Divinity; and Wi. Prynne, Barrister at Law, were censured for their libels against the Hierarchy of the Church &c.'; in the 30 June entry he confirms: 'The above-named three libellers lost their ears.'[57] In 1637 Laud became in turn the target of numerous libellers for various reasons, including the recent Star Chamber proceedings, the St Giles riot, and the increased strength of the '*Popish* Faction,'[58] for which the archbishop was held responsible. Reviled in the numerous libels that suddenly appeared,[59] chiefly in manuscript form, a very agitated Laud excuses an interruption in correspondence with Strafford in 1637: 'the Truth is, I have been so exercised with Libellings and Star-Chamber Business, and the Consequences which have followed upon them'; 'a little more Quickness in the Government would cure this Itch of Libelling.'[60]

Far from silencing them, the sentence merely increased the determination of Prynne, Burton, and Bastwick to publicize their viewpoints. From the time he ordered their public punishment, Laud found their defiance very unnerving: 'But what say you to it, that *Prynne* and his Fellows should be suffered to talk what they pleased while in the Pillory, and win Acclamations from the People, and have Notes taken of what they spake, and those Notes spread in written Copies about the City, and that when they went out of the Town to their several Imprisonments, there were thousands suffered to be upon the way to take their Leave, and God knows what else?'[61] That the three should have their words recorded proved even more disturbing. In the coming weeks and months, Laud would continue to be plagued by written attacks of whose materiality and circulation he was also painfully aware.[62] Peter Heylyn noted that Laud collected the libels and the broadsheets that poured off the presses,[63] some of which he recorded in his *Diary*: July 7: 'A note was brought to me of a short libel pasted on the cross in Cheapside: that the Arch-Wolf of Cant. had his hand in persecuting the saints and shedding the blood of the martyrs. Memento, for the last of June';[64] Aug. 23: 'Wednesday, My L. Mayor sent me a libel found by the watch at the south gate of S. Paul's: That the devil had let that house to me, &c.'; August 25: 'Friday, Another libel brought me by an officer of the High Commiss., fastened to the north gate of S. Paul's: That the Government of the Church of England is a candle in the snuff, going out in a stench';[65] Aug 25: 'The same night, my Lord Mayor sent me another libel, hanged upon the standard in Cheapside. My speech in the Star Chamber, set in a kind of pillory, &c.,' a 'pillory in ink.'[66] The eventual release of Prynne, Burton, and Bastwick would mark 'a triumph for the unauthorized interpretation of [their] trial,'[67] while spawning the literary campaign against Laud. 'At midnight,' writes Laud on 11 May 1640, 'my house at Lambeth was beset with 500 of these rascal routers ... Since [then] I have fortified my house as well as I can; and hope all may be safe. But yet libels are continually set up in all places of note in the city.' Then in an abrupt turn, Laud reports: 'My deliverance was great,' though the libels, nevertheless, continued to penetrate the unscalable walls of the fortress.

Laud's short-lived 'deliverance' ended with his arraignment and imprisonment in December 1640.[68] He was committed to the Tower three months later. As in Strafford's case, Laud's examination, sentencing, and punishment spilled over into the court of public opinion. Anti-Laudians marked the occasion with numerous satirical pamphlets and dialogues, which often cited or copied each other, thus demonstrating their popularity. Though the circulation of pamphlets was difficult to control, the large number of satires in dramatic form indicate that dramatists-turn-pamphleteers were addressing a parliamentary Puritan city audience and not a royalist one. The frontispiece woodcut in *Lambeth Faire* (see figure 3) features the pope with his mitre, crosier, and elaborate garments, but bent over under the weight of despair and of printed attacks, 'Ore-prest with griefe to thinke on *Lambeth Faire*.' The 'prologue' or preface 'To the Reader' explains that Parliament has dismantled the popish stage, and the pamphleteer as satirist and iconoclast takes this opportunity to itemize the bishops' wares at the fair. In the absence of Laud – the 'Master of the Fayr' committed to the Tower (A2v) – a cryer is called to open the ceremonies at which all the wares are displayed. Identified as the 'last *Act* upon the *English* Stage' (B2r), the fair is interrupted by a Messenger who announces that an act of Parliament has ordered the show to end: 'The *Parliament* hath pul'd your pride to th' ground, / and by the *House* three times y'are *voted down*' (B2r). At the conclusion of the last Romish 'Act,' a different sales pitch is made: I 'have it here to sell; / Come buy the *Faire* of me, and so farewell' (B2r). In the sequel, *New Lambeth-Fayre* by Richard Overton, a large part of which is devoted to repeating the contents of the first *Lambeth Faire*, the pope sails from Rome to England where he consecrates a new fair. As the author of the pamphlet, Overton gets into the act by annotat-

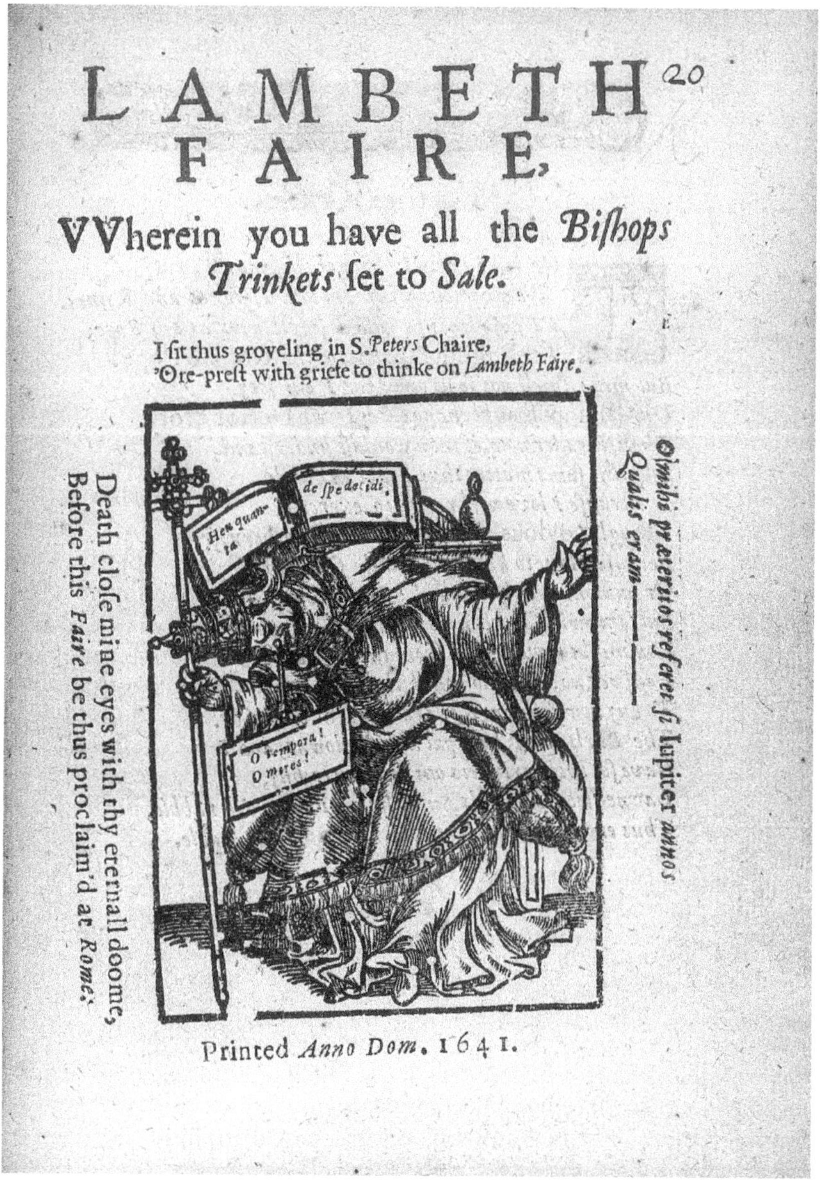

Figure 3. *Lambeth Faire.* 1641. © Copyright The British Museum.

ing his playlet with brief and often satirical notes about the history of the items or relics for sale. At the end of the pamphlet, he expands the account of Parliament's judgment, sentencing, and planned hanging of the bishops described in the earlier *Lambeth Faire*, though he closes with the same invitation to prospective consumers and readers of his work: 'Come buy the *Fayre* of me.'[69] The tract's success in the marketplace becomes a factor in assessing the efficacy and legitimacy of Overton's attack on Laud.

Further demonstrating his adeptness in exploiting print and the dramatic mode in the cause of polemical and political critique, Overton produces another sequel to *Lambeth Faire*, titled *A new Play called Canterburie His Change of Diot*, which invokes 'Lambeth great Faire.'[70] A mock reenactment of Laud's sentencing of Bastwick, Prynne, and Burton turns into a revenge fantasy for all Laud's victims.[71] In Act 2 of this four-act pamphlet-play, Laud, who approaches a carpenter about sharpening his knife to sever the ears of the accused, is himself picked up and held to the grindstone. The carpenter's wife in the next act bids her husband to 'put these *Cormorants* [Laud and Father Robert Philips, the Queen's confessor] into this Cage, They that have cut of eares at the first bout, God knowes what they may cut off next' (A4r). The woodcut found at the start of Act 3 is taken from the frontispiece, and features Laud and Father Philips, the Jesuit Confessor, in a bird cage with Archie Armstrong mocking their folly and repeating his famous question, 'who is the foole now' (A3v), a line from *Archy's Dreame*.[72] The pamphlet contains the trappings of live theatrical productions through its caricatures, its dialogues (including that between the jester and the king in Act 4), and its folksong snatches and jig in the epilogue. The satirical effect of the pamphlet depended on its readers' (and prospective audience's) familiarity with acted plays[73] but also with the acts on the political and judicial stages.

The extrajudicial, unauthorized proceedings certainly left their impression. In a letter designed at once for council and confession, Laud advises the vice chancellor of Oxford to maintain his distance from politics: 'affairs of State being theatres, on which whosoever acts his part, though it appear to him comical in the beginning, the end will produce his own tragedy, if he look not with the greater care to his performance.' Laud's own fate was inscribed in the libels: '[No] man hath had so many scandalous abuses cast upon him; none ever (considering my calling) having been made so notorious a subject for ridiculous pamphlets and ballads.'[74] His concerns about paper-contestations are evidenced through his early 1640s correspondence: 'I must tell you further, that from the time that the Earl of Strafford was first brought to his answer in Westminster-Hall, [22 March 1641] the bitter and fierce libels of factious people came daily out, to keep up and increase the people's hate against him.' One of them, he continues, features Strafford falling into 'great and passionate expressions' against Laud.[75] Laud and Strafford, who were friends, correspondents, and now objects of ridicule, encountered each other on the scaffold as well. On his last walk to Tower Hill, Strafford paused outside Laud's window and asked his blessing. Laud lifted his hand and then fell to the ground in a swoon (12 May 1641).[76] While Strafford is condemned and executed, Laud is judged.

In July 1641 Star Chamber and the High Commission were abolished, leaving no one authority to control the press.[77] As pamphleteers pursued their relentless assault on the episcopacy, Bishop Joseph Hall complained to Parliament about the eruption of print that threatened the sacred church government. In *An humble remonstrance*, a powerful defence of episcopacy, which provoked a retort from Puritan divines who wrote under the name of Smectymnuus, Hall sharply contrasts the quiet resolve of the Church of England with the 'many spurious and malignant spirits [that] every where have burst forth into sclanderous [*sic*] Libels, bitter Pasquines, railing Pamphlets? (under which more Presses then one have groaned).'[78] Another who took offence at the paper-contestation was John Bond. Surveying the previous year's malicious pamphlets, Bond's *The Poets Knavery Discovered* adds anti-Laudian libels to the anti-Straffordian satires mentioned earlier in this tract. These include *The Discontented Conference, Canterburys Dreame, Lambeth Faire, The Bishop's Potion*, and *Canterbury's Will* (A2v). In an argument resembling that of Thomas Herbert, Bond insists that if Laud be 'culpable, & peccant, the Law is sufficient to curb him, & he ought to suffer according to its censure'; but pamphleteers have taken matters into their own hands: 'to see his grave made before his eyes with lying libels: or to encounter such extreams, as the blasting tongue of infamy, is an act of higher suffering, then the just censure of Law may permit' (A2v).

The paper-contestations eventually led to the very high-profile courtroom trial, which began, after numerous delays, on 12 March 1644. John Maynard, who had been a counsel at Strafford's arraignment, headed the prosecution. Laud himself did most of the legal research for his defence, and the notes taken by John Browne, clerk of the Parliament, generally confirmed the accuracy of Laud's version in *The History of the Troubles and Tryal of ... William Laud*. Laud's defence, the gallantry

of which was acknowledged by supporters and opponents alike, undermined the parliamentary 'show trial' which, as in their case against
Strafford, ultimately 'failed to demonstrate what it had intended to
prove.'[79] The last day of trial was 11 October 1644, and the prosecutors
then handed Laud over to the judges for sentencing. The Lords, however, did not agree about the charge of treason against Laud. As in the
trial against Strafford, tensions between the Commons and the Lords
mounted. On 2 January 1645, the Commons resorted to their legislative
power, short-circuiting the justice process. The Lords' resistance ended
two days later, and they assented to the Ordinance of Attainder – a declaration of the two Houses without the king's consent. John Cleveland
conveyed his opposition to the proceedings in 'On the Archbishop of
Canterbury': 'The Law is dead, or cast into a trance, / And by a Law
dough-bak't, an Ordinance.'[80]

On learning his fate, Laud ended *The History of the Troubles* and prepared his scaffold sermon, one that reaffirmed his commitment to Protestantism. Image-conscious even at the moment of his execution, Laud
handed a copy of the sermon to his chaplain, Dr Richard Sterne, and
informed the public shorthand writer: 'he desired him not to do him
wrong in publishing a false or imperfect Copy.'[81] In *The Archbishop of
Canterbury's Speech,* John Hinde reports that after Laud's first prayer on
the scaffold, the archbishop, recognizing the power invested in the
printed word to vindicate him, appealed to Hinde to 'have no wrong
done me' through the falsification of his final speech.[82] Laud was in fact
well 'studied in the Art of Dying,' Heylyn later confirms; 'finding the
way full of people who had placed themselves upon the Theatre to
behold the Tragedy, he desired he might *have room to die*, beseeching
them to let him have *an end of his miseries which he had endured very long.*'[83]
The 'laudable Act' of execution was performed, Prynne states, on 10
January 1645 in the view of thousands 'by that *Axe of publike Justice.*'[84]
Without further adieu, newsbook writers seized the opportunity to pro-
file the event: the entry for 11 January 1645 of *Mercurius Aulicus* prints
Laud's speech from the scaffold and laments the act of 'studied Mur-
ther' committed against the archbishop, while *A Perfect Diurnall* of the
same week presents a rendition by the Puritan partisan, Samuel Pecke,
of Laud's final speech, interpolated with Pecke's criticisms. In discrediting Laud's last act, Pecke insists on the fairness of Laud's trial while
making the reader complicit in the act of judging and condemning
Laud for the fallacies, omissions, and misuse of scriptural comparisons
that characterize his scaffold speech.[85]

The newsbook accounts of Laud's final moments provoked various counterresponses, including Heylyn's *A Briefe Relation of the Death and Sufferings of ... Canterbury*, which transforms the ephemeral material of the newsbooks into a tragedy: 'It is a preposterous kinde of writing to beginne the story of a great mans life, at the houre of his death; a most strange way of setting forth a solemne *Tragedie*, to keepe the *principall* Actor in the *tyring-house*, till the *play* be done, and then to bring him on the *stage* onely to speake the *Epilogue*, and receive the Plaudites. Yet this must be the scope and method of these following papers' (1). When Laud was already imprisoned in 1643, William Prynne, as he himself recorded in the previously mentioned *Breviate of the Life* (a1v), seized Laud's personal diary, documents, and books, and used them for his 1644 account of Laud's religious policy and trial. Henry Wharton, who, like Heylyn, sought to redeem the image of Laud, described Prynne's *Breviate* – a corrupt edition of Laud's *Diary* – as barbarous. Consequently, Wharton published a corrected version as an introduction to his edition of Laud's self-defence, *The History of the Troubles and Tryal of ... William Laud.*

Canterburies Doome, Prynne's own account of Laud's trial, appeared in the year following Laud's execution. 'I presume,' Prynne states in his dedicatory epistle, 'the setting forth of this *History of his Tryall* will soon *Un-Martyr, Un-Saint*, Uncrown this *Arch-Imposter*, by presenting him in his *Proper Colours*, stript of all *Disguises*' (a2). Much of the extensive front matter is devoted to his efforts at defending his objectivity and counteracting the damage done by Laud's '*Sophistry, Oratory, Subtilty, Protestations*' and '*verball Apologies*' and by the 'late lying *Legends* of his death, [as] *A most Glorious Martyr*' (a1). Prynne thus arraigns Laud again – properly this time, he insists. Since the evidence presented at Laud's arraignment was 'pressed at the tryall, though not all fully read' (a2v), Prynne uses his painstakingly detailed account to reveal the truth and offer a 'fuller discovery of [Laud's] Popish intentions' (a3). After excusing his delay in compiling these materials, he recommends *Canterburies Doome* to the Christian Reader, who is encouraged 'to collect some profitable Meditations for [his] Spirituall advantage' (b4).

Perhaps the most dramatic account of Laud's public and personal trials is the broadside, *England and Irelands sad Theater of William Laud heretofore Arch-Bishop of Canterbury, his Trance and vision*, which features the 'droomgesicht,' that serves as the final theatre of judgment examined in this chapter (see figure 4). The scenes in the broadside are presented as a series of panels depicting in an allegorical mode a decade's worth of

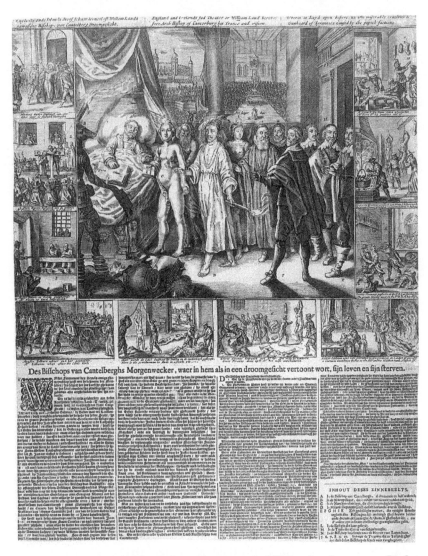

Figure 4. *Englants ende Irlands drees schaw tooneel oft Willem Lauds gewessene Bischop van Cantelberg Droomgesicht. England and Irelands sad Theater.* [Amsterdam], 1645.
© Copyright The British Museum.

historical events and of popular interpretations of those events. Here the public display of justice and injustices in the panels is again converted into a private case of conscience, filtered through Laud's internal strife as recorded in his *Diary*. The setting is a dreamscape, the last act of the tragedy, in which all the players, including those discussed throughout this chapter, appear as ghosts on the stage in an antimasque or 'sad theater.' Sleeping in his prison, Laud is approached by a naked Truth carrying the New Testament. Truth is pushed forward by Time, and accompanied by the ghost of Strafford, who bears a torch. Behind are six of Laud's victims, who had their ears severed or were imprisoned for their anti-Laudian writings. At the foot of Laud's bed is a wolf, representing corrupt monopolizers and 'popery,' as stated in chapter 1. The backdrop for this stage features scenes of judgment and punishment: the Tower, Laud kneeling before Parliament, and the execution, thus locating the trial of conscience in a narrative of justice restored. Framing the centre panel on three sides are ten separate scenes depicting cruelties committed against Laud's victims who include Prynne, Burton, Bastwick, and Lilburne.

Some copies of *The Sad Theater* include an inscription in English which accords in most but not all respects with the text on the broadside or the accompanying Dutch description. The inscription consists of exchanges between Laud and a cast of ghostly figures who call him to repentance. The broadside thus serves as an alternative last dying speech in which Laud confesses his guilt and is pursued by his conscience like the king in the *Great Eclipse*. Following Laud's opening self-incriminating soliloquy, in which he identifies the company that will appear in this drama of personal trial and justice, the Ghost of the Deputy attempts to awaken Laud to report that he too is still tormented by 'all those ills through thy bad counsell vented' that ravaged the land.[86] The broadside reinforces the commonplace identification of Laud with Catholic despotism in terms of an exchange between the pope and his obedient son, who has slavishly followed and enforced 'popish doctrine' and now implores his father for assistance. Thereafter a speech containing a wake-up call from the ghost of Thomas Scott, author of *Vox Populi*, details Laud's atrocities as illustrated in the designs surrounding the centre panel. Among the other victims who confront him – Peter Smart, Henry Burton, John Bastwick, Alexander Leighton – is the imprisoned John Lilburne, who enters the stage momentarily and likewise denigrates his jailer. The spirit of Strafford then informs Laud that his guilt has raised the 'restless ghost' and that time has run out: 'through thy throte an axe sharpe whet / Shall glide, thy time is short, the day is set' (1:299). Truth and Religion appear on the scene and prepare the way for Time, which ends the drama by prophesying the end of popery and the restoration of unity: 'Now Laud thy hope is lost, no teares, nor strife / Can alter time, with mee I'le take thy life, / And then will England, Scotland Ireland tie / In bonds of never ending unitie' (1:300). The envisioned union of the three kingdoms that Strafford and Laud were accused of disbanding concludes the trial of justice.

Englante ende Irlands drees schaw toonell oft Willem Lauds ... Droomegesicht offers an adventure in interpretation, involving both a diachronic and synchronic viewing and reading experience. As image and text, the broadside appeals at once to the visually and verbally literate. It reproduces stock symbols, allegorical images, and speeches from earlier prints – including *A new Play called Canterburie His Change of Diot*, which tried Laud in print several years beforehand – and incorporates intertextual references and dramatic elements designed to facilitate identification, encourage active engagement, and incite judgment. In late February 1645 *A Charme for Canterburian Spirits* reported that Laud's ghost again appeared in multiple diabolical shapes throughout London, as popular writers exploited the combined effects of the performative nature of print and the dramatic qualities of trial literature to complement, advance, or emend the work carried out by the judicial system.

An examination of the theatres of judgment and of the 'unauthorized' versions of the two famous 1640s trials enables a study of the practices of textual revolt and collective identification that generate alternative interpretive communities, produce cultural and political ruptures, and intensify the social and political dramas on the English stage. The official and unofficial forums in which information was exchanged exhibit the various kinds of stagecraft in which English society was involved. Performance is thus associated with the production of texts and with the actions carried out by texts *as* events in the period in which they are generated. Most important in the context of this study, performance refers to interpretive practices, especially acts of writing and reading, through which textual communities evolve, intersect, and resist each other. As we discover in the following two chapters, the royalists seize the opportunity to 'write back,' as the king himself outperforms the entire company on the public stage and in the 'private' pages of *Eikon Basilike*, and as Interregnum writers deploy theatrical discourses and dialogues to generate alternative cultural and political relationships.

Chapter 3

The 'Stage-work' of Charles I

God preserved and prospered [*Eikon Basilike*] to revive [Charles I's] honor, and redeeme hys Majesty's name from that grave contempt and abhorrence, or infamy, in which they aymed to bury hym. When it came out, just upon the King's death; Good Good! what shame, rage and despite filled hys Murtherers! What comfort hys friends! How many enemyes did it convert! How many hearts did it mollify, and melt! ... What preparations it made in all men's minds for this happy restauration ... In a word, it was an army, and did vanquish more than any sword could.

John Gauden, 21 January 1660/61

Prologue

A counterfeit *Mercurius Pragmaticus*, which imitated the incisive rhetoric of Marchamont Nedham, appeared on the morning of 30 January 1649 to set the stage for the greatest of early modern English tragedies:

'Yes, the feat is now done, and Law and Equity must both give way: the Trayterous Tragedians are upon their *Exit*, and poor King CHARLES at the Brinke of the *Pitt*; The *Prologue* is past, the *Proclamation made*, His Sentence is given, and we daily expect the sad *Catastrophie*; and then behold! The Sceane is *chang'd*;

> *England* but now a glorious *Monarchy*
> Degraded to a base *Democracy.*

The *Play* thus done, or rather the *WORKE Finish'd*; the Epilogue remains, to wit the Epitaph of a slaughter'd King; which I reserve to another Opportunity; hoping Heaven may prevent you ere your sceane be finish'd, (as you did those poor Players lately in the middle of their's).'[1]

The writing of the king's epilogue as epitaph began before the execution, as the timely appearance of *Eikon Basilike* and of the numerous royalist accounts of Charles's final performance attests. My investigation in this chapter and in chapter 4 of the literary response to the regicide – the 'memorable scene' on the 'tragic scaffold'[2] – situates this most important and controversial event in seventeenth-century English political history in relation to a transmigrated theatre culture and emergent print culture explored throughout this book.

As John Milton acknowledged, Charles, who was deprived of the 'force of Armes,' strategically resorted to print to continue the battle. Milton, moreover, recognized the affective power of Charles's motto, *Vota dabunt quæ Bella negarunt,* and the king's book generally,[3] which would result in its becoming the most popular text of the century. The remarkable performance of *Eikon Basilike* as image, book, and material object is attributable not only to its wide circulation but also to its appeal to the collective imagination of an audience in a stage-play world.

Readers of *Eikon Basilike* are offered privileged access to the king's internal drama in a work that, like the cabinet-literature and closet drama of the period, relied on the revelatory power of image and print. The publication of Charles's 'solitudes and sufferings' was provocatively intended to expose the truth, invite a reinterpretation of the tragic events in the political theatre, and secure the nation's commitment to kingship. While the experience of reading the book might be regarded as a private act, the extensive engagement with *Eikon Basilike* and its many offshoots/prints generated a discursive community.[4] Furthermore, the propaganda triumph of Charles's book not only completed his public performance on the scaffold but prepared the way 'in all men's minds for th[e] happy restauration,' as Gauden proclaimed.[5]

In examining Charles's 'Stage-work' and the polemical debate it ignited, I return to the concept of the trial and execution as 'social dramas,' that is, sites of competing performances which spilled over into the new political/theatrical arena of print. To Charles's theatrical politics and his memorable performance on the 'tragic scaffold,' we must add the part played by the king's book on England's political stage and in the material culture of the period. Also of importance are the (other) actors or characters in the social and political drama – the spectators at the trial and execution[6] and the consumers and readers of the king's book in its various incarnations. The most famous reader of *Eikon Basilike* is Milton whose critique of the king's 'Stage-work' (E, *CPW*, 3:530) is the subject of *Eikonoklastes* and, as I demonstrate in the epilogue to this book, is carried over into his closet drama, *Samson Agonistes*. The battle in which political opponents of the time are engaged is a battle both over the control of the press, which now 'acts' in the silence of the stage, and over the politics of reading through which the terms of authority are played out, continually renegotiated, and contested.

I

Conscious of the fact that theatrical performances, rituals, and spectacles shaped communal life, Parliament introduced an ordinance against play-acting, the resistance to which I also discuss in chapter 4. This antitheatrical prejudice did not, however, prevent the Rump Parliament from recognizing the advantages of staging 'acts of justice' when the decision about the king's fate was determined. Coopting the discourses, structures, and expectations of the theatrical performance, the Rump brought the king to justice before a live audience. The political rituals of judgment and punishment were intended both to display the power of the governing party and to create consensus in the community.[7]

A suitable stage had to be chosen for the trial. A debate by the members of the High Court of Justice determined that not the enclosed precincts of Windsor (among two other possible locations – St James and the Guild-hall) but rather the famous Westminster Hall should serve as the site. Westminster Hall was regarded as 'a place of publicke resort';[8] but it was also the setting of Strafford's and Laud's arraignments (see chapter 2) – where these traitors had been brought to justice. The people could therefore be expected to interpret the spectacle of the king's punishment accordingly.

The court sought to persuade the people that the proceedings were being conducted on behalf of the public. *A perfect Narrative of the whole Proceedings*, the main account of the trial, reports that 'the great gate of the said Hall [at Westminster] was set open, to the end that all persons, without exception, desirous to see or hear, might come into it'; the prisoner is described as looking down on 'the multitude of spectators on the right side of the said great Hall.'[9] Yet the trial – a political forum rife with dramatic potential – was at the same time carefully scripted and managed. By holding the proceedings at the extreme south end of Westminster Hall, the spectators in the body of the Hall would in fact be prevented from taking in very much of the event. Even so, railings, partitions, and soldiers were put in place to control the crowds in this theatre of justice.

The actors in the drama were identified and assigned specific parts. The House of Commons named about 135 commissioners to act as both judges and jurors. The Commons, which instituted the High Court of Justice, assumed an unprecedented judicial power in arraigning Charles because all justice in English law had traditionally proceeded from the king. Moreover, the cases of Edward II and Richard II notwithstanding, there had in fact been no precedent for the trial and execution of an English king in the name of a sovereign power invested in the people on whose behalf the Rump Parliament claimed to be acting.[10] The king was brought to justice 'In the name of the Commons in Parliament assembled and all the good people of England.' The prosecutor at the trial informed an acquaintance 'I am serving the people,' to which the man replied: 'There's a thousand to one will not give you thanks.'[11]

Not all the parliamentarians who were named would, however, be willing to play their parts – in fact fewer than half of the judges showed up for the trial. Information about any opposition to the proceedings was reserved for royalist commentaries. Following a detailed account of the 'secret consults' of the parliamentarians who debated among each other about the fate of the king, the earl of Clarendon reported: 'it fell out, however, that they among them who wished the king best, and stood nearest to the stage where these parts were acted, did not believe that there were those horrid intentions that shortly after appeared' (*ST*, 4:994n). While the text of the trial was published in full and the king's words not suppressed – something that the government very soon regretted – references to interruptions from spectators or members of the High Court were omitted from the accounts, and royalists were altogether prevented from reporting the trial. The Presbyterian polemicist Clement Walker, in his gloss on the ellipses appearing in the courtroom transcription, explains: 'I hear much of the Kings Argument is omited, & much depraved, none but licensed men [were] suffred to take Notes.'[12] The government also broke up demonstrations against the proceedings, thus requiring objectors to devise alternative strategies for communicating their dissent. Presbyterian clergy resorted to condemning the trial from the pulpits, while printers illegally produced proroyalist materials that were circulated from hand to hand.

Enacted before a multitude of spectators, the trial scripted a particular role for the king, but one he used in order to stage a counterperformance – an extension of his politics of silent defiance, which was compared to that of Christ before Pilate.[13] From the start of the wars, Charles sat above the debates generated by the pamphleteering, having enlisted the earl of Clarendon to represent him in print by preparing his numerous declarations and manifestoes. Inside Westminster Hall, Charles repeatedly refused to recognize the High Court or to answer the charges against him, insisting that he could not be subject to a human tribunal.[14] Judgment of the king would largely be reserved for the readers of the book *Eikon Basilike*, in which his words acquired an extratextual status and lent the dead king the aura and mystique of a martyr. The overheard conversations with his addressees and confidants, God and Charles II, were designed to validate his saintliness.

The courtroom drama which resulted in the sentencing of the king was transferred to the scaffold/stage. The execution scene, which would seize the king's enemies with amazement and bring the House down (see the epilogue to this book), became a site of competing performances. The route that Charles took to the scaffold was the same one he would have taken to a masque. The scaffold was erected in the open street around Whitehall, the location of the executions of his ministers, whose tragedies anticipated his own. In his final speech, which he delivered eloquently upon suddenly losing his life-long stutter, Charles affirmed his innocence, defended the rule of kings, and set himself up for martyrdom.[15] The paradoxical nature of his last address is captured in his first utterance: 'I shall be very little heard of any body here, I shall therefore speak a word unto you here.'[16] This appeal to a private-public interpretive community is a tactic Charles uses in *Eikon Basilike*, as shown in section IV. After reciting his dying speech, Charles spent some time in devotion; each chapter in *Eikon Basilike* correspondingly concludes with Charles in prayer. Then, having performed his part, Charles was beheaded in front of his beloved Banqueting Hall at Whitehall Palace. Heightening the theatrical quality of the occasion, the executioner and his assistant wore masks, false hair, and disguises resembling those of antimasquers. In an attempt at crowd control, which reenacted Parliament's closing of the theatres to discourage the assembly of spectators, soldiers were called in after the execution to disperse the people who would otherwise have gazed too long on the horrid spectacle.[17]

On-site parliamentary shorthand reporters took notes of the execution since the stage management of the ritual of judgment and punishment 'allow[ed] the lessons implicit in the spectacle of execution, and explicit in the last dying speeches, to be diffused more widely by the popular press.'[18] The writers even checked their versions of Charles's address against his 'script,' the record of his last verbal performance, the copy of which Bishop Juxon remitted following the execution. Again royalist accusations that the government had misrepresented the king were for the most part forestalled by the detailed reporting of his words.

But the Rump Parliament's staging and documentation of this social drama was strategically preempted. The power manifested in the drama of justice was eclipsed by the king's own counterperformance – an act of self-dramatization and self-memorialization, for which he had long been rehearsing. Charles's own departure was 'a studied performance of kingly self-possession designed to stamp his unchanged identity into the minds of all spectators at the execution.'[19] In this stage-play world, royalists, defenders of the Commonwealth, and even dissenters then appropriated the language of dramaturgy to represent the event as the greatest of tragedies. The stage performance of this tragedy would be reenacted in a wide array of genres, ranging from newsbooks like *Mercurius Pragmaticus* (quoted in the epigraph to this chapter) to countless pro-royalist sermons, poems, prayers, plays, pamphlets, meditations, epitaphs, elegies, and songs. A lasting impression was, then, being manufactured behind the scenes in the form of printed materials but also of images and icons – all relics of Charles's last act.

The 'memorable scene' was sealed with the word 'remember,' presumably intended for the prince. Milton cites Juxon's explanation of the injunction (which the bishop had allegedly offered under duress): '"The king had bidden me, if I could reach his son, to carry him this last injunction from his dying father, namely, that if he were ever restored to his kingdom and sovereignty he should pardon you, the authors of his death. The king again and again commanded me that I should remember this"' (*Second Defence, CPW*, 4:645). Seventeenth-century commentators interpreted the command as a recollection of Christ's admonition to his followers, which Charles now directed at his son. However, Patricia Fumerton – in a Miltonic move? – identifies an alternative source, namely Shakespeare, and specifically the cry of the ghost of Hamlet's father 'remember me.'[20] Parliamentarians had earlier in the decade connected Hamlet and Charles as tragic figures haunted by their consciences. Portraits of Charles as a character tormented by his complicity in past and present death sentences are often accompanied by images of Strafford's ghost 'that doth follow after the King and his Cavaliers ... it is worse then *Hamlets* Ghost; for it will haunt him every where.'[21] Certainly, Charles's 'remember' was not intended to raise Hamlet's ghost, though this association would have underscored the interrelationship of political and theatrical performances which antiroyalists exploited in discrediting the monarchy.

Milton recognizes the part that *Eikon Basilike* played in deciphering the vexed, political significance of the command to Juxon: "'long since had Charles enjoined on his son this mandate, among others, in the *Eikon Basilike*, a book which, it is sufficiently clear, was written so that this secret might with diligence be revealed to us a little later, even against our will, as ostentatiously as it had been fabricated"' (*Second Defence*, *CPW*, 4:646). The elusive 'remember' would in reality return to haunt the regicides when the king was etched into memory through *Eikon Basilike*, the appearance of which caught the antiroyalists as much off guard as the king's 'Stage-work' on the scaffold. The commemoration of the tragedy through the timely publication of the king's private-political narrative effected a seamless connection between the two performances. Rather than dramatizing the execution, a Messenger's / nuntius' (or shorthand writer's) account might have enabled the Rump Parliament to control the response of the people more effectively. As it was, however, the spectators were captivated by the performance and transformed into a receptive, ready-made audience/readership for *Eikon Basilike*.

II

An outpouring of texts commemorated the 'royal actor' and Christian martyr according to the model established by *Eikon Basilike*, which was probably in circulation as early as the execution day. All parties were in fact surprised at the sudden appearance of so complete and masterly a publication of the king, the existence of which had not been suspected nor could be explained except by a few behind the scenes; and their exact roles in producing the text remain open to question in our own day.[22] Charles's epilogue had been written on the authority of the king himself whose 'redressive' action[23] of rendering the scene memorable enabled him to take the lead role in the social drama both on and off the 'tragic scaffold.' More than that, the final performance was produced as the first act of a tragicomedy – a distinctly royalist genre which would dominate the Restoration theatre, if not also help set that stage, as the epigraph to this chapter announced.[24] 'Doe not we suppose that King *Charles* his life may be the period of our temporall happinesse, and his death the first act of that *tragicall Woe* which is to be presented upon the *Theatre* of this *Kingdome*, likely to continue longer than the now living Spectators?' asks the author of *The Subject's Sorrow*, who identifies Charles's passion with Christ's.[25]

The king's book presented the execution as an event in a succession

process, making it a manifestation of political power. Charles copro-
duces a drama of personal and political history, which elevates monarchy above military success and failure. Though advertising itself as a
private genre, the text performed the rhetorical and political work of
conditioning the imaginative possibility of a restored Stuart monarchy,
to which end chapter 27 (addressed to the Prince of Wales) is especially
directed. '[T]he private reflections of my conscience and my most
impartial thoughts ... may also give you [the Prince] some directions
how to remedy the present distempers and prevent, if God will, the like
for time to come' (EB 158), Charles/Gauden advises the future king,
who momentarily displaces God as addressee.

   The creation of *Eikon Basilike* relied on print as a medium for the
iconic, theatrical, and political, and specifically for 'a posthumous royal
performance' which effected a transference of power to the royalist
cause.[26] Having repeatedly resisted subjection to the judges' 'arbitrary
jurisdiction,' Charles became 'the best advocat and interpreter of his
own actions' in *Eikon Basilike* (E, *CPW*, 3:340). In this court of his making, the defendant appealed to a higher form of justice, and through
acts of self-examination and devotion – for which James I, John Donne,
and George Herbert had provided guides – Charles staged a personal
trial more intense than his state trial.[27] The two kinds of trials were
nevertheless connected figuratively and editorially, as in *The Proceedings
of the High Court of Justice ... Whereunto is added his prayers* (1655).

   The public spectacle of punishment was thus complemented by
Charles's closet drama. James I had maintained that those who judge
the king 'by the outward appearance' would discover his motives, which
serve as 'trunche-men, to interprete the inwarde disposition of the
mind.'[28] In *Eikon Basilike*, Charles transposed the relationship between
the king's two bodies by presenting his meditations as an index for reading his public identity. This act of revelation (through publication)
exploited the belief that access to the private sphere and theatre of
inwardness leads to the truth;[29] and, moreover, that print could provide
privileged access. *The Princely Pellican* captures *Eikon Basilike*'s strategic
negotiation between the private and public spaces; the king 'ingenuously laid Himselfe open ... in a *private addresse* for the *Publick interest*.'[30]
The confessional mode adopted by Charles, in which the reader becomes privy to a private conversation between the king and God, is an
audience-conscious one. At the same time, *Eikon Basilike* detextualizes its
textuality by operating as ritual and prayer, what Charles described as
'the soul's more immediate converse with the Divine Majesty' (EB 95).

Casting himself as a penitent sinner as well as a national martyr, the king established the authenticity of his tragic narrative for the seventeenth-century reader accustomed to viewing the world as a stage and regarding the Christian *mythos* as the basic pattern of life.[31] The book's pious, biblical significance was foregrounded, and correspondingly it was interpreted in poems and sermons alike as a holy relic and 'Golden *Manuall* ... a stately building of Meditations ... raised upon emergent occasions'[32] – a testimony of a sacred, exemplary performance that also recalled Donne's devotions and art of dying.

While displaying a lively portraiture or an artificial miracle, *Eikon Basilike* also took on a life of its own as a material object and as an event in the print culture and political culture of the period. The book was widely distributed in many shapes and sizes and at a wide range of prices from 2*s* 3*d*. to 15*s*.[33] Thirty-five to forty clandestine editions were released in London within one year of its initial appearance in the face of Parliament's efforts at suppressing the book; twenty-five more during the same time in Ireland and abroad. Richard Royston, for whom John Grismond and Roger Norton printed the first edition, and William Dugard, who printed the edition that first contained the King's Prayers, were summoned before the Council of State and arrested soon after the appearance of their respective editions. Thereafter the publisher John Williams defied the ban on publication by producing pocket-size editions, which allowed *Eikon Basilike* readers to carry the image of the king with them – literally and not just imaginatively. At least forty-seven different frontispieces to various editions were issued, thus enabling the text to reach the illiterate through its iconography. The controversy about the king's inscription of Pamela's prayer from Sir Philip Sidney's *Arcadia* only increased the demand for editions, which often contained different numbers of the king's devotions.

The responses generated by the wide distribution of *Eikon Basilike* did not always correspond in a straightforward manner with the ideological alignments of its individual readers. Nor could the identities of the book's readers necessarily be established along predictable political lines. Even parliamentary supporters like Ralph Josselin confess to being moved by the tragedy: 'I was much troubled with the blacke providence of putting the King to death, my teares were not restrained at the passages about his death.'[34]

The matter is further complicated when interpretation is understood as a communal activity enabled through the performative nature of texts as well as through their publication practices and reception histories.[35]

Charles's testimony and textually preserved aesthetic created sympathiz-ers while also contributing to the formation and cementing of royalist communities. *An Elegie upon the Death of Our Dread Sovereign* acknowledges 'Thy *Book* is our best Language; what to this / Shall e're bee added, is Thy *Meiösis*: / Thy *Name's* a *Text* too hard for us: no men / Can write of it, without *Thy Parts* and *Pen.*'[36] As political actors, royalists have more often than their parliamentary counterparts been judged as acting indepen-dently rather than collectively. A revisionary narrative of royalist literary history, in this case in reference to *Eikon Basilike*, heightens our aware-ness of the aesthetic they developed to communicate and strengthen allegiances in the literary/political world during the wars and Interreg-num, as I discuss further in chapter 4.[37] Material culture also shaped roy-alist politics through the iconographic tradition which *Eikon Basilike* exploited. 'Portraits of king and courtiers evoked memories, doubtless sustained royalist communities, and retained mystical, iconic power with plain folk,' Kevin Sharpe explains in his recent study of the failure of republican culture.[38] The iconophobic new regime which held fast to its antitheatrical prejudice could simply not compete, and yet it was pre-cisely this challenge that awaited Milton.

III

Through the print revolution, debates over political authority and king-ship took on a new direction. The discovery of Charles's letters, which were captured at Naseby on 14 June 1645, first unsettled the relation-ship between Charles's private self and outward self-presentation, and furnished Parliament with evidence of the king's behind-the-scenes negotiations. The editor of the king's correspondence uses a theatre metaphor in advertising the publication of the letters in *The King's Cabi-net Opened*: 'the King himselfe has not appeared with an open face in the busines [of Protestant-Catholic conflicts], now by Gods good provi-dence the traverse Curtain is drawn, and the King writing to *Ormond* and the Queen, what they must not disclose, is presented upon the stage.'[39] Milton in turn casts Charles as a 'cheif actor ... overrul'd onely by evil Counselers' (E, *CPW*, 3:594), and charges him with deferring to his 'manly' wife even in political affairs; the letters 'reveal'd his endeavours to bring in forren Forces, Irish, French, Dutch, Lorrainers, and our old Invaders the Danes upon us, besides his suttleties and mysterious arts in treating: to sumn up all, they shewd him govern'd by a Woman' (E, *CPW*, 3:538). As a political contriver, Charles was worse yet, Milton alleges, an imitator of female performances, including that of his Catholic grandmother, Mary Queen of Scots who had exploited the rhetoric of martyrdom (E, *CPW,* 3:597). The contents of the *King's Cabinet* were printed in 1645, but now in *Eikon Basilike* the pivate cabinet was reopened to reveal an inner chamber, the heart and soul of the king. Charles's opponents would have to demonstrate that the chamber was empty or that it was filled with skeletons; to succeed, they would need to subject it to the judgment of a discriminating readership.

The government's preoccupation with justifying political and penal practices in early 1649 resulted in the production of the *Declaration of the Parliament of England.*[40] This treatise was part of a concerted campaign to censor and write over the king's book, which was leaving its imprint on the English cultural and political imagination. While the popularity of texts can be assessed by the extent of efforts made to restrict their circulation, royalists were inclined to exaggerate reports of the censoring of *Eikon Basilike* in order to discredit their enemies: 'these Jewes raged against his Majesties Book, the issue of his Divine Soul, and laboured by all meanes to suppresse it.'[41] *Mercurius Pragmaticus* likewise denounces the Rump Parliament's 'daily search and inquiry at all *Book-sellers* and *Printing-houses,*' and the use of 'more then [*sic*] ordinary violence' against persons found in possession of the book.[42]

The main contest with *Eikon Basilike* materialized in a pamphlet war, ignited by *Eikon alethine,* 'the truthful image.' The authors of *Eikon alethine* and *Eikonoklastes* both insist that they were required to produce their texts, perhaps in response to the king's claim that he was forced to do the same. The frontispiece to *Eikon alethine,* which depicts Charles's behind-the-scenes activities, shows a curtain drawn away by a hand to reveal a divine impersonating the fraudulent king. Charles's image and his history are the fabrications of the divine, who authored the royal actor's allegedly autobiographical text, the *Eikon Basilike,* his 'blacke Babe': 'Presumptuous Preist to skip into the throne, / And make his King his Bastard Issue owne.' As the king's authorship of *Eikon Basilike* is questioned, so is his authority contested. Prefatory verses addressed to the Doctor in *Eikon alethine* identify the ghostwriter as the ever popular Catiline: 'For when I read thy Book, in every line / Appear'd the genius of curst *Catiline* ... I make no doubt the knowing in our Age, / (As fooles did his) will hisse thine off the stage.' The epistle dedicatory censures the gullible people, calling them 'Fooles,' 'Geese,' and 'lame and blinde *Jebusites*' who, having been duped by a clerical forger, now idolize the dead king.[43]

Eikon e piste is a royalist response to this controversy of authorship. The frontispiece again presents a stage scene, but this time a curtain is drawn away to unveil a cavalier placing a jester's cap on the head of the author of *Eikon alethine*, who attempts to 'Murder the issue of the Kings owne braine' by taking credit for the text.[44] The jester grasps the crown of the seated monarch whose authorship of *Eikon Basilike* is authenticated and whose identity is verified: 'Do not then say one skips into his throne; / The Doctor and the King may both be one' (ll. 11–12). In the *Eikon E Piste* frontispiece, both the cavalier and the hand that draws the curtain expose the plot of the king's enemy (see figure 5). Like *Eikon alethine*, *Eikon e piste* dramatizes the revelation of the truth; the introductory line in the verses contained in the two *Eikons* is identical: 'The Curtain's drawne; all may perceive the plot.' Moreover, both texts include the Horatian phrase, 'Spectatum admissi risum teneatis' (Being admitted to the sight, could you restrain your laughter). In *Eikon alethine*, the phrase is used as a caption, whereas in *Eikon e piste*, the words curl around and indict the jester. In both texts, however, the authors create a theatrical space to invite critical readings of the activities behind the curtains of the political stage.

The printing of *Eikon e piste* led the government to take even stricter measures against illegal journalism, but further action yet was required to perform the feat that the regicides had failed to complete; indeed 'the head was not strook off to the best advantage and commodity of them that held it by the hair' (E, *CPW*, 3:346). Commissioned to advance their work, Milton unsheathes his pen to defend the commonwealth.[45] He assumes the role of a governmental agent, as highlighted on the title page of the first edition of *Eikonoklastes* on which the phrase 'Published by Authority' is printed in red ink. Milton seeks in turn to contest the authority and authorship of the king's book. He proceeds deliberately and methodically, along the lines of *Eikon alethine*, to interrogate *Eikon Basilike* point by point, uncovering Charles's borrowed robes and words and his on- and offstage performances.

Eikonoklastes opens – as *Samson Agonistes* would also – by presenting the aftermath of a tragedy, that is, by 'descant[ing] on the misfortunes of a person fall'n from so high a dignity,' despite the unpleasantness of such an endeavour (E, *CPW*, 3:337). Milton analyses the closet drama of the royal actor, appropriating the dramatic terms he used to elevate himself. Thus readers of *Eikonoklastes* (and *Eikon Basilike*) are reminded that 'the general voice of the people almost hiss[ed] [the king] and his ill-acted regality off the Stage' until he was exhorted against his will to

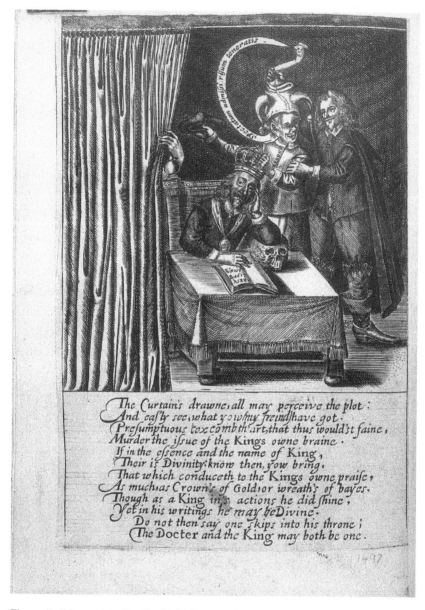

Figure 5. *Eikon e piste. Or, The faithfull pourtraicture of a loyal subject in vindication of Eikon basilike* [London], 1649. © Copyright The British Museum.

summon what would become the Long Parliament (E, *CPW*, 3:355). Milton also condemns the 'licentious remissness of his Sundays Theater' (E, *CPW*, 3:358), and charges Charles with stealing lines from Shakespeare's Richard III, who cheated his way to power by 'speaking in as high a strain of pietie, and mortification, as is utterd in any passage of this Book' (E, *CPW*, 3:361). Stage performance masquerades as piety, Shakespeare being 'the Closet Companion of these his solitudes' (E, *CPW*, 3:361). In a similar vein, John Cook, solicitor for the Commonwealth, argued that Charles would have been vindicated if only he had 'studied Scripture half so much as *Ben: Johnson* or *Shakespear*.'[46] Cook's remarks recall *Mercurius Britanicus*'s accusation, quoted in the prologue to this book, that the ostensibly devotional books of an Anglican minister near Wantage, which were torn apart by Haselrig, were in fact '*Shakespeares* Workes.'[47]

Accepting the challenge to retry Charles in print after death had exonerated him, Milton enlists his readership and posterity in an act of textual exegesis. His faith in his readers and specifically in their ability to judge the king is, however, at best inconsistent throughout *Eikonoklastes*. Like the Commonwealth government, Milton relied on a 'paradoxical conjunction of cooperation and censorship' in his efforts at crowd pleasing and crowd management.[48] On the one hand, Milton casts the people as 'not less then Kings' (E, *CPW*, 3:542) and encourages them to be active interpreters of the images of kingship. He also attempts to transform the mesmerized spectators and idolaters into critics who could make 'the Book thir own rather then the Kings' (E, *CPW*, 3:338). On the other hand, Milton expresses deep resentment at those who have fallen prey to the text's iconography and conceited portraiture, its fictive and representational qualities, and the posturing of a king whom they have vindicated. The people who rallied to Charles's cause are labelled 'fools and silly gazers' (E, *CPW*, 3:342), members of a 'mad multitude' (E, *CPW*, 3:345), a 'fatally stupifi'd and bewitch'd' herd (E, *CPW*, 3:347), and an 'inconstant, irrational, and Image-doting rabble' (E, *CPW*, 3:601). David Norbrook cautions us not to literalize Milton's attacks on the people;[49] yet Milton's disillusion with the multitudes continues to surface in most of his texts thereafter.

The struggle of the people against the authorities had been propelled by the language of *Areopagitica*, but now Milton's defence of freedom of expression and rational thinking is intended for nonconformists who require protection from the public itself. The self-governed 'need not Kings to make them happy, but are the architects of thir own happiness;

and whether to themselves or others are not less then Kings' (E, *CPW*, 3:542). Milton assigns the fit though few a role as enlightened readers of Charles's last great show and rhetorical performances: 'For in words which admitt of various sense, the libertie is ours to choose that interpretation which may best minde us of what our restless enemies endeavor, and what wee are timely to prevent' (E, *CPW*, 3:342). With this proposal, Milton urges a reinterpretation of Charles's text. A critical reading of the theatrics of kingship becomes an act of textual analysis, political intervention, and justice.

Eikonoklastes was issued in two versions in 1649; it was revised and enlarged in the following year, translated into Latin and French, and answered by Joseph Jane's text *Eikon Aklastos* in 1651. *Eikon Aklastos* itself posed no threat to Milton; Edward Hyde did not consider it worth translating into French, though such a translation could have helped the royalist cause in counteracting the effect of Milton's treatise. Still Jane's text did testify that the cause of royalism was gaining momentum through the king's book, as it casts a critical eye on those who misjudged and condemned Charles: 'Upon the comming foorth of the booke, they found what they feared, that many, whose passion kept them from a right judgement in the heate of Action, saw their owne errours in that booke.'[50] *Eikon Aklastos* implies, moreover, that Charles had been vindicated and memorialized through his book: 'His Majest:booke hath passed the censure of the greatest part of the learned world, being translated into the most spred Languages, and strangers honour his Memory, and abhorre his murtherers.'[51] The presses, then, served to advance the cause and victory of royalism; this was anticipated by Jane, among others, who wrote in support of the restoration of kingship.

IV

The general public did not share the view of the situation which Milton, Parliament's most celebrated writer, had championed. While *Eikonoklastes* was being written, a collective memory, fed by a material and print culture which achieved a kind of social control, kept Charles's image in circulation. At a time when the printed book became identified with the corpus carrying the life and spirit of the author, *Eikon Basilike* in whole and in parts began the process of resuscitating royalism.[52] The reprints and representative editions of the book bore a synecdochic relationship to the whole, just as the king's relics were invested with a life-giving power.

Like his book, the king's material possessions were stamped with their owner's identity and also judged as immutable – even in the market-place. *New-Market-Fayre*, which satirizes the sale of the king's property by greedy, self-destructive Grandees, reinforces this idea. The 'royalist' playlet opens with a cryer at Westminster advertising the king's mer-chandise as 'Jewels of wondrous price':

> Here be Cabbinets with *letters*,
> To instruct all your *betters*;
> His *Meditations* and *Prayer-Booke*,
> In which all Nations may look;
> Here is his *Haire*, and *royall blood*,
> Shed for his Subjects *good*;
> Here be his *Liberaryes* and *books*,
> And Pictures that contain his *looks*;
> Here you may all things *buy*
> That belong to *Monarchy*.[53]

Despite itemizing the king's possessions seized from his cabinet, the cat-alogue resists any random distribution of the goods, and in fact trans-forms them into keepsakes, memorabilia, and relics intended for the edification of the people. On the streets of London, however, royalist vendors with an entrepreneurial spirit capitalized on profits made from the beheading. Even the soldiers took advantage of the demand for rel-ics. Meanwhile, Richard Royston, Francis Eglesfield, John Williams, and a fourth publisher, probably Henry Seile, who between them handled nearly all the English printed editions of *Eikon Basilike*, worked together and traded in each other's productions. The king's book had become one of the relics.

Eikon Basilike was compared to a treasure chest of the king's hidden valuables. The text was in fact designed to be a type of cabinet-literature or 'bookish "cabinet[]" contain[ing] spiritual and literary jewels,' which relied on a strategic and 'paradoxical partnership of secrecy and publica-tion.'[54] Abraham Wright's poem on *Eikon Basilike*, 'Upon the Kings-Book bound up in a Cover coloured, with His Blood,' compares the king's book to a treasure of which the frontispiece portraying the king's spiritual preparation for passion and martyrdom is the book's crowning jewel: 'although thou [Eikon Basilike] be / A Book, where every leafe's a Library / Fil'd with choise Gems of th'Arts, Law, Gospel; yet / The chief-est jewel is the Cabinet.'[55] The poem also commends the closet performance of Juxon, who serves as the king's counsellor and then as the treasurer of his precious book. 'Upon the Kings Book bound up on a Cover coloured with His Blood,' another poem in Wright's volume, reinforces the significance of the frontispiece: 'although thou [*Eikon Basilike*] be / A Book, where every leafe's a Library / Fil'd with choise Gems of th'Arts, Law, Gospel; yet / The chiefest Jewel is the Cabinet.'[56] The king himself referred to his conscience as an 'incommunicable jewel' (EB 53), which he, 'contrary to what is heer profess'd,' puts on display through the publication of his private communion with God (E, *CPW*, 3:459).

The theatrical imagery on the frontispiece of *Eikon Basilike* and the performance of the frontispiece as a material object in the marketplace go hand in hand. As an emblematic 'Masking Scene' (E, *CPW*, 3:342), the frontispiece achieved the same effects as the art works of the Caroline court which commemorated the dead king. Nigel Smith explains how the political work of the masques was furthered after the regicide: 'The masques ... famous for amplifying the reputation of Charles as peacemaker and absolute power in the kingdom, *froze* the image of the King in order to glorify his earthly power. Now dead, not unrelated art forms turn the really frozen King (in *rigor mortis*) into pieces of literary memory for the future.'[57] But the visually preserved performance in *Eikon Basilike* – which through its change of title from '*Suspiria Regalia*, or The Royal Plea' foregrounded the visual over the verbal – manages to present the king to the people in a way that the masques could not. Turgid and overrehearsed, the masques imposed a barrier between court and kingdom by enabling the king to occupy a fantasy world in which he was represented as the ideal ruler at a time of nation-wide upheaval. Milton had this kind of performance in mind when he remarked cynically: 'quaint Emblems and devices begg'd from the old Pageantry of some Twelf-nights entertainment at *Whitehall*, will doe but ill to make a Saint or Martyr' (E, *CPW*, 3:343). The last masque performed by Charles's court was Sir William Davenant's *Salmacida Spolia* on Twelfth Night, 1640. The final act showed Henrietta Maria coming from the heavens to calm the Fury, and Charles descending from his golden throne to restore harmony on-stage and offstage where his rule was failing miserably.[58] But another stage was required to enact a restoration of order and the scaffold became that stage, one on which Charles made his last appearance. The script for the performance was *Eikon Basilike*, through which the performance would also be read.

Besides the frontispiece, the most influential parts of *Eikon Basilike* were the devotions and chapter 27 'Intitil'd to the Prince of Wales.' Combining the dual purposes of the book as a prayer book and political manual, *The*

Princely Pellican refers to the *Eikon Basilike* as 'a *Living Memoriall* of Princely piety, and devotion, to all Posterities recommended' (1). That *Eikon Basilike* had captured the political imagination of its readers was acknowledged in royalist writings. *Eikon Aklastos* noted that the devotions and instructions in the king's book proved threatening to his opponents (10); and *An Elegie upon the Death of Our Dread Sovereign* reacts against the book's suppression: 'Are Thy *Devotions* dangerous? Or do / Thy *Praiers* want a Guard? These faultie too?' (ll. 44–5).[59]

Separate editions of the devotions and chapter 27 were also produced. Reprints of the prayers appear in *His Majesties Prayers Which He used in time of his suffering* (1649); *The Divine Penitential Meditations and Vowes of his Late Sacred Majestie at Holmby House, Faithfully Turned into Verse* (1649); *The Proceedings of the High Court of Justice ... whereunto is added his prayers* (1655); and Richard Watson's *The Royall Votarie* (1660) which consists of short paraphrases in various metres of the prayers in the first nineteen chapters of *Eikon Basilike*. The king's devotions lent themselves not only to private readings; they were in fact read out loud and even sung after being translated into verse and set to music in Thomas Stanley's famous *Psalterium Carolinum. The Devotions of his Sacred Majesty*, published just before the Restoration. Milton presumably refers to the *Psalterium* in *Eikonoklastes* when he observes that the King's book 'might perhaps be intended a peece of Poetrie ... there wanted onely Rime, and that, they say, is bestow'd upon it lately' (E, *CPW*, 3:406), in which case Stanley's manuscript draft must have been completed before October 1649.

Chapter 27 was reprinted in texts, such as *King Charles His Farewell. Left as a Legacy to his deare Children* (1649), *The Kingly Myrrour, Or King Charles His last Legacy to the Prince His Son* (1649), and *Eikon Basilike Or, The True Pourtraiture Of His Sacred Majestie Charls the II* (1660). *King Charles His Farewell* contains both the prayers and chapter 27. The frequent printing of these two sections of *Eikon Basilike* in particular shows how – and why – the king's book was read as a private-public document. As a devotional text, *Eikon Basilike* succeeded in enshrining the king's memory in the hearts of the people; as a mirror for magistrates, it envisioned a future for monarchy that was reserved not only for a post-temporary period.

Numerous texts like *Eikon Basilike, or The True Portraiture of His Sacred Majesty Charles II* were made in the image of the 1649 *Eikon Basilike*. Charles II's *Eikon Basilike* bore the impression of Charles I, including the famous frontispiece. Other texts were redesigned to remember the king and *Eikon Basilike*. A 1636 edition of the *Book of Common Prayer*, used by

Charles for worship, later became an 'Eikon Basilike' which memorialized the king himself and provided a gloss for reading his private devotions. This specific edition of the *Book of Common Prayer* was rebound by Charles II (and evidently not sold at New-Market-Fayre). John Boyle's 1731 inscription in the text underscores the correspondence between Charles's closeted activities and his public affairs which the king sought to reinforce through print: 'This was King Charles the 1st's Common Prayer Book: which he used in his Closett, and which was carried by him wherever he travell'd, even to the Day of his Death.' The frontispiece from *Eikon Basilike* serves as the new cover for the *Prayer Book*, and several woodcuts by the artist W. Faithorne (dated 1653) are placed throughout the rest of the book. They include scenes from the life of Christ, pictures of all the apostles, and representations of the Virgin Mary. But the king's portraiture now headed the gallery exhibition.[60]

Through the publication of *Eikon Basilike* and its numerous offshoots, Charles's private and public selves were reconciled, while the king's natural body – onto which the nation's divisiveness became inscribed – was reunited with the body politic. The work of re-membering was advanced by royalist iconography, in which the severed head was usually put back in place, and even in parliamentarian defences, in which it was placed just out of view. By contrast, the early Restoration iconography and printed texts that portrayed the executions of the regicides foregrounded dismemberment, as is the case with the broadsheet *A True and Perfect Relation of the Grand Traytors Execution, as at severall times they were Drawn, Hang'd, and Quartered* (1660).[61] A scene littered with body parts is juxtaposed with an illustration of the king on the scaffold solemnly beckoning to Bishop Juxon, perhaps to give him the famous, cryptic injunction 'remember.' In body, spirit, and image, the king transcended anatomization.

Eikon Basilike had displaced the king's body and yet bore a synecdochic relationship to the author, thus validating Milton's observation in the *Areopagitica* that books are infused with the 'pretious life-blood of a master spirit' (*CPW* 2:493). The alleged ritualistic burning of *Eikon Basilike*, for which sectarians even into the Augustan period would be charged, was judged as a reenactment of the execution:

Soon as the Blood-hounds have by Symbol kill'd
The *King* afresh, and their curs'd Stomachs fill'd,
To shew they're worse than *Heathens, Jews* or *Turks*,
They in Derision burn his pious Works.[62]

Eikonoklastes was likewise burnt by the common hangman in 1660 as a symbolic, sacrificial offering and as a sign of the restored monarchy's triumph in war and words. Yet the inefficacy of the text had already been established; it proved to be no match for *Eikon Basilike*, and could not stem the tide of proroyalist sentiment to which the king's book contributed. The failure of the commonwealth, together with the work undertaken by the royalists to keep kingship alive, established the conditions for the Restoration. While *Eikon Basilike* had imagined the events of 1660 rather than actually determining them, the book was accorded the victory; in the year of the Restoration *Virtus Rediviva* proclaims the king's noble triumph through his 'Royal Portraicture, drawn by himself.'[63]

As a private-public performance, an icon, and as an event in the writing of royalist history, the king's book transcended the medium of print on which it relied. Moreover, the power invested in the text by the conditions of its circulation and interpretation rendered it impervious to the critique to which even its most famous reader subjected it. Milton's final response to royalist culture and politics thus takes the form of a dramatic poem unintended for stage performance, which appeals to a select, like-minded readership. *Samson Agonistes* attempts to advance the political and aesthetic work of *Eikonoklastes*, *Eikonoklastes* being an event in Milton's development towards the time he would write *Samson Agonistes* as an alternative closet drama and drama of justice.[64] Like *Eikonoklastes*, *Samson Agonistes* protests against stage acts, which are identified with royalist culture. Milton makes aestheticism part of the larger program of cultural and political 'purification' when he attacks the mixing of genres in the prefaces to both texts. Impurity of genre characterizes the king's book and marks it as a motley composition, in effect, a tragicomedy, a genre with which Milton would continue to do battle in the Restoration. In its immediate, material context, *Samson Agonistes*, as I briefly discuss in the epilogue, would, however, be no more successful in upstaging Restoration tragicomedy than *Eikonoklastes* was in dismantling Charles's 'Stage-work' in *Eikon Basilike*. In the years between the publication of *Eikonoklastes* and that of *Samson Agonistes*, the royalists, as we observe in the following chapter, would resuscitate and sustain an underground theatre culture and community, and thereby advance the work performed by Charles on 30 January 1649 of reclaiming the political stage.

Chapter 4

'Yet we may Print the Errors of the Age': Tyranny on Trial

> But whilst you reign, our low Petition craves
> That we, the King's true Subjects, and your Slaves
> May in our Comick Mirth and Tragick Rage
> Set ope the Theatre and shew the Stage;
> The Shop of Truth and Fancy, where we vow
> Not to act any thing you'l disallow ...
> Your Tragedies more real are exprest,
> You murther men in earnest, we in jeast ...
> Since ye have sat, your play is almost done,
> As well as ours, would't had ne're been begun;
> But we shall finde, e're the last Act be spent,
> *Enter the King, Exit the Parliament,*
> *And hey then up go we, who by the frown*
> Of guilty Members have been voted down.
> Yet you may still remain, and sit, and vote,
> And through your own beam see your brothers mote,
> Until a legal tryal shew how
> Y'ave us'd the *King, and hey then up go you,*
> So pray your humble slaves (with all their powers)
> That when they have their due you may have yours.
>   Thomas Jordan, 'The Players Petition to the Long Parliament'

The theatre had traditionally served as a charged territory and as a site of affiliation and social formation.[1] Developing alongside theatre culture was an antitheatrical prejudice, which became the subject of paper-contestations throughout the late sixteenth and early seventeenth centuries, culminating in William Prynne's *Historiomastix*. Nevertheless, the concerns about the social and moral dangers posed by the theatres during the seventeenth century were resolved to some degree by the establishment of more private playhouses and the greater respectability attributed to play-going. Moreover, the possibility that the theatres might give way to reformed stages and stage productions was also entertained, though Prynne remained sceptical. In the place of drama performances, he extols in *Historiomastix* the virtues of dramatic verse, which he judges as '*usefull and commendable among Christians*, if rightly used.' Prynne went on to identify various exemplary ancient and modern poets and playwrights, including Gregory Nazianzen and George Buchanan, whose use of the dramatic mode he approved. In such cases, readerly engagement with drama is not only permissible but the only appropriate response to the playwrights whose works 'were never acted but recited onely, they being composed for Readers, not for Spectators, for private studies, not publicke Playhouses, as our present Stageplayes are.'[2]

This transference of the theatre experience into the writing, printing, and reading of plays to which Prynne alludes was already enacted in the productions of the anticourt Senecan tragedies of the Sidney circle – inspired by Buchanan's antipersecution drama. Play-reading served not only as a way of ensuring the 'wholesome' consumption of dramatic works but also as an act of textual revolt and political resistance. In the mid-seventeenth century, the predominantly royalist dramatic political allegories and satires which aimed, as Thomas Jordan's poem suggested, to restore justice to the royalist cause encouraged play-reading as a politically charged activity.[3] Building, then, on discussions of performance and its migration from the stage to the printed page in the antiestablishment drama of the new Parliament and the mock-tragedies and political dialogues produced by royalist supporters, this chapter investigates the realignment of the dramatic and tragic modes as well as the practices used by writers to prompt politically partisan acts of reading that arraign those who managed to evade 'publick Trial.'[4] As sites of judgment, these writings, which serve as a type of closet drama – a private-public genre – enabled meaningful interventions in political discourse: while parliamentary-sponsored tragedies anatomized tyranny through classical and biblical models, royalist mock-tragedies looked ahead to tragicomedy, which would dominate the Restoration theatrical and political stages.[5]

Parliament was certainly conscious of the role dramatic productions could perform in shaping political and communal identities, even though the issuing of the August 1642 *Special order ... concerning Irregular Printing, and ... the suppressing of all false and Scandalous Pamphlets* and the subsequent closure of the theatres (and bear gardens) were likely motivated by an urgent need to quell civil unrest and sedition.[6] The printed version of the 2 September 1642 ordinance appeared as part of a two-page document, titled *A Declaration of the Lords and Commons ... For the appeasing and quietting of all unlawfull Tumults and Insurrections ... Also an Ordinance of both Houses for the suppressing of Stage-Plays.* Instability in Ireland and internal unrest in England, which is described in some detail in the first declaration, called for a period of solemnity and not mirth. The question of the moral content of plays remained unaddressed while the order concentrated instead on the inappropriateness of festivities during a period of crisis: 'while these sad Causes and set times of Humiliation doe continue, publicke Stage-Plays shall cease, and bee forborne. Instead of which, are recommended to the People of this Land, the profitable and seasonable Considerations of Repentance, Reconciliation, and Peace with God.'[7]

Though primarily a security measure to forestall riotous assemblies, Parliament's closure of the theatres after the outbreak of war did indeed gratify the antitheatre lobbyists while also inhibiting the dramatizing of popular grievances and spreading of royalist propaganda by court companies. The management of theatricalized political discourse initially involved curtailing the activities of the theatre and the playwrights. But, as we discover more explicitly in the 1648 Ordinance against stage performances, spectators themselves proved to be a threat to the regime and were punished accordingly.

I

Having passed the first ordinance against play-acting, state officials nevertheless conceded that reformed dramas might be permissible under the conditions like those outlined by Prynne or in the case of government-sponsored works like *Tyrannicall-Government Anatomized.* Parliament ordered the printing of this translation of George Buchanan's *Baptistes* by the House of Commons Committee Concerning Printing in 1642/3. It may even have allowed actual performances of plays as stately and lofty as this, but the appeal of the play resides primarily in the topicality of its dramatized political and polemical commentary, which is overlaid with biblical history.

While mainly reserved for royalist textual performances, this chapter begins by reviewing the received tradition of *Tyrannicall-Government Anatomized*[8] under the rubric of *closet drama*, printed plays designed to be read rather than (or as well as) staged,[9] which served as vehicles for the formation of alternative interpretive and political communities. I situate this rare example of a parliamentary-sponsored play not only in relation to its literary inheritance but also in the cultural and political moment in which it was printed, and the reading experience it conditioned. I conclude with observations on the contested but intriguing attribution of *Tryannicall-Government* to John Milton[10] as polemicist and author of *Samson Agonistes* (1671) – the subject of the epilogue to this book. In the Restoration when the commercial theatre became the dominant royalist venue for drama in terms of both status and popularity, Milton, an admirer of Buchanan's poetics and politics, produces an antiestablishment closet drama that offers 'an internalised, read-only, version of that collective experience'[11] enabled by the theatre.

The sixteenth-century Scottish humanist, poet, and reformer George Buchanan was the most famous author of Christian tragedies in his day, and among the first writers of Senecan tragedies. Buchanan's plays imitate the structure of those of Euripides, whose *Alcestis* and *Medea* he rendered into Latin. Between 1541 and 1544, he produced his first biblical tragedy, *Baptistes Sive Calumnia*, a blank verse tragedy on the arrest and death of John the Baptist, which was performed in Bordeaux in the 1540s, presented in manuscript to Daniel Rogers in 1566, and then printed in 1577. The frontmatter for *Baptistes* includes Buchanan's 1 November 1576 dedication to James VI in which he recommends the use of the stage in imitating the classics, inspiring morality, and denouncing tyranny. The dedication is followed by a prologue which includes the commonplace lament about the protean nature of audiences who indiscriminately attack theatrical productions. The true judge of his play is one who applies skill and moral sense ('aestimator candidus'), Buchanan maintains, and who recognizes that he as the playwright is aspiring to a higher or purer form of literary expression in staging the tragedy of the Baptist. The thrice repeated reference to 'calumnies' in the Latin prologue links the description of the fickle audiences to the murderers of the Baptist, and thus connects the trials of the playwright (and the historical Buchanan) to those of the Baptist as martyr. While originally intended for performance by Buchanan's pupils, including Montaigne, *Baptistes* was judged to be a closet drama by

Stephen Gosson, among others, who claimed that the moralizing and didactic effect of Buchanan's *Baptistes* depended upon the reading experience it conditioned.[12]

Though Buchanan was not connected to the Sidney circle, his play has much in common with the overtly political, anticourt productions by members of this group.[13] The classicizing dramas examine theories of monarchy, tyranny, and rebellion by treating the evils of absolutism and the duties and corruption of kings and royal favourites. Generic features include the trappings of Italianate Senecanism; the primacy of speech and narrative over action; long rhetorical monologues and philosophical and moral discourses; the casting of women as heroes and villains; and the inclusion of a nuntius, as well as of a chorus that speaks from a limited rather than an authoritative position. The closet drama, moreover, provides an effective medium for staging the conflicts of a social rebel. The reader's assignment to assess the heroic nature of this controversial figure is inevitably frustrated by the play's resistance to any conclusive judgments about the protagonist.

The appeal of *Baptistes* extended beyond its dual function as a play and readerly text. Readily lending itself to allegorization, *Baptistes* also served as political commentary, and was interpreted variously as a warning against Henry VIII's marriage to Anne Boleyn, a condemnation of Henry for his execution of Sir Thomas More, and an admonition to James VI of Scotland (Buchanan's pupil) about the evils of tyranny, specifically, his attachments to the Scottish Catholic nobility. When brought before the Lisbon Inquisition in 1550, Buchanan under oath took poetic license in declaring that 'in qua quantum materiae similitudo' (so far as the likeness of the material would permit), the tragedy was about Sir Thomas More, Anne Boleyn, and Henry VIII, a statement which Buchanan might have offered to appease the authorities. Buchanan's explanation about the political subtext remained unknown until the publication of the Lisbon documents in the 1890s; but even when this interpretation surfaced, it did not settle the question about the play's significance.[14] Since he had become a Protestant by the time of his trial, it is all the more curious that Buchanan now cast his protagonist as a Catholic martyr rather than the Protestant reformer he was assumed to be. Still Buchanan's latest interpretation would have met with approval from the authorities on the Continent. No evidence exists of the extent to which Buchanan's inquisitors were satisfied with his response or whether they had even read the now lost manuscript play.[15] What we do know, however, is that *Baptistes*' status as a printed work, its association with Buchanan as the Scottish champion of Protestantism, and its amenability to political allegorization facilitated its entry into seventeenth-century political culture and literary history.

While *Tyrannicall-Government Anatomized* – the English translation of *Baptistes* – is a rare, if not unique, example of a parliamentary-sponsored play, we should not assume that MPs unilaterally opposed drama. Certainly the examinations in chapters 2 and 3 of Parliament's staging of the three famous trials of the 1640s offer extensive evidence of the government's reliance on theatricality in negotiating judicial and political relations. But dramatic conventions are also commonly featured in parliamentary-issued writings, which serve in turn as alternative playtexts and include legal proceedings, parliamentary speeches, trial accounts, pamphlets, and satires. The release of *Tyrannicall-Government Anatomized* itself followed shortly after Parliament first printed speeches and newsbooks. Taken together, these various writings shifted the theatre to the political stage, the courtroom, and the court of public opinion. The ensuing war of words was played out in writings with dramatic conventions and performative effects, many of which 'staged debates and posed questions, bringing to print culture the dialogic genre and space of drama in which, in the end, the reader or auditor has to choose and perform.'[16] As Kevin Sharpe notes, a large number of the Thomason Tracts raise questions and present arguments and cases in dramatic forms. These new politicized playtexts were designed to combine playreading with critical participation, for which *Tyrannicall-Government Anatomized* was likewise intended.

Translated into a theatricalized readerly prose text, *Tyrannicall-Government Anatomized* omits the frontmatter to *Baptistes*, including Buchanan's 1 November 1576 dedication to James VI and the Prologue on the protean audience. The parts into which *Tyrannicall-Government Anatomized*, unlike *Baptistes*, is divided, make it more conducive to reading while inviting an interpretation of the work as a drama. Simultaneously exposing and disguising the text's original verse form, the translator renders his intentions unclear. The motives for reissuing the play are, however, apparent when considered in relation to events on England's political stage; these events open the text up to new meanings. The issue of justice is explored through the exposition of interiority, particularly that of Herod, to which a readerly text best lends itself. The role of judge is ascribed to readers who are privy to the play's central irony: tyrants are most tormented when they seem most powerful. *Tyrannicall-Government Anatomized* thus dramatizes the trial or case of conscience – what William Ames in the seventeenth century defined as 'a practical question concerning which the conscience may make a doubt.'[17] Popularized by parliamentarians and royalists alike, this mode was used to publish the struggles of conscience or (mock) confessions of political opponents, thus legitimizing past or proposed acts of justice. Trials of conscience corresponded in various ways with the scripted final speeches criminals on the scaffold/ stage were expected to recite during spectacles of punishment.

The publication of the translated *Baptistes* thus involved the translation of sixteenth-century political history into seventeenth-century events. Buchanan, it seems, had been right about the ongoing relevance of the attack on tyranny dramatized in *Baptistes* and about the play's reliance on allegorical associations which catered to popular political interpretive practices.[18] Curiously the 1643 title page indicates the translation was 'Presented to the KINGS most Excellent MAJESTY by the Author,' in this case the son of the monarch to whom *Baptistes* was dedicated. Perhaps Parliament was mentoring Charles's tutor, in light of the tutorial role that Buchanan played for James. Read as seventeenth-century political allegory, *Tyrannicall-Government Anatomized* casts Charles as Herod, Henrietta Maria as Herod's wife, and Parliament as John himself. The tyrant and his female accomplice are now allied with Catholicism, while the protagonist is properly Protestant again. In the eighteenth century, Francis Peck develops the allegorical correspondences by identifying Herod with Charles I; Herodias and her daughter with 'the one character of Q. HENRIETTA MARIA'; Malchus with Archbishop Laud; Gamaliel with Bishop Williams; John the Baptist with William Prynne; the nuntius with the 'rumor' that is generated 'to surmise the intended making away of PRYNNE'; and the Chorus of Jews with the Chorus of English puritans.[19]

The afterlife of *Baptistes* is also evidenced in other classical, Senecan dramatic writings that made occasional appearances in the Interregnum. *The Tragedy of That Famous Roman Oratour Marcus Tullius Cicero* is perhaps the best example thereof. Printed during the Commonwealth in 1651 by Richard Cotes – appointed the official printer to the City of London in 1642 – the play created a mythic vocabulary for and was used to validate republicanism, while also continuing the tradition of the Greville circle's antityrant drama.[20] In the play, the poet, Laureas, assigns to the historian, Tyro, the nuntius's task of 'tell[ing] ... the Tragick story' (E3v). The account of Cicero's demise is presented as a dialogue, in accordance with the conventional use of a nuntius in classical tragedies and in their early modern counterparts, including

Tyrannicall-Government Anatomized and *Samson Agonistes*. In *The Tragedy of
... Cicero*, the tragic hero ultimately opts for death rather than the
destruction of his *Philippics* – his political writing. Reporting the dismemberment of Cicero, Tyro describes the amputation of the hands
'that wrote those glorious *Philippicks*,' to which Laureas responds: 'Those
illustrious hands / Which once held up this tottering Common-wealth, /
And set her on her feet, when she was falling / From her proud orbe
into a gulph of Fire' (E4r). The composition of the prorepublican work
which outlives its author is, like the production of *The Tragedy of... Cicero*,
not just an act of textual revolt but of political engagement.

The most renowned apologist for republicanism in the period, one
whose antiregicide treatises were featured in a book burning by the
restored monarchy, was Milton. His contribution to the antityrant discourse in both the political and literary spheres is formidable. Among
his models was George Buchanan, and long before composing his readerly drama, *Samson Agonistes* – interpreted here as a product of the 1660s
– Milton situated himself in a canon of his own making that included
Buchanan. In his attack in the *Second Defence* on the excesses of popular
tragedy, Milton invokes Buchanan's art as the expression of a counterculture: 'Now, poets who deserve the name I love and cherish, and I
delight in hearing them frequently. Most of them, I know, are bitterly
hostile to tyrants, if I should list them from the first down to our own
Buchanan' (*CPW*, 4:592). Poetics and politics go hand in hand for Milton. Moreover, like Buchanan, Milton recognized 'the radical politics of
his own reading' and the role of the reader in securing revolution.[21]
And while play-reading specifically would be lent a sense of deficiency
after the waning of humanism and certainly after the reopening of the
royalist theatres in the Restoration,[22] Milton would insist on the restor-
ative nature of this form of critical and political engagement for his like-
minded readers, whom he distinguishes from the audiences captivated
by Charles I's 'Stage-work.' The readership 'hypothesized' by Milton or
'postulated' by *Samson Agonistes*, for example, would be familiar with the
Aristotelian theory of catharsis; the philosophy of Cicero and Plutarch;
the works of Seneca and Martial; and with the Renaissance tragedies of
Italian playwrights who adhere to the models of the ancients. The best
judges of *Samson Agonistes* would, moreover, not be unacquainted with
the greatest Greek playwrights, Aeschylus, Sophocles, and Euripides –
'the three Tragic poets unequall'd yet by any' who offer models for the
design of the plot.[24]

Milton's commitment to classically educated readers and dramatic prescriptions is not the only satisfactory explanation for his composition of a closet drama. *Samson Agonistes* needs to be examined in light of Milton's concern to problematize closeted performances and encourage critical reading as an alternative practice. While its lofty style and classical sources distance the poem from the vulgar, *Samson Agonistes* nevertheless speaks to an antiestablishment culture through its visionary politics, its redefinition of authority and heroic performance, and the conflicting interpretations it presents. *Samson Agonistes* might accordingly be said to perpetuate the tradition of *Baptistes* and its 'Englished' counterpart, *Tyrannicall-Government Anatomized*. Though the attribution of *Tyrannicall-Government Anatomized* to Milton has all but been dismissed, it continues to be cited by contemporary critics of the play,[24] and informs the received tradition of both *Baptistes* and *Samson Agonistes*. More important, however, an examination of the interrelated production and reception histories of the three closet dramas demonstrates the transgressive nature of play-reading as a classical as well as an early modern cultural, polemical, and political practice.

II

While party politics may not have been consolidated until the Restoration, it did materialize in a 'nexus of customs and cultural practices.' Because kingship was so firmly entrenched as a cultural phenomenon, royalism emerged as an ideological phenomenon that resisted the representation and delegation of power by the Cromwellian government.[25] During the mid-century, disempowered promonarchists and defenders of the Established Church deployed the language of drama and theatrical performance to signal political transgression and develop coteries and communities defined by an awareness of shared discourses.[26] Often identified as retreating in the years of the Civil War and the Interregnum, royalist writers in fact turned to alternative dramatic modes, satire, closet dramas, and political allegory in prose and verse (not to mention romance and historical fiction) to register their response to current events and thus to engage the public, political world from which they allegedly withdrew.[27]

Royalist writers' interactions with readers are central to the success of their ideological struggles, as well as their art of political critique. Their engagements are played out most directly in the front matter of dramatic texts. Edmond Rookwood's contribution to the front matter, 'For Plays,' in *The Queen, or the Excellency of Her Sex* states: 'And Crimes escap'd all other laws, have been, / Found out, and punish'd by the curious Scene,' the exposure of vice being one of the theatre's main roles. In a second dedication to Alexander Goughe in the same play, the publisher announces: 'in the Theatre men are easier caught, / Then by what is in clamorous pulpits taught.'[28] Identifying the printed play as an alternative to staged performances, R.C.'s commendatory dedication to Goughe casts the reader as judge to whom the issue of the 'guiltles presse' is presented:

> Is it unlawfull since the stage is down
> To make the press act: where no ladies swoune
> At the red coates intrusion: none are strip't;
> No Hystriomastix has the copy whip't
> No man d'on Womens cloth's: the guiltles presse
> Weares its own innocent garments: its own dresse,
> Such as free nature made it: Let it come
> Forth Midwife *Goughe*, securely; and if some
> Like not the make or beautie of the play
> Bear witnes to 't and confidently say
> Such a relict as once the stage did own,
> Ingenuous Reader, merits to be known. (A3r)

The front matter thus politicizes theatrical discourse and the language of tragedy, theatrical performance having become a metaphor for political transgression. The publication of royalist tragic modes was similarly and provocatively intended to expose the truth and invite a reinterpretation of the tragic events in the political theatre. The execution of Charles, as royalists regularly lamented, had made the production and staging of tragedies impossible.

But theatrical performances continued, as suggested by the appearance of the government's ordinance '*to suppresse Stage-playes, Interludes, and common Playes.*' Like its 1642 predecessor, the 1647 Ordinance was contained in a two-part document. The first part declared the appointment of city officials in plague-stricken Chester, while the second part focused on the restoration of civic order in London, which entailed the arrest of all actors on charges of roguery. Reinforced restrictions on public performance put a greater emphasis on reading as resistance. While the experience of reading a text, as opposed to viewing a performance as part of an audience, might be considered a solitary undertaking, the reader's participation in interpreting a common set of codes facilitated the development of discursive communities. Published by the 'guiltles presse,' playtexts also exposed the hidden thoughts and motives of the playwrights and the behind-the-scenes activities not shown to audiences of staged plays. In such cases, the cabinet-literature and closet drama – printed plays that were not (or no longer) intended for performance – relied on the revelatory power of print. In his address to the reader in the 1647 Beaumont and Fletcher volume, Humphrey Moseley, the royalist publisher of the volume, declares the victory of print over stage performances: 'When these *Comedies* and *Tragedies* were presented on the Stage, the *Actours* omitted some *Scenes* and Passages (with the *Authour's* consent) as occasion led them ... But now you have both All that was *Acted,* and all that was not; even the perfect full Originalls without the least mutilation.'[29] Referring to '*this* Tragicall Age *where the* Theater *hath been so much out-acted,*' James Shirley in a Preface to the Beaumont and Fletcher volume wrote: '*thou has a liberty to reade these inimitable Playes*' (A3). Through prefaces, prologues, epilogues, dedications, provocative stage directions, dramatic signals, and metadramatic remarks – which Roger Chartier identifies as textual 'machinery'[30] – the playwright organized prescribed reading while also negotiating his/her relationship with readers – the visible, the invisible, and the imagined. Transforming the volume into a readerly text, the added postscript underscores the interest in reader orientation: 'We forgot to tell the *Reader,* that some *Prologues* and *Epilogues* (here inserted) were not written by the *Authours* of this *Volume;* but made by others on the *Revivall* of severall *Playes*' (G2). The relegation of plays to print also called for a renegotiated relationship between playwrights and editors, as well as between popular and elite cultures since the elite now also read unproduced or badly produced plays.

The play as book thus became an increasingly important concept. Among the other collections appearing at this time were that of James Shirley (1647, 1653), William Cartwright, (1651), Massinger in 1655, and Brome in 1653 and 1659. Richard Meighen issued in 1656 *Three Excellent Tragœdies,* second editions of Thomas Goffe's plays. The new edition offers the reader a different kind of interpretive experience that invites comparative analysis. The printed plays 'come forth together from the Presse,' Meighen explains, 'neerer allyed ... in this their second birth.'[31] Attached to the edition is a list of books sold by Gabriell Bedell and Thomas Collins in 1656, which includes plays in quarto by Jonson, Davenant, Fletcher, and Shakespeare. Somewhat less enthusiastic about the move from performance to print and the circumstances that precipitated it, '*A Prœludium to Mr. Richard Bromes Playes*' announces: 'Then we shall still have *Playes*! and though we may / Not them in their full Glories yet display; / Yet we may please our selves by reading them, / Till a more Noble Act this Act condemne.'[32] An edition of five additional Brome comedies, printed in 1659, complicates the relationship between readers and play-goers: the preface, 'To the Readers,' begins with a qualification: 'Or rather *to the Spectators*, if the Fates so pleas'd, these *Comedies* exactly being dressed for the *Stage*.'[33] While acknowledging that the plays are not designed for performance, Alexander Brome, editor of the volume, caters to the consumers' interest in 'new' releases: 'We suppose we bring what in these dayes you scarce could hope for, *Five new Playes*. We call them *new* because 'till now they never were printed.' The edition of Brome's works, moreover, shields readers from the harsher realities of the political stage: 'They are all *Comedies*, for (a man would think) we have had too many *Tragedies*. But this Book knew them not' (A3v).

As anonymous and cheap productions, play books and playlets could be readily dispersed to wide audiences. The pairings of works, representing an alternative 'second birth,' increased their popularity. Examples of two-part individually produced playlets include Samuel Sheppard's *The Committee-Man Curried* (1647) and *The Second Part of the Committee-Man Curried* (August 1647); Mercurius Melancholicus's *Craftie Cromwell: or: Oliver ordering our New State. A Tragi Comedie* (February 1648) and Pragmaticus's *The Second Part of the Tragi-Comedie called Craftie Cromwell* (February 1648); the 1649 *New-Market-Fayre* and the more ambitious and theatrical, *Second Part of the Tragi-Comedy, called New-Market Fayre* (1649). The latter attempts to make 'proud *rebels* rage, / To see themselves thus acted on the Stage,'[34] and this dramatic exposition of the rebels' tyranny was also carried over to the two editions in the which sequel was reproduced.

The various playlets and their sequels are often connected through their common codes. The rhetoric of the divided body politic and of feminized changeability used by pro-parliamentarians to discredit kingship in the Civil War years was, for example, channelled into royalist satires. In their political dialogues, pamphlets, and closet dramas, royalists staged mock trials and used imagery of grotesque physicality to portray female characters who recited false confessions and published their crimes by vomiting or bearing appropriately monstrous offspring. Diurnals, including *An Exact Diurnall of the Parliament of Ladyes*, *The Ladies Parliament*, and *A Parliament of Ladies, with their Lawes newly enacted*, and royalist mercuries, particularly *Mercurius Melancholicus, Pragmaticus,* and *Elencticus,* satirized the sexual rapacity of parliamentary leaders and the ludicrousness of female jurors granting pardons to political traitors while also publishing their own crimes. They thus continue in the spirit of the anti-Straffordian and Laudian pamphlets, which depict haunted perpetrators who are arraigned by their own consciences, though the tables have now turned on the parliamentarians themselves. The 'Mistress Parliament' dialogues that appeared, which fanned the flames of this ideological warfare, multiplied at a rapid rate. Among the best known was *Mistress Parliament Brought to Bed of a Monstrous Childe of Reformation,* a quasi-dramatic political work, appropriately designated by W.W. Greg as the first act of a play. *Mistress Parliament Presented in her Bed* – which opens with 'Act Two' – is the sequel.[35] The former political dialogue serves also as the opening act for three 1660 female Parliament dialogues, *Mris. Rump brought to bed of a monster, Famous tragedie of the life and death of Mris. Rump,* and *The life and death of Mris Rump,* in which the post-1648 atrocities and monstrosities of Cromwell and the Rump are staged. 1659 would see the production of *The Rump, or the Mirrour of the late Times* by John Tatham, whom Lois Potter identified as 'the most successful dramatist of the period, when it came to dealing with politics and getting away with it.'[36]

Still months away from actually metamorphozing into a Rump in December 1648, Parliament issued new legislation against theatrical productions and theatre attendance in February 1648. An extended and more severe version of the 1647 Ordinance, the 1648 *Ordinance of the Lords and Commons ... for The utter suppression and abolishing of all Stage-Playes and Interludes. With the Penalties to be inflicted upon the Actors and Spectators, herein exprest* called for the complete demolition of playhouses, the punishment of actors as 'incorrigible Rogue[s],' and the penalizing of spectators.[37]

Antiparliamentary remarks on theatre closure filled royalist papers. *Pragmaticus* reports: 'and to witnesse unto the world how perfectly they hate a *King,* they are resolved for the time to come, after the *Tragedy* of this, never to admit of one, so much as in *Comedy* again. And therefore on *wednesday* last the grand *Ordinance* against *Stage-playes* was hastened into the *House,* which ordains, that all *Players* shall, for the first offence, be *committed & and Fined,* and for the second, be *whipped'* (8–15 February 1648). *Mercurius Bellicus* also lashes out and accuses the parliamentarians of taking to the political stage their performance of *Catiline* – the primary figure of rebellion from Roman history: 'But now farewell Playes for ever, for the Rebels are resolved to bee the onely Tragedians, none shall act *Catiline* but themselves.' Later when the trial of Charles was imminent, *Melancholicus* likewise observes the displacement of stage tragedy by political tyranny: 'But it seemes our deformers will have no Tragedie presented but that of their own; I confesse they are exquesite [*sic*] Tragedians, and play their parts to the amazement of all mankind; they have worn the Buskins so long, that they have changed the face of beauteous Britain into a charnell or Golgotha, yet were there any love of learning in them they would not be so eager for the suppressing of plaies, the lustre and glory of our Nation' (25 September to 2 October 1648).[38]

The occasion of the 1648 Ordinance also called for a new play. *Craftie Cromwell: or: Oliver ordering our New State. A Tragi Comedie* reminds playwrights and pamphleteers how they might bypass the reinforced restrictions: 'An Ordinance from our pretended State, / Sowes up the Players mouths, they must not prate / Like Parrats what they're taught upon the Stage, / Yet we may Print the Errors of the Age.'[39] Just as playtexts reveal parts of the original play not performed on stage, so does the printed pamphlet expose the 'Errors of the Age' not exhibited on England's political stage. *The Second Part of the Tragi-Comedie called Craftie Cromwell* also invokes the recent legislation: the Plebians who 'hate those Lines, [that] doe from the learned flow[] / Have Voted downe all Plaies, on this pretence / Their Sceans are lavish, and to God offence.'[40] Under such circumstances, the work of 'whip[ping] the crimes of this Licentious Age' (A2) is relegated to print. The arraignment of the criminals thus involves a dramatic textual reenactment of strange metamorphoses intended to delight and provoke the reader: '*Burligh's* illegall Triall (wonderous thing) / *Oliver*, Metamorphiz'd, to a King. / With various passages, that will invite / Your sense at once to wonder and delight' (A2).

The pamphlet dialogue, *Rombus the Moderator: or, The King Restored*, sentences the antiroyalist supporters to the fate of endlessly rehearsing the scene of their trial and judgment. The magistrates and grandees are cast as actors in *The English Gipsee, and her damned Crue*, which, Rombus explains, 'shall be capable of enlargement, for variety, but never loose [*sic*] the Tittle.'[41] Fairfax is assigned the role of directing the company of players in this drama of a tyrannical government anatomized:

of this Company you [Fairfax] shall be *Rex*, King of the vagabonds; Oliver shallbe your *malus genius*, or evill Counsellour. *Lenetall*, the Prologist, and Treasurer. *Martin*, the Humorist, or Mad Lover. *Marshall, Annanias*, or the While Devill. *Rainsborough*, the Intelligencer, or Scout. *Hamon*, the Door-

Keeper. Madamoiseille Fairefax, the Gipsee, or Stigan Proserpine. And *Chaloner,* though exempt from publick Trial, shall likewise passe upon his part, and play the Fool egregiously, Your Scean shall be the banks of *Acheron;* you shall Act in Hell, and be bound to fix your Stage there, *from everlasting, to everlasting, world without end, Amen.* (12–13)

Rombus the Moderator enacts a legal and divine judgment on William Lenthall, Henry Martin, Thomas Rainsborough, and Thomas Chaloner, an advocate of classical republicanism in this period. The sentence is carried out for an audience whose witnessing of the tragic demise of the rebels is extended to include judging and affirming the justness of their trial by print: 'You that have seen the fall of these Miscreants; that have heard their triall, or shall hereafter reade it; for I imagine, so famous an Occurrence, will hardly escape the Presse.' The restoration of justice is intended in turn to prepare the way for the restoration of Charles (13).

References to the theatre and theatre productions, as *Rombus the Moderator* demonstrates, were now politically charged, prompting readers to interpret the world of the stage and the stage of the world allegorically and politically.[42] [Samuel Sheppard's] play-pamphlet *The Famous Tragedie of King Charles I,* written in the aftermath of Charles's execution, is another popular case in point.[41] Together with its sequel, *Cromwell's Conspiracy. A Tragi-Comedy* (1660), *The Famous Tragedie* bridges the gap between Interregnum mock-tragedy and Restoration tragicomedy. *The Famous Tragedie* is rife with references to theatre culture; 'The Prologue to the Gentry' observes that 'refined Soules' can appreciate the great playwrights of England's past – who are individually named in the opening lines – while the plebeians would 'raze our Theaters to the ground' (A4r). *The Famous Tragedie* may have in fact been performed; in any case it reached a large audience through play reading[43] and certainly it registers its status as a readerly text. E.D.'s 'To the Author, on his Tragedy' states: 'I wisht thy Play had been more largely writ / Or I had ne're seene, or perused it ... He that can read thy Play, and yet forbear / For his late Murthered Lord, to shed a tear, / Hath a heart fram'd of *Adamant*' (A3r). The front matter enables a reconstruction of a readership that is educated and versed in the language of political allegory and topical references, as well as being unambiguously proroyalist. In the play's dedication to Charles's eldest son, then 19, *The Famous Tragedie of King Charles I* is given an aristocratic frame (see figure 6): the dedication performs the political work of stereotyping parliamentarians in terms of villains, manipulators, and demons, while imaginatively conditioning the

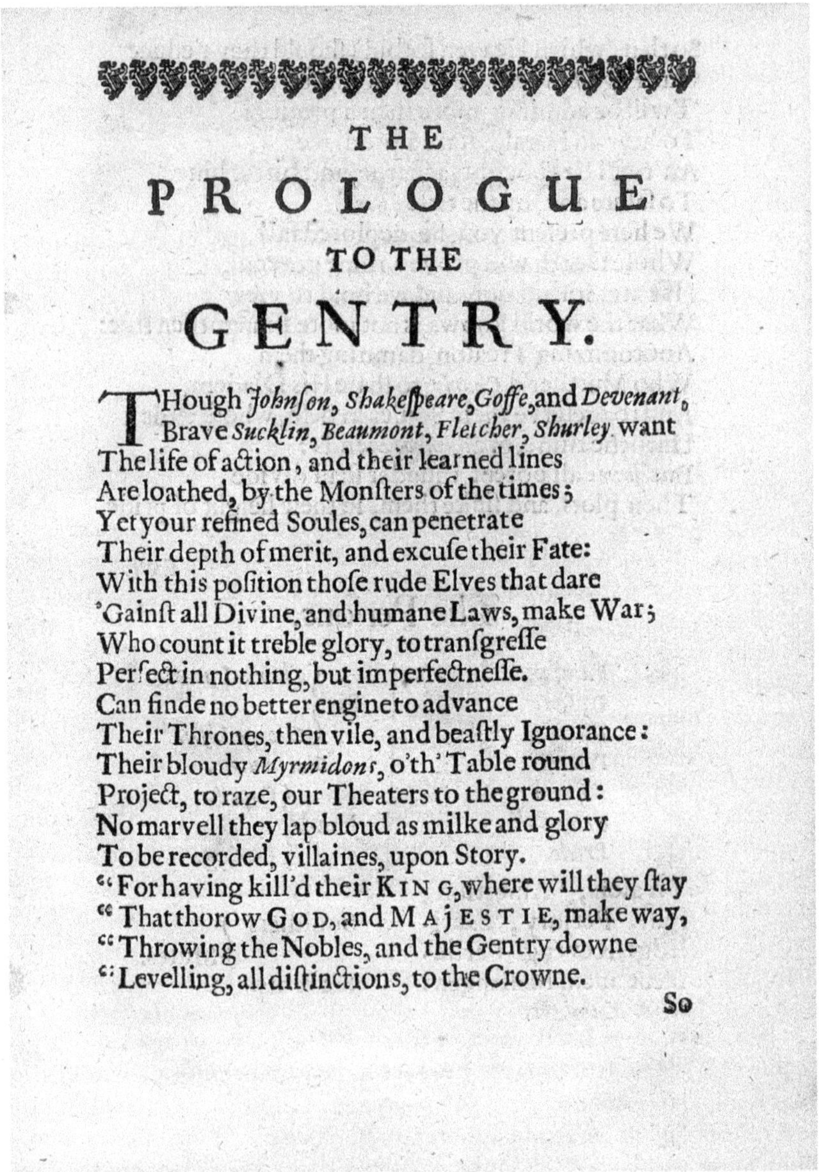

THE
PROLOGUE
TO THE
GENTRY.

Though *Johnſon*, *Shakeſpeare*, *Goffe*, and *Devenant*,
Brave *Sucklin*, *Beaumont*, *Fletcher*, *Shurley* want
The life of action, and their learned lines
Are loathed, by the Monſters of the times;
Yet your refined Soules, can penetrate
Their depth of merit, and excuſe their Fate:
With this poſition thoſe rude Elves that dare
'Gainſt all Divine, and humane Laws, make War;
Who count it treble glory, to tranſgreſſe
Perfect in nothing, but imperfectneſſe.
Can finde no better engine to advance
Their Thrones, then vile, and beaſtly Ignorance:
Their bloudy *Myrmidons*, o'th' Table round
Project, to raze, our Theaters to the ground:
No marvell they lap bloud as milke and glory
To be recorded, villaines, upon Story.
"For having kill'd their KIN G, where will they ſtay
" That thorow G O D, and M A j E S T I E, make way,
" Throwing the Nobles, and the Gentry downe
"Levelling, all diſtinctions, to the Crowne.

So

Figure 6. *The Famous Tragedie of King Charles I.* [London?], 1649. © Copyright The British Museum.

possibility of a restoration. The front matter is entirely written in verse form while the remainder of the play is in prose. Since *The Famous Trage-die* is less concerned with Charles's tragedy than with the corruption of culture, rhetoric, and political power, as the Latin epigraph on the title page underscores, the shift from verse to prose is fitting.

Based on major events in the Second Civil War, specifically the siege at Colchester, the play opens with Cromwell lauding the achievements of Hugh Peters – who is addressed with a mock-epic epithet suggestive of the relationship between Faust and Mephistopheles: 'My fine *facetious Devill*, who wear'st *the Liverie of the Stygian God*, as the white *Embleme* of thy *innocence*' (B1r). Peters is hailed for his mastery of language, his 'insinu-ating perswasive art' and oracular-sounding 'absurd Syllogisme, or eare-deceiving paradox,' which cures 'that perilous disease, call'd *Speaking truth*' (B1r, B2r). Cromwell characterizes the Parliamentary victory at Colchester in terms of the triumph over Troy, the Greeks having been aided by the magic of Calchas, that is, false persuasive rhetoric. The vic-tory is Peters's, who manufactures lies both 'at Presse and Pulpit' (B2v) and is crowned by Cromwell as poet laureate with 'a Grove of Bay to shade [his] learned skull from [Apollo's] all-piercing Beames' (B4r). The portrait of Peters reminds us of John Birkenhead's character sketch of 'The Assembly-man': 'Nor can we complain that *Playes* are put down while he can preach, save only his *Sermons* have worse Sense, and lesse Truth. But he blew down the Stage and preach'd up the Scaffold. And very wisely, lest men should track him, and find where he pilfers all his best Simile's.'[44] Indeed Peters derives his similes from the world of the theatre as he compares Cromwell to Alcides, Tamburlaine (B1v), and 'Third *Richard*' (B4r). Act I of *The Famous Tragedy* ends with a soliloquy by Peters who ironically deconstructs his own laudatory language by demonizing Cromwell and confirming the righteousness of the king.

In Act 3 royalists Sir Charles Lucas and Sir George Lisle are executed, but not before each utters some last dying words. A shift into verse form (D2r) used in Lisle's prayer for the restoration of justice and in Lucas's appeal to Jove distinguishes these speeches from the rest of the main text of the prose play. Art, culture, and aesthetics die with the royalists; Lucas 'make[s] his *exit* first' (D2r):

Here then I bid farewell, unto this Stage of misery, my life hath been but one continued Scene, woven with perturbations and anxieties – but stay, whether must now my fleeting Soul take wing: into you Starry mansion, or steep *Tartarus*, up to the Milkie way, she'l take her flight

Where Soules of Heroes doe enjoy their blisse,
Where all Celestiall comforts, meet, and kisse;
Mankinds Redeemer, oh *Emanuel*!
Who in Mans shape on Earth were pleas'd to dwell. (D4r–v)

Lisle follows Lucas's lead, bringing Act 3 to a close. The actors left on the stage are mock performers coded as antiroyalists. Act 4 opens with Cromwell returning from chasing the Scots to woo the wife of John Lambert. Mrs Lambert reluctantly plays her part at the instigation of Peters, whose roles as rhetorician and pimp are thus aligned. Cromwell calls for a masque of 'six prime Westminsterian Senators,' the allegorical counterparts of which are ambition, treason, lust, revenge, perjury, and sacrilege (F1v). The setting for the final act of Cromwell and Mrs Lambert's performance is 'the Chamber of delight' (F2r). In Act 5 Peter as nuntius interrupts the bedroom scene and reads Ireton's letter about the king's execution, which mentions the enragement of the vulgar, the 'thousands of ... Spectators of His Tragedy' (F4r). Ireton commits to continuing his reign of terror; and the play closes with a Chorus pronouncing a judgment on the monstrous Rebels in a speech that includes various stage directions as literature performs the work that royalist political history leaves incomplete in 1649.

The juxtaposition of *The Famous Tragedie* with early Restoration plays like *Cromwell's Conspiracy: A Tragy-Comedy* provides evidence of the readers and of the received tradition of *The Famous Tragedie*, while also underscoring the use of the dramatic mode in the restoration of poetic/dramatic justice and even political and national order. The Prologue of *Cromwell's Conspiracy* – the play's only front matter – suggests that Cromwell outperforms even Catiline, and it also sets the stage for Cromwell's damnation. Act 1 repeats the encounter between Cromwell and Peters printed in the *Famous Tragedie*, with some notable differences. Besides the obvious omissions of the historical events of the late 1640s, including the siege at Colchester, the extended discussion of Hughes's and Cromwell's corruption of language is left out. Moreover, by the second page of Act 1, prose gives way to verse, in effect reversing the stylistic transformation of verse into prose that characterizes *Tyrannicall-Government Anatomized*.

In Acts 2 through to 5, the author of *Cromwell's Conspiracy* takes much greater liberty in rereading *The Famous Tragedie*. Following Peters's monologue at the end of Act 1, *Cromwell's Conspiracy* wastes no time arriving at the bedroom scene when Peters serves as a pimp for Cromwell, informing Mrs Lambert of her duties to both men. Act 2.4 rehearses Charles's execution, and includes a brief epitaph by Juxon. A scene concurrent with the regicide opens Act 3, which raises the curtain on Cromwell and Mrs. Lambert. Recalling the executions of George Lisle and Charles Lucas in *The Famous Tragedy*, the trials of two historical enemies to the Cromwellian regime, Dr John Hewet and Sir Henry Slingsby, are staged in Act 4. Cromwell's daughter, who was married by the historical Hewet in November 1657, intervenes on the condemned man's behalf; but in a scene that epitomizes the dissolution of order at every level, she is dismissed, though not without first cursing her monstrous father. Thereafter, John Lisle presides over the trial of Hewet at 'the Pretended High-Court of Justice,' during which the accused confronts his prosecutors by challenging their jurisdiction in terms reminiscent of Charles I before the parliamentary judges (D3v–E1v). The historical Hewet insisted on his right to be tried by a jury[45] and then announced his plea, one that Prynne had prepared and which would be printed in the following year as 'Beheaded Dr. John Hewytt's Ghost pleading.' Like his historical counterpart, the fictional Hewet is nevertheless sentenced and becomes a royalist martyr. As in Charles I's case, Hewet's last dying words were immediately printed and circulated. Moreover, the mourning rings given to Hewet's friends apparently contained an inscription that recalled the theme of *Tyrannicall-Government Anatomized*: 'Herodes necuit Johannem';[46] though here of course the biblical account of Herod and John the Baptist is put to use in the service of proroyalist history.

Act 5 of *Cromwell's Conspiracy* overturns the parliamentary victory and dramatizes the internal battle of a haunted, damned Cromwell who experiences a now familiar trial by conscience. A brief appearance by Richard Cromwell is soon overshadowed by General Monk who responds to the people's wishes for 'a King, a Monk, a Free Parliament' (F1r).

The main performer on the English political stage in the seventeenth century, Charles I, had reinforced the tragic nature of the age. Yet at the same time, his performance paradoxically set the stage for a comic or romanticized ending to seventeenth-century royalist history. Literary culture captured this complex negotiation of history, tragedy, and comedy. Edmund Gayton's *Pleasant Notes upon Don Quixot*, a valuable source of information on the period, uses the language of the stage-play world in working through these relationships. In a defence of plays and romances, Gayton observes: 'For want of these chimera's, (which had no more harm in them, then their impossibility) reall phantasmes, and strong delusions have succeeded and possessed not a few, who transported with their owne imaginations, doe not write Romances, but act them, and fill the world with substantiall Tragædies.'[47]

Richard Brathwaite's *Panthalia: or the Royal Romance* (1659), published under a pseudonym in August 1659, captures the pivotal historic moment. *Panthalia* exhibits the characteristics of the romance as a hybrid genre of fiction structured on diversity. Though this romance was probably completed in the summer of 1658, the Advertisement in the front matter and the Postscript at the end of the text were added in 1659 to reflect the changes on the national stage, including Richard Cromwell's departure from Whitehall in July 1659. The subtitle anticipates the intertwining of politics, theatre, and romance in *Panthalia*: 'A DISCOURSE Stored with infinite variety in relation to STATE-GOVERNMENT ... And presented on a *Theatre* of Tragical and Comical *State*, in a successive continuation to these Times.'[48]

The concluding episodes in *Panthalia* present a tragicomedy-in-progress, featuring a king who must yet make his way onto the political stage. We encounter Charicles (Charles II) following the Battle of Worcester in 1651 as he is rescued by Candiope. Candiope is likely the historical figure, Jane Lane, who disguised herself as her servant, William Jackson, in accompanying Charles II from Bentley to Abbots Leigh and Trent; or she may represent Juliana/Judith Coningsby, who accompanied the king in the journey from Trent.[49] Candiope hears a voice from the grove, perhaps suggestive of Mary Magdalene's encounter with the risen Christ whom she mistakes for the gardener. But Charicles speaks of tragedy at this stage: '*O Heavens! When will these cloudy dayes close with a clear evening? ... Must Theatres be erected onely for acting our tragedies? Must the fame of our family be quite razed forth of the Annals of posterity?*' (258). Only divine intervention can convert tragedy into comedy and restore the king to the throne, Brathwaite suggests: 'there remained no hope of a new being or breathing to the revivall of their Phænix ashes, unless some invisible hand *far above all humane expectance* should interpose it selfe, and in mercy raise it from the rubbish of division, and by degrees restore it' (270; italics mine). Charicles, who appears '*beyond all expectancy*' (254) in the narrative, is now the '*new being*,' the instrument of the invisible hand which interposes itself 'far above all humane expectance.'

The Restoration, which Brathwaite could only hint at in *Panthalia*, was realized in the following year, thus transforming tragedy into divine comedy (or at least tragicomedy) for royalists. In 'The Stationer to the Reader' of John Webster and William Rowley's play, *The Thracian Wonder. A comical History* (1661), Francis Kirkman observes that the winter of discontent has now passed, though the extraordinarily tragic nature of recent events relegates history to the realm of fiction or romance. Using the imagery deployed by royalists in the experience of defeat, Kirkman declares: 'We have had the private Stage for some years clouded, and under a tyrannical command, though the publick Stage of *England* has produc'd many monstrous villains, some of which have deservedly made their exit. I believe future Ages will not credit the transactions of our late Times to be other than a *Play*, or a *Romance*. I am sure in most Romantick Plays there hath been more probability, then in our true (though sad) Stories.'[50] Here Kirkman underscores the entanglement of history with romance, which materialized as tragicomedy on the Restoration stage.

Restored to power, the new monarchical regime assumed control over not only the representation and delegation of political power but also the (ideological) power of representation. Conversely, the marriage of comedy and tragedy in royalist drama helped prepare the stage for the new king. Tragicomedy took political and literary culture by storm to mark the occasion of the *astræa redux*. But if the public playhouses of London provided a locus for celebrating the restoration of the monarch en masse, they also offered an opportunity for critique. The king himself was a ready-made subject for satire for Restoration dramatists, who mocked the sexual politics and antics of the court in comedies, often featuring Cavaliers as effeminate fops. A discussion of the nature of ideological and political battles waged on the Restoration stage is reserved for a place and time 'beyond the fifth Act,' prior to which we turn to the drama of a counterculture that developed alongside that of royalism.

Chapter 5

Trials of Authorship and Dramas of Dissent

The dramatic arraignment of parliamentarians and the Rump by the royalists discussed in the previous chapter extends to religious dissenters who, since the time of their emergence, were tried not only in the courtroom but also in print. By no means resigned to such a fate, seventeenth-century radicals produced their own counterculture and communal identities through which they also parted company with the Rump. The communities they formed were partly textual in nature. Dissenters set considerable store in universal literacy as a means to popular emancipation, which their claims to spiritual and religious equality had justified. Elitist discourses, including that of the law, traditionally discouraged participation in the political and legal spheres. Maintaining that God revealed his message to the poor, dissenters insisted that the nation's laws be rendered accessible to all, thus challenging the authority of officials like lawyers and judges.[1] John Lilburne even goes so far as to empty the judges of their authority, thus reducing them to 'ciphers' by ascribing to jurors the right to act as judges of law.

The creation of communities of dissent through alternative (dramatic) performances and the social drama of the trial is the subject of this chapter.[2] In an account of the records of Quaker legal proceedings, particularly the oath trials of the 1660s, ethnographer Richard Bauman observed that Quakers 'attached great importance to the trials, and their content makes clear that the trials were indeed [what Victor Turner called] social dramas,' that is 'symbolic enactments in which social conflicts are personified, placed on view, and publicly played out.'[3] The social dramas display characteristics of theatrical dramas in being framed, public, formalized, agonistic, and symbolic; but unlike theatrical dramas that mimic social life, the trial '*is* social life.' The trials on which Bauman concentrates are recorded, in this case, in transcriptions of courtroom proceedings that were taken down in shorthand.[4] The intersecting scenes of speech, writing, and political action examined in this chapter present a series of speech-acts, acts of witnessing, and palimpsests of communicative actions. The result is a new stage for the performance and politics of dissent.

The application of speech-act theory involves analysing the interrelationship between political agency and various forms of communication through language. Performing actions through language has long been an integral part of language use. As George Yule explains, 'in attempting to express themselves, people do not only produce utterances containing grammatical structures and words, they perform actions via those utterances.' Speech-act theorists identify five types of speech acts: declarations, those statements that 'change the world via their utterance'; representatives, which 'state what the speaker believes to be the case or not'; expressives, which 'state what the speaker feels'; directives, which are used to get someone else to act; and commissives, which speakers use 'to commit themselves to some future action.'[5] Of the five classes, declarations are the strongest in terms of producing tangible results. While expressives and representatives indicate the speaker's efforts to make words fit the state of the world, declarations are unique in changing the world to fit their words.

Among the many different kinds of genres, legal documents, which include courtroom transcriptions, trial histories, contracts, and wills, best exhibit speech-act principles and practices at work in the written word. Legal discourse has the power to effect genuine change, and is largely declarative; the word-centred religious culture of the radicals in the seventeenth century in fact encouraged the production of legal accounts and records.[6] The social drama of the trial, which occasioned the application of legal discourse, presented a site of convergence for speaking and writing and for dramatic performances, interspersed with scenes of public reading. This chapter examines several trial accounts featuring the Leveller, John Lilburne; the Fifth Monarchist, Anna Trapnel; and Quakers, James Nayler, Margaret Fell, and George Fox. All of the trial scenes exhibit, though in different ways, a renegotiation of power relations, constructions of authority, and the creation of alternative juries and arenas for judgment. In each case, the radicals on trial performed their political role through their textual accounts and in dramatic productions for popular audiences, who were given active parts to play.

The protean nature of Puritanism, particularly of the radical historical and literary tradition, readily lent itself to dramatization. In his memorable statement on the origins of the Puritans and sectaries, R.H. Tawney explained, 'In the furnace of the Civil War ... Presbyterian and Independent, aristocrat and Leveller, politician and merchant and utopian gazed with bewildered eyes on the strange monsters with whom they had walked as friends.'[7] Dissenters were known for their multiple, if not shifting, affiliations. George Fox located the origins of many Friends' groups in 'shattered Baptist communities';[8] and Fifth Monarchists were never entirely separated from the Baptist and Independent congregations from which they emerged. The Leveller, Gerrard Winstanley, became a Quaker,[9] as did John Lilburne. The fluidity that characterized the dissenters' individual and communal identities was also a function of their resistance to established social structures, their eccentric behaviour, their tolerance for diversity; and their propensity for dramatic performance or 'readiness for dramatic action.'[10] The political prophet Anna Trapnel was, for example, labeled a Quaker; and Quakers themselves were frequently identified with the demonized minority at the opposite end of the religious and political spectrums – Roman Catholics.[11] Yet it is precisely these (Protestant) sectarians and heretics who advance God's work and raise his temple, Milton maintained in *Areopagitica* (*CPW*, 2:555; see chapter 1).

I

The Levellers were among the dissenters most intent on staging scenes of judgment and recording them in legal discourses and documents infused with dramatic discourses. Contemporary historians credit these left-wing politicians and populist radicals for anticipating the fundamentals of modern democracy, English trade unionism, Chartism, and American republicanism. Visions of alternative social and political systems and a fervent belief in the universality of grace and human rights underwrote their defence of political liberty and of popular representation. Levellers also possessed a strong sense of community,[12] despite the distinctions among the spokespeople: John Lilburne, Thomas Prince, and John Wildman were constitutional Levellers, while Richard Overton, William Walwyn, and Thomas Rainsborough promoted more radical social and economic changes, and thus can be considered true Levellers.

Nigel Smith argues that while the effort to contextualize the Levellers' ideas has sometimes rendered them lifeless, they should be regarded as 'clever manipulators of media opportunities.'[13] Levellers advanced their ideas though pamphlets, tracts, and petitions until they became a threat to the New Model Army – a confirmation of the material and political work performed by their paper-contestations and acts of textual resistance. In this chapter, I consider the dramatic features of their writings, their work as material objects, and their consequent effectiveness in arraigning their critics and accusers. I demonstrate as well that the Levellers' practices of media manipulation extend beyond print culture to include oral speech acts and other public performances.

Particularly well known for his use of dramatic modes of representation, Richard Overton published many pamphlets in the early 1640s that attacked the foundations of English religious, political, legal, and economic life. His satires targeted governmental officials, monopolies, the legal system, and episcopacy, represented primarily by the figure of William Laud. The government was hardly unaware of Overton's writings: his theological work, *Mans Mortalities* (1644), and Milton's *Doctrine and Discipline of Divorce* (1644) provoked Parliament's investigation of unlicensed printing.

Overton's most popular assault on the Presbyterian members of Parliament was the *Araignement of Mr. Persecution*, which was issued in two editions, the first of which was printed twice. Characteristic of Overton's writing is his 'semi-dramatic discourse' and his legalistic reproduction of the actual documents in confronting governmental authorities.[14] The title page of his *Araignement* defends the cause of toleration and justice by boldly confronting persecution: the printer of the text, Martin Claw Clergie, locates his bookshop on '*Toleration Street*, at the *Signe* of the *Subjects Liberty*, right opposite to *Persecuting Court*.' The front matter consists of a mock authorization and casts the reader as the main judge of the satirical morality play that unfolds: 'Thus (Reader) that *Court* being compleat, for thy more speedy progression through the matter intended, suppose the transaction of many passages in these *Assizes* here in this *Relation* omitted ... Thus then the *Grand Inquest* (the matter being thus far brought) falls into debate' (4). The *Araignement* goes on to allegorize the trial of 'Mr. Persecution' by the 'Prosecutour,' identified as 'Mr. Gods-Vengence' (6). The execution of Laud in the same year represented a major setback for persecution and intolerance, but Overton persisted in writing or cowriting pamphlets and newsbook commentaries calling for reforms as part of the Levellers' program.

Conventional dramatic features in Leveller writings are largely confined to Overton's satires, though Walwyn's writings also included monologues. But it was John Lilburne who became the most famous performer among the radicals, particularly in the courtroom. As Nigel Smith has observed, 'Lilburne seems to have functioned as a perform- ing "text" for the movement, a figurehead and centre of attention, rather like George Fox was to become for the early Quakers.'[15] In 1638 Lilburne was tried for allegedly engaging in subversive acts: helping to print anti-prelatical works in Holland and facilitating their distribution in England. Archbishop Laud complained that while Lilburne was being punished for his crimes, he 'audaciously and wickedly did not only utter sundry scandalous Speeches, but likewise scattered divers copies of seditious Books amongst the people that beheld the said exe- cution.' Consequently, Laud ordered Lilburne's warden to 'take special notice' during Lilburne's imprisonment 'of all letters, writings, and books brought unto him, and seize' them.[16] *A Worke of the Beast* (1638) reveals that Lilburne proudly admitted to tossing banned books into the crowd while in the pillory for distributing such unauthorized works: 'And for mine owne part I stand this day in the place of an evill doer, but my conscience witnesseth that I am not soe. And here about I put my hand in my pocket, and puld out Three of worthie *D. Bastwicks Bookes* and threw them among the people and said, There is a part of the bookes for which I suffer, take them among you, and read them, and see if you finde any thing in them, against the Law of God, and the Law of the Land, the glory of God, the honour of the King or state.'[17] Some of the people with whom he communicates while in the prison, includ- ing the porter, John Hawes, requested books from him for their own personal use (*Beaste* 24–5). As for *A Worke of the Beast*, the tract from which this information is derived, marginalia indicates that Lilburne was successful in attracting his intended reader, one who despised the prelatical popish 'Beaste' with which Laud was generally identified: the British Library copy of *A Worke of the Beast* includes a hand pointing to the identification of the Bishops as '*Jure Diabollico*' (14), and to the cita- tion of Rev. 16:13–14 (15). The reader's imperative 'NOTE THIS WELL' appears beside Lilburne's reference to 'Prelates, and their Crea- tures in their printed Books,' whose authority originates in Rome (15). In 1641 Lilburne would be pardoned by the Long Parliament along with Burton, Bastwick, Prynne, and Leighton. Thereafter he is avenged, as we have seen in chapter 2, in the 1645 *Sad Theatre* in which Laud is tried in print.

Until 1646 Lilburne sided with the Puritans and the Independents in particular; and all during this time, he contributed to the political education of the people by writing numerous tracts, which detail his trials and interrogations.[18] *An Alarum to the House of Lords* defends Lilburne against the accusation that 'his Bookes tend to Rayse sedition in this Realme' (8), and questions how it could now be '*seditious* and *dangerous* for any man to publish his minde.' Overton warns that God will see justice restored: 'God will provide, above hope: out of the thicket shall come a Ransome for this his beloved *Isaac* ... for God cannot suffer so abominable wickednesse: He can turne the hearts of a whole *Presbyterian Jury*, (if it should come to that,) in an Instant, and make them to see their owne *Liberties* burning at the stake in him; That his Sufferings are but a *Preface* to their *Tragœdy*.'[19]

Lilburne's performances in print and in the courtroom helped keep him alive. But his writings also endangered his life, and often by assuming a life of their own. Such is the case with *An Agreement of the People*, which appeared in October 1647, and is the best-known statement on toleration in the period. The *Agreement* defended liberty of conscience as a God-given right to all people, while denouncing state authority: the 'matters of Religion, and the wayes of Gods Worship, are not at all intrusted to us by any humane power, because therein wee cannot remit or exceed a tittle of what our Consciences dictate to be the mind of God.'[20] The document also condemned conscription and insisted that Parliament itself be held accountable to the justice system. The imagined readership of *An Agreement* is inclusive insofar as the petition is aimed at the citizens and the officers in the army and even royalist supporters. As a restrained version of the more militant *The Case of the Army*, the *Agreement* was still intended to secure Cromwell's support.

The first *Agreement* was read and opened for discussion in a meeting of officers and agitators on 29 October 1647 as part of the Putney debates. The victors in the first Civil War debated the form of government that should be established in England. The role of the English people became a central issue in these debates, and differences of opinion about this role heightened tensions between Independents like Henry Ireton, who wanted the franchise to be restricted to property holders, and radicals, including John Wildman and Thomas Rainsborough who, along with the Levellers, demanded universal suffrage.[21] Denied access to the political theatre, royalists nevertheless wasted no time in fighting back with paper-contestations: Mercurius Pragmaticus's (Marchmont Nedham's) *The Levellers levell'd. Or, The Independents Conspiracie to root out Monarchie. An Interlude* (1647) is a case in point. The opening song introduces the main actors by calling for 'Roome for these Traitors, *now they come / To Act upon the Stage.*'[22] The Prologue that follows refers to the Interlude's brief stage history after declaring its status as a readerly work: 'These sonnes of Belial, you must onely read; / And yet this Play was acted once indeed' (A1v). The political allegorical figures, consisting of the Levellers, Apostasie, Conspiracie, Treacherie, Democracie, and Impietie, plot the murder of Charles after swearing their allegiance to Cataline (A3v). The link between the regicidal plot and the Levellers' mandate is established by the reference to the *Agreement* in the exchange between Patricide and Regicide, who declares: 'the Adjurators of five Regiments ... have broke the Ice to our Designe, and op't a gap for Liberty to enter; sever'd themselves from their Coleagues, drawn up a manifesto to the Kingdom, divulg'd that they intend to purchase absolute freedom, and break in sunder the heavy yoake of Kings, and as perswaded of a happy Issue, that all the Vulgar will joyne as one man, they call it an AGREEMENT OF THE PEOPLE' (B1v). Closing the scene, Pragmaticus reiterates the motives of the conspirators to kill the king, a plan that is frustrated by the end of the Interlude.

The royalist press judged and vilified the dissenters in numerous other dramatic works, including *The Second Part of the Tragi-Comedie called Craftie Cromwell* and *Rombus the Moderator: or, The King Restored*, by linking the Rump and the Levellers, and also regicide and 'levelling' – though Levellers were generally united with royalists in their opposition to Charles's execution.[23] Still in the postregicidal *Famous Tragedie*, Rainsborough – identified on the title page as a conspirator who will get his due – denounces Sir Charles Lucas and Sir George Lisle, who are martyred in Act IV. The character of Rainsborough then proceeds to attack royalists at large: 'Why spend we time in Dialogue with these Miscreants ... who fight for Yoakes and Fetters ... and wish profusely for to spend their blouds to please a Tyrants lust.'[24] Two acts later, Rainsborough is haunted by a ghostly vision of the mangled bodies of Lucas and Lisle (F3r). He dies at the hands of Blackburne after uttering some parting words that fulfil the prophecy on the title page that he will receive his 'just reward': 'Let all those that have fought [for] their Soveraignes ruine looke upon me and my deserved destiny' (F4r).

In the meantime Gerrard Winstanley and his coauthors defiantly advanced the radical position in a collective document, titled *The True Levellers Standard Advanced: The State of Community opened*. Printed days before the third *Agreement*, *The True Levellers Standard* defended the cause of the common people: 'the Earth [must] become[] a Common Treasury again ... for all the Prophesies of Scriptures and Reason are

Circled here in this Community, and mankind must have the Law of Righteousnesse once more writ in his heart, and all must be made of one heart, and one mind.'[25] Both wars had in fact been fought over the rights of the people in the nation and their place in its government, Winstanley and the others maintained. Following on its heels, the collaborate undertaking that constituted the third *Agreement*, titled *An Agreement of the Free People* (1 May 1649), outlines the final form of the Levellers' program. The authors, who were at this time in prison, commented further on the constitutional issues debated at Putney, and defended the rights of the people. Composed of thirty articles, *An Agreement of the Free People* revealed the authors' confidence in the judgment of the voting public. In turn, they demanded annual parliaments, insisting that Parliament's authority be curtailed by the replacement of its court of law with a court of justice. Ultimately, military power must be made answerable to civil authority.[26] The Levellers' program was intended to restore civil liberty, while the act of levelling itself was associated with rioting insofar as parliamentary representatives who caused disturbances or disagreed with the *Agreement* were reduced to 'levellers.'

Pamphlets and newspapers of the day frequently cited the *Agreement*, which was printed in 20,000 copies. Its intentions were peaceful, but the explosive historical events that coincided with its appearance and that greatly influenced its initial reception and its controversial afterlife rewrote the document. At the time that the tract was produced, mutiny broke out in the army, and the Levellers intervened to defend the rights of disgruntled soldiers who opposed the parliamentary commanders. The regiment was quickly suppressed, and Robert Lockyer, one of the ringleaders, was executed; this led to further uprisings. The imprisoned Lilburne and Overton continued their protest to Fairfax from the Tower, while William Thompson outlined the grievances of the soldiers in a manifesto, titled *Englands Standard Advanced*, which included the *Agreement* as part of the petition. Thompson reminds the reader about the subtitle (and subtext) of the *Agreement* as 'a Peace offering,' while insisting that his 'annexing' of the document to *Englands Standard Advanced* confirmed his resolve 'to pursue the speedy and full accomplishment thereof.'[27] This textual revolt was followed by yet another mutiny and, in reaction, the issuing on 14 May of a new parliamentary act that would see mutineers charged with treason.

The government introduced corresponding measures to regulate the press, though the controls were less than effective. Overton's 1649 *The Baiting of the Great Bull of Bashan Unfolded* and the anonymous, though thematically related, playlet of the same year *A New Bull-Bayting* both turn attack dogs loose on Cromwell. The theatres, which earlier replaced the bear gardens (next to which *A New Bull-Bayting* is purportedly printed), are now themselves upstaged by dramatic texts that satirize or 'bait' their dangerous foes. Writing from prison, Overton refers to his *Arraignment of Mr. Persecution* in *The Baiting of the Great Bull,* and essentially casts Cromwell in the role of Mr. Persecution in this playlet. But Overton also chastises the reader of his text, particularly in his remarks on the public's response to the *Agreement.* 'Yee have not danced up so roundly and so sprightly a tune' as the *Agreement* merits, he states. In fact, he claims, the *Agreement* 'lyeth half dead in the streets.'[28] *A New Bull-Bayting,* a politically allegorized playlet produced several months later, again invokes the *Agreement,* but this time as a liberationist document 'slighted by a bloudy *Juncto*' (5) under Cromwell's command. *A New Bull-Bayting* passes judgment on Cromwell by featuring the (imprisoned) Levellers, Lilburne, Overton, Prince, and Walwyn as 'Bear-wards' who train their attack dogs (each suggestively named) to gorge the bull, Cromwell. The arraignment and sentencing of Cromwell, who '*Bull'd* poor *England,*' occur simultaneously.[29] In justifying the war on tyranny, the author – in the voice and character of Overton – inserts a lengthy genealogy of the bull featuring an account of current political history and attacking various Cromwellian acts: the erection of 'a Court of *Mock-justice* by his own Authority, against the peoples will'; the execution of the king; and the establishment of 'a Monstrous *Government,* without *head* or *tayle*; *rule* or *President*; *law* or *Reason*' (7). This proradical playlet relies on some of the same anti-Cromwellian arguments and images that appeared in royalist literature, including the Rump pamphlets discussed in chapter 4.[30] Characteristic of radical and royalist satires alike, this playlet concludes with Cromwell's 'His last Will and Testament' in which his body is dismembered and tyranny is anatomized. The 'Bear-wards' also succeed in tearing Cromwell apart rhetorically, as he casts judgment upon himself by itemizing and bequeathing his various parts to the devil.

Acts of textual resistance, particularly the production of the *Agreement,* were not left unpunished by the Rump. On 12 October Parliament ordered Lilburne's prosecution for the treacherous act of having written, published, and circulated among the soldiers various pamphlets designed to '*raise force against the present Government, and for the subversion and alteration of it.*'[31] The trial was held before a jury of London citizens upon Lilburne's insistence that the doors of the courtroom be opened to the public. The famous printed version of the trial, intended to publicize the event even more, draws attention to the crowds in attendance. *The Triall, of Lieut. Collonell John Lilburne ... Being as exactly pen'd and taken in short hand, as it was possible to be done in such a croud and noyes ... that so matter of Fact, as it was there declared, might truly come to publick view* (see figure 7), moreover, theatricalizes the courtroom scenes, first of all by printing the names of the participants as featured in playbills. The relationship between the audience-conscious Lilburne and the spectators in the courtroom is represented as sympathetic. In his remarks on the arraignment of Lilburne, the transcriber invites the reader to reenact the drama: 'The Reader is desired to take notice, that in the Indictment it selfe, there was a great many other things then in this is expressed, as particularly, divers passages out of a book called Mr. *Lilburnes*, Intituled, *The Legall Fundamentall liberties of* England *revived, & c.* as also out of another book Intituled, *A preparative to an Hue and Cry after Sir* Arthur Haslerigg, *& c.* as also out of *The Agreement of the People* of the first of *May* 1649' (65). The trial in fact consists of the prosecution confronting Lilburne with quotations from his pamphlet writings which are read aloud: 'Here they began to read over his Books,' reports a witness at the trial, 'which pleased the People as well, as if they had acted before them one of *Ben Johnsons* Playes, for their excellency.'[32] The officials anatomize / analyse his works and judge his motives, claiming that 'the whole Course of all his pens writing, that been to this purpose,' that is, to bring the Cromwellian government into disrepute as '*a tyrannicall Government*' (92), a characterization, as we observed in chapter 4, that was used by Parliament to discredit the royalist government. The court ordered public readings of various texts: *An impeachment of high Treason against* Oliver Cromwell, *and his Son in Law Henry Ireton* (92), *The legall fundamentall Liberties of the people of* England *revived,* (96; also see 98), and *The Agreement of the People*, which, they concluded, 'strikes ... at the very root of all Government' (102). Judging that writing could incite readers to rebellion, Lilburne's accusers unwittingly acknowledged the power of print and public opinion.

The presence and authority of the people at the trial was as much on the mind of the officials as it was on Lilburne's. The judges proceeded cautiously to preserve themselves from the charge of denying Lilburne his rights; they were, according to one Lilburne biographer, eager to demonstrate not only that they were impartial, 'but to be quite sure their audience knew they were fair.'[33] Lilburne all the while repeatedly emphasized the jury's jurisdiction, and defying legal precedent, attrib-

Figure 7. Frontispiece, *The Triall, of Lieut. Collonell John Lilburne …. Being as exactly pen'd and taken in short hand, as it was possible to be done in such a croud and noyes … that so matter of Fact, as it was there declared, might truly come to publick view.* London, 1649. © Copyright The British Museum.

uted to the jury the authority to act as judges of law and not just fact: '[I] cast my life, and the lives of all the honest free-men of *England*, into the hands of God, and his gracious protection, and into the care and conscience of my honest Jury and Fellow-Citizens, who I again declare by the law of *England*, are the Conservators and sole Judges of my life, having inherent in them alone, the judicial power of the law, as well as fact.' Lilburne goes even further by divesting the judges of the power they had monopolized, thus rendering them redundant: 'you Judges that sit there, being no more, if they please, but Ciphers to pronounce the Sentence, or their Clarks, to say *Amen*, to them, being at the best, in your Original, but the Norman Conquerours, Intruders' (140–1).[34] Support for this legally unprecedented position is evidenced, according to *Truths Victory*, by the enthusiastic response of the crowds in attendance who applaud Lilburne's self-defence and his defence of the people's rights (141).

Lilburne's success at crowd management threatened the court officials, who again raised concerns about the seditious nature of the 1 May 1649 *Agreement* (143–4). 'Mr. *Lilburn* hath been very free in his writing, in his speaking, in his printing, and it now riseth in judgment against him, and the law must now give him his due, which you my Lords, are sole Judges of, and from whom the Jury, and the Prisoner both must receive' (144), the prosecution declared in judging Lilburne's tract as a provocation to rebellion. 'This Agreement,' the prosecution charged, 'shall be the Center, the Banner, and the waved Standard unto which they shall flock, and to send Agents into several Countries to put this into execution' (144). Throughout the trial, Lilburne continually appealed to the jury, which eventually returned a verdict of not guilty, thus causing 'the whole multitude of People in the Hall' to shout for half an hour, leaving the judges pale (151; *Truths Victory*, 6–7).

Released on 8 November 1649, Lilburne sought to publish his own version of the courtroom drama. *The Man in the Moon* reports in November 1649 that with 'both his heels at liberty,' Lilburne 'is now very busy in Printing a Book of all the Particulars of his *Arraignment*.' In hot pursuit, the authorities hunt for the printer of this document, which they intend to suppress, the *Man in the Moon* continues. This newsbook account of Lilburne is followed immediately by a critique of the unjust 'bespatter[ing]' of another controversial text that appeared in the same year, *Eikon Basilike*; but, assures the journalist, 'the more such *doggs* bark against this *Picture* of *King Charls*, the more venoration will be given it.' The Man in the Moon also declares his verdict on the trial of authorship which 'bespattered' the received history of *Eikon Basilike*: 'We still Adore that Book, because 'tis good, / Writ by King Charls, and sealed with his Blood.'[35] Though again they make strange bedfellows, the author of *A New Bull-Bayting* joins forces with the *Man in the Moon* by including the 'Dogge' of this royalist-supporting journalist among the hounds sent by the Leveller-'Bear-wards' to attack bullish Cromwell (4). For those at opposite ends of the political spectrum, Cromwell was a figure of treachery, whose representation in these terms occasioned a meeting of minds of radicals and royalists, particularly in the year of the regicide. Leveller and royalist meet not only in *A New Bull-Bayting* but also in the relatively sympathetic response to *An Agreement* in *A Tragi-Comedy, Called New-Market Fayre*,[36] as well as in their shared support for Lilburne during and following his arraignment.

As significant contributors to the radical traditions, female dissenters were among those who pleaded on behalf of Lilburne in 1649 and again in 1653 when he was rearrested. Protesting their exclusion from the world of letters and law, about 10,000 Leveller women signed a petition in April 1649 demanding justice from the authorities. Women also justified their intervention in the public sphere in other political petitions presented to Parliament, including *To the Supream Authority of England ... The Humble Petition of divers wel-affected woemen* (5 May 1649). This plea for the release of 'the Four Prisoners our friends in the Tower' identifies the most severe act of repression with the denial of 'all liberty of Discourse.' The 1649 petition was followed up by *To the Supreme Authority ... severall Wives and Children*, 1650; *To the Parliament ... the humble Petition of divers afflicted Women*, 1653, and *Unto every individual Member of Parliament: The humble Representation of divers afflicted Women-Petitioners*, which also appealed for Lilburne's release, this time from his 1653 sentence.[37] But the most noteworthy example of female petitioning occurred in 1659 when Quakers and women from other radical congregations joined in protest against tithes. In the preface to the reader in *These several Papers was sent to the Parliament* (1659), the compiler, Mary Forster – a Quaker activist and polemicist – acknowledges that 'It may seem strange to some that women should appear in so publick a manner, in a matter of so great concernment as this of Tithes,' but the petition includes about 7000 signatures, headed by Margaret Fell's name (see figure 8).[38] The publisher was likewise a female Quaker, Mary Westword; and the petition at large serves as testimony of female political activism and collective resistance. In light of such evidence, Hilary Hinds reminds us, it is necessary 'to think of women not as an adjunct to the

(7)

We who are of the Seed of the Woman , which bruiſeth
the Serpents head, to which the Promiſe is, Chriſt Jeſus
in the Male and in the Female, which is the Everlaſting
Prieſt, not after the Order of *Aaron*, which took Tithes,
nor of the Tribe of *Levi*, but of the Tribe of *Judah*,
and who is a Prieſt for ever, made by the Oath of God,
after the Order of *Melchizedech*, and remains a Prieſt continually ; And therefore can we ſet our hearts and hands
againſt *Aarons* Order, which is diſannulled, and the Law
changed, and do bear our Teſtimony, that Chriſt Jeſus
the Everlaſting Prieſt is come.

Margret Fell, ſenior	Eliz. Kitchin	Agnus Brown.
Margret Eell, junior	Anne Wilſon	Mabel Wiſon
Bridget Fell	Elin Newbie	Iſabel Garnet
Iſabel Fell	Eliz. Newbie	Rebecca Storey
Sarah Fell	Agnus Newbie	Jane Thomſon
Mary Fell	Elin Newbie	Agnus Wilſon
Suſanna Fell	Jane Cheſter	Iſabel Berk
Rachel Fell	Elin Muckelt	Elizabeth Newbie
Mary Askey	Margret Idle	Dorothy Ducket
Eſter Benſon	Iſabel Stephenſon	Elizabeth Simpſon
Jane Jakes	Margan Shepherd	Mabel Moor
Mabel Warner	Anne Rawes	Eliz. Moor
Elizabeth Walker	Jane Lancaſter	Margret Moor
Jenet Jeats	Iſabil Grave	Elin Rigge
Agnus Sponder	Eliz. Sewart	Elizabeth Heline
Mary Peper	Margret Thomſon	Mabel Game
Elin Towenſon	Anne Brigs	Dorothy Lorimer
Anne Colinſon	Agnus Thomſon,	Margret Wharton
Anne Bateman	Iſabel Wilſon	Iſabel Storey
Dorothy Maskew	Margret Clark	Eliz. Lonſdal
Margret Deniſon	Jane Halehead	Eliz. Rigg
Agnus Bank	Janet Bateman	Margret Thompſon
Anne Dogſon	Dorothy Bateman	Eling Came
Margret Deniſon.	Mary Bateman	Eliz. Rigge
	Dorothy Bateman	Margret Thompſon
		Elin

Figure 8. Forster, Mary, comp. *These several Papers was sent to the Parliament ...
Being above Seven Thousand of the Names of the Hand-Maids and Daughters of the Lord
... Who Witness Against the Oppression of Tithes and Other Things.* London, 1659.
© Copyright The British Museum.

radical sects, but as centrally formative of all aspects of the sectarian phenomenon: their congregational composition, the writings and prophecies produced from within their ranks, and the ways in which they were perceived by others.'[39]

Scholarship on print culture offers new avenues into studies of subjectivity and gender, though the development of gendered identities in relation to interpretive communities and reading practices has received limited critical attention, particularly in analyses of nondramatic seventeenth-century literature. In attempting to address that gap, I focus in this section of the chapter on a particularly unusual example of female authorship and identity formation as documented in the works of the dissenter, Anna Trapnel. The representation by and of Trapnel offers insights into the trials of authorship and into the writing and counter-performance of the female subject, including negotiations of the private and public self in a judicial system.

I begin by rephrasing Joan Kelly's famous question, 'Did women have a Renaissance?' and Margaret W. Ferguson's follow-up discussion about whether women had a Reformation to ask instead whether women experienced a revolution during this time of political upheaval and cultural change. Patricia Crawford has recently argued that while the Revolution 'did not alter any of the fundamental constraints on women's lives,' it did offer some opportunities for personal and collective expression justified and authorized through claims to spiritual equality.[40] The record of women's personal and political disillusion, including that triggered by the failure of God's national cause, constitutes in particular a significant part of the radical literary tradition. Sectarians, such as Mary Cary, Anna Trapnel, Elinor Channel, Elizabeth Poole, Hester Biddle, and Margaret Fell, relied heavily on the printed word to spread political and dissenting opinions and to produce narratives of self and community formation. Certainly, however, women's literary renaissance and revolution was also double-edged: though their output doubled during the mid-century, it still constituted only about 1 per cent of all writings that were generated. Of the material that was produced, much dealt with the personal experiences of trial and defeat.[41]

The experimental nature of autobiographical writings is intensified in the works of visionaries and prophets of the period. A common characteristic of the record of personal experience of the period is a consciousness of the writing process, and both the opportunities and the obstacles it presents. Another element is an avowed concern with the truth, often provoked by an 'almost legalistic desire for self-defence.'[42]

Through writings and utterances, prophets developed both a collective identity and a symbolic, double-voiced language and dramatic self-portraiture that eschewed traditional forms of representation and interpretation.[43] In the process of constructing and articulating identity through the act of writing, self-other relations are constantly renegotiated. The prophet moves between self-affirmation and self-annihilation; through the act of ventriloquism or the projection of another's voice – that of God – she brings forth the Word. Her utterances are in turn subject to various conflicting interpretations: prophetic statements could be read as divine or satanic and could appear either self-effacing or self-aggrandizing. The prophet could gain a privileged status in society by way of the anxious respect she aroused, or her performance as an author or public actor might merely reinforce the stereotype of women as irrational, even hysterical creatures, or as passive instruments of external powers.

This ambiguous response to female visionaries and their works is evidenced in the critical reception of Anna Trapnel, a Fifth Monarchist who defended the millenarian doctrine of the imminent establishment of God's kingdom and the destruction of competing worldly powers, as prophesied in Daniel and Revelation. Her dramatic entry into the political arena is reminiscent of Lilburne's. The connection between Lilburne and Trapnel is implied, for example, in correspondence of 25 July 1653 in which an account of Lilburne's detention at Guildhall is juxtaposed with a report of a new actor on the political stage, who is introduced as follows: 'There has started up an audacious virago, or feminine tub-preacher, who last Sunday held forth for almost two hours in the late Queen's mass chapel at Somerset House, Strand, and has done so there and elsewhere several Sundays of late. She claps her Bible and thumps the pulpit cushion with almost as much confidence (I should have said impudence) as honest Hugh Peters himself.'[44] Trapnel's performance included the publication, likely by her Fifth Monarchist friends, of four texts in 1654 after the dissolution of the Barebones Parliament in Cromwell's assembly: *The Cry of a Stone*, *A Legacy for Saints* (consisting of letters Trapnel produced while incarcerated in Plymouth and which were printed to publicize her cause while she was in Bridewell), *Anna Trapnel's Report and Plea*, and *Strange and Wonderful News from White-Hall*. Of particular interest is *The Cry of a Stone*, which is produced in a 'declamatory autobiographical-prophetic-political-historical-spiritual mode,'[45] and is a transcription of the rapturous prophetic verses and prayers she uttered while in a trance at Whitehall. In

January 1654 Trapnel and others were awaiting at Whitehall the outcome of the hearing of Vavasor Powell, a Welsh preacher, who predicted the demise of the Protectorate.[46] *The Cry of a Stone*, which reinforces Powell's message, is at the centre of controversy at Trapnel's 1654 trial that follows her arrest in Cornwall and is recorded in *Anna Trapnel's Report and Plea*. Trapnel's trials are, then, multiple and interrelated; they refer to her challenges first as a female public speaker and author in the early modern period; second as a political visionary; and third as a defendant in the courtroom drama in which her performances and writings were used as evidence against her and in which she was thus forced to play various parts, one she dramatizes in her *Report and Plea*.

Both in her transcribed and her self-authored writings, Trapnel subsumes her individual identity in a communal identity. The title of *The Cry of a Stone* refers to the apocryphal Second Book of Esdras (2 Esdras 5:4–5), Habakkuk 2:11–12, and Luke 19:40, thereby locating Trapnel in the line of biblical prophets who were unjustly silenced or persecuted. Lilburne had cited the same tradition for his bold defence during his trial, 'I will not hold my peace,' he informs the fat lawyer; 'Alas if men should hold their peace in such times as these, the Lord would cause the verie Stones to speake to convince man of his cowardlie basenesse' (*A Worke of the Beast*, 20, 23). While resisting structures of authority, Trapnel goes still further, bypassing male forms of mediation and interpretation by relocating the power of prophecy in the female. The autobiographical fragment she includes in *The Cry of a Stone* alongside her biblical genealogy reveals that in her deathbed speech, Trapnel's mother prayed to God to double his spirit on her child (3). According to Charlotte Otten, this request recalls that of the prophet Elisha who asked Elijah for a double portion of his spirit in 2 Kings 2:9.[47] But Trapnel's tract of the same year, *Report and Plea*, transfers the exchange of power between males and identifies a more immediate source for her mother's prayer: Elkanah's presentation to his beloved though barren wife, Hannah, a double portion of the sacrifice he makes to God (1 Samuel 1:5). The name Anna is a variant of Hannah, a connection Trapnel reinforces in *Report and Plea* with passages from 1 Samuel – including Hannah's distress about her barrenness and Eli's false accusation of Hannah's intoxication.[48] Relations between Hannah and Elkanah ('Now Elkanah knewe Hannah his wife'; 1 Samuel 1:19), which led to Samuel's birth, are translated in *Report and Plea* into Trapnel's relationship with Christ who 'maketh fruitful, and removes barrenness' (A3). In fact it is Christ whom she was urged to marry after her mother's death,

Trapnel states in her *Legacy for Saints*.[49] Thus she deflects criticism about her dramatic self-portraiture and mysterious utterances by locating herself in a line of holy women as well as men who defend the truth in the face of persecution: '*If ye suffer for righteousness sake, happy are ye*' (A1). Trapnel's power of expression and gift of prophecy confirm that her prayers and her mother's have, like Hannah's, been answered.

This personal testimony, like the literature of dissent generally, has a public function and communal context. Maureen Bell observes in fact that 'what marks the activity of ... prophets and visionaries, and of other sectarian writers, is a clearly stated sense of the community, an interconnected group of preachers, writers and readers.' Consequently, 'categories of "private" and "public" prove to be false distinction.'[50] Like Mary Cary's *Little Horns Doom*, which incorporates a ready-made support group, *The Cry of a Stone* and *Report and Plea* imagine a community of readers and witnesses. In *The Cry of a Stone*, Trapnel names the Fifth Monarchists, Henry Jessey and William Greenhill, the Fifth Monarchist sympathizer, Hanserd Knollys, and the Independent ministers, John Simpson and Ralph Venning as witnesses who were prepared to confirm her story. The account is also a conversion story for the sceptics in her audience: 'I was judged by divers friends to be under a temptation' (5); while others, whom she specifically identifies, 'waited till they saw it accomplished, and then admired' (7).

Trapnel's trials of authorship are relocated in a courtroom setting during her hearing in Plymouth, presented in *Anna Trapnel's Report and Plea*, which recounts her prophetic mission to the South-west and her imprisonment. Appealing in her account to a wide readership of 'all sorts of people, high and low,' Trapnel imagines a cross-section of sympathetic readers who comprise a community of spectators, judges, and converts to the testimony of the persecuted prophet (A4). The autobiographical work also acquires the properties of a public testimonial through its dramatic features. The recorded courtroom drama, in which Trapnel assumes the roles of the male transcriber and 'relator' from *The Cry of a Stone*, is intended to vie with the 'the worlds stage of Reports, and Rumors' which transformed her into 'a Monster or some ill-shaped Creature' (49).

Though not a Quaker, Trapnel incorporates features of the social drama of the trial as described by Richard Bauman. In doing so, Trapnel develops an alternative site of judgment and justice in which she arraigns her accusers. Reenacting the drama of justice, Trapnel in *Report and Plea*, for example, mixes direct and indirect speech and presents marked exchanges between herself and the authorities who interrogate her about the authorship of *The Cry of a Stone*:

> Then *Lobb* said, *Tender her the book which was written from something said at* White-Hall: so the book was reached out to me: and Justice *Lobb* said, *What say you to that book? will you own it? is it yours?*
> A.T. *I am not careful to answer you in that matter.*
> Then they said, *She denies her book.* Then they whispered with those behinde them. Then spake Justice *Lobb* again, and said, *Read a vision of the horns out of the book:* so that was read: then Justice *Lobb* said, *What say you to this? is this yours?*
> A.T. *I am not careful to answer you in that matter, touching the whole book, as I told you before, so I say again: for what was spoken, was at* White-Hall, *at a place of concourse of people, and neer a Counsel, I suppose wise enough to call me into question if I offended, and unto them I appeal;* but though it was said, I appealed unto Caesar, and unto Caesar should I go; yet I have not been brought before him which is called Caesar: so much by the by. (Report 25)

The public reading ordered by Justice Lobb of Trepnel's apocalyptic, political vision of the horns – in which the identification of Cromwell as the little horn of the Beast displaces the allegorization of Charles I in like terms by the Fifth Monarchist, Mary Cary, several years before-hand,[51] provokes another evasive response from Trapnel. Trapnel again refers in the passive voice to '*what was spoken ... at* White-Hall' (25). The circumstances of the production and reception of *The Cry of a Stone*, of which she reminds the court, complicate questions about the (gender) politics of translating Trapnel's speech into print and thus about the authorship of this contested work. Recorded by a male amanuensis, who acknowledges that he transcribed only as much as he could with his 'very slow and unready hand,' and who admits to omitting some of her utterances (*Cry* a2v; see also 19, 42), *The Cry of a Stone* is at several removes from the speaker and her speech community, which received the mediated prophecy first-hand. The affirmation Trapnel received from this audience is translated in *Report and Plea* into a statement about the spectators' and readers' reactions to her testimony. The avowed concern with the truth, often provoked by a concern for self-legitimation that characterizes women's autobiographical writings, is transferred to the 'rude multitude' – the unofficial jury in her rescripted trial. The multitude, Trapnel explains, is persuaded by her and renders the verdict: '*Sure this woman is no witch, for she speaks many good words, which the witches could not.* And thus the Lord made the rude rabble to justifie his appearance,' Trapnel resolutely declares (28).

Neither Trapnel nor her supporters, however, had the final word. The critical reception of the prophet and her writings intensified the trials of authorship as the drama of justice spilled over into print culture and popular culture. Henry Walker's *Severall Proceedings of State Affaires* offers a detailed account of Trapnel's physical condition, her attendants, the manner in which she delivers her trances, and their political signifi-cance. As a sympathizer to millenarianism, Walker's report was mixed rather than being wholly derisive, and he conveys the range of re-sponses that Trapnel's performances engendered:

> A Breviate of *Hannah* whom some call a Prophetesse, in *White hall*, ... to whom many hundreds do daily come to see and hear, who hath now been there about a fortnight: Those that look to her, and use to bee with her, sayes she neither eateth nor drinketh, save onely sometimes a Tost and drink, and that she is in a Trance, and some say that what she doth is by a mighty inspiration, others say they suppose her to be of a troubled mind, and people flocking to her so as they doe causeth her to continue this way, and some say worse, so every one gives their opinions as they please. But this is visible to those that see and hear her ... Her prayers are in exceeding good method and order, good language, and such as indeed all that come doe much admire what they hear from her, excellent words, and well placed, such as are not ordinary.[52]

Trapnel's criticisms of Cromwell, Walker continues, were well-inten-tioned and in parts also well-founded.

While Walker surveys the varying reactions of the audience that Trap-nel's performance provoked, the majority of other commentators take the matter of interpretation and judgment into their own hands by either discrediting her entirely or attacking her duplicity. In his corre-spondence to Cromwell on 7 February, Marchamont Nedham, report-ing on a recent 'confluence of silly wretches,' names Trapnel as one 'who played her part lately at Whitehall at the ordinary.' He accuses Trapnel of contriving a 'twofold design,' involving both the printing of her diatribe against the Cromwellian regime and the proclamation of her views '*vivâ voce*,' and he concludes that the havoc she wreaks is nationwide. Worse yet is the fact that her audiences are receptive: 'The vulgar dote on vain prophecies.' Some of her prophecies wound up, he explains, 'in the hands of a man who was in the room when she uttered them day by day in her trance, as they call it.' If the transcriber fulfills his promise to lend Nedham the scripts, 'I will show you them,' Nedham promises Cromwell; 'They would make 14 or 15 sheets in print.'[53] Nedham's *Mercurius Politicus* claims that 'Mr. *Langdon*, and Mr. *Bauden*, two Members of the late short-lived Parliament ... endeavored to make a learned Defence for her, but it was not suffered'; they then presented bail, that is, 'entered into Bonds of three hundred pounds.' Trapnel's intent, according to Nedham, was to 'vent her Prophesies, and thereby disaffect the people to the present Authority.'[54] Another Fifth Monarchist assigns a different motive – or 'twofold design' – to Trapnel's performances: Arise Evans, who is featured in a news report in *The Grand Politique Post* alongside a story about Trapnel's Whitehall trances, produced Elinor Channel's *A Message from God, [By a Dumb woman]* in a manner resembling that of Anna Trapnel's relator. Evans, however, distinguishes between the two prophecies, concluding that 'though [Channel's] be but short,' Cromwell 'shall find more truth and substance in it, than in all *Hana Trampenels* songs or sayings, whom some account of as the *Diana* of the English, *Acts* 19.34.'[55] In Acts 19, the Ephesians reject the apostles' testimony in favour of their pagan goddess, Diana, whose image they reproduce and sell at a great profit (Acts 19:26). What we discover, then, in reviewing this drama of dissent is another revealing example of the 'appropriation' of courtroom performances and writings by different audiences and interpretive communities that remained at odds about their reading of this female actor, who in turn had defiantly rescripted the roles in which she was originally cast.[56]

II

Speech acts and open silences that characterize performances and literature produced in response to judicial dramas all resist interpretation by presenting sites and spaces for conflicting readings. They thus afford opportunities for actors, directors, and especially audiences, to 'settle upon and enact specific meanings and effects,' an opportunity that is conventionally associated with the experience of play-going.[57] Trapnel's strategic manipulation of communicative codes and her use of silences and evasions in her trials are a case in point. They also offer a foray into another drama that unfolded in the 1650s, though this time for the members of the Quaker sect and specifically for James Nayler, the rebel Quaker leader. Roger Farmer, in *Sathan Inthron'd in his Chair of Pestilence*, recounts the 1656 entry of Nayler into the city of Bristol in imitation of

Christ's triumphant entry into Jerusalem prior to his crucifixion. Attending Nayler in the procession are Dorcas Erbury, Hannah Stranger, and Martha Simmon(d)s – Nayler's greatest disciple and, according to Farmer, the instigator of his tragic fall: 'Now here you see this *Martha Simonds* is much complained of by *Fox*, as one that disturbes the scaene, and *spoils the play* ... And truth is, it is not altogether ground-lesse to conceive of her [as a witch], as will appear when you have the story of her prevailings upon *Nailer at the first*, according to her own confession.' These remarks introduce a cross-examination of Nayler by the authorities, which concludes with the charge against Simmonds for bewitching the emasculated Nayler and potentially George Fox as well.[58] Central to this and most versions of the Nayler drama is the disputed significance of the procession by Nayler and his company. While Quaker supporters and deriders, including George Bishop, William Dewsbury, John Perrot, George Fox, John Deacon, and James Parnell, all conveyed their fascination with the Bristol episode, it became particularly popular among critics, who used it as incriminating evidence against Nayler and Quakerism in such tracts as *The Quacking Mountebanck*, *The Deceived and Deceiving Quakers Discovered*, and *Quakery Slain Irrecoverably*.

All subsequent reenactments of Nayler's trial reveal a fascination with the performances of the actors in the sensational drama, which 'engaged Cromwell's parliamentarians in one of their most searching debates.'[59] The proceedings involved unravelling the elusive identity of the actor and of interrogating Nayler about the epithets by which he was known to his female disciples: 'The Fairest of Ten Thousand,' 'The Only-begotten Son of God,' 'The Prophet of the Most High,' 'The King of Israel,' 'The Everlasting Son of Righteousness,' 'Prince of Peace,' and finally, 'Jesus.'[60] The officials also confronted Nayler and his company about their reenactment of Christ's journey. Publicly read letters are used as evidence against him, and after heated exchanges, the judges sentenced him for 'horrid Blasphemy.' The question about imposing the death penalty on Nayler becomes the subject of more lengthy debates by Parliament in which Cromwell also participates.[61]

The *True Narrative of the Examination, Tryall, and Sufferings of James Nay-ler* consists of a series of contesting accounts and voices assessing and disputing the evidence and the procedures used to arraign Nayler. The first section consists of a text of the examination, accompanied by a marginal gloss which questions each detail. Journal entries describing from a pro-Nayler perspective the events of each day of the trial and punishment constitute the middle section of the *Narrative*, which takes advantage of the James-Jesus connection that Nayler played up. Nayler's memorable sufferings at the pillory – when two women stood at his side and a sign saying 'This is the King of the Jews' was placed above him – were apparently witnessed by 'many thousands of people' who were in awe over his fortitude (41–2). The final components of *A True Narrative* are petitions presented on Nayler's behalf. The work thus offers a defence that the courtroom drama had denied the accused. Nayler himself valued written documentation and pleaded that his testimony be recorded accurately. The author of the *True Narrative* reports, 'That he told those Ministers, he saw they had an intent to make him suffer (though innocent) as an evill doer; and therefore denyed any to be present that might be indifferent Judges betwixt them and him, (or words to that purpose.) And therefore he shold not say any thing, unlesse, what passed, might be writ down, and a Coppy therefore given him to keep, or left with the Goaler, signed by them' (58). The examiners assented, and made arrangements to record the interrogation. But they later burnt their testimony, thus failing to keep their promise (40). The *Narrative* ends by questioning the jurisdiction of the examiners, who become the sole reporters of the case to the judges. The author of the document also challenges the credibility of the testimony, that is, both the verbal accounts and the correspondence used as evidence against Nayler. Finally, he asks why Nayler's original request could not have been honoured: 'Whether it were not a very reasonable desire of James Naylor's ... that Questions might be sent him in writing from the Parliament, and he might have liberty to return his Answers in writing; for the avoiding of misinterpretation of his adversaries' (60).

John Deacon's *The Grand Imposter Examined* seeks to undermine Nayler's performance further. A preface to the reader comments on the recorded exchanges between Nayler and his judges, and accuses Nayler of playing Christ.[62] The account of James Naylor's *Examination* is preceded by another address to the readers in which the famous ride into Bristol is recalled. Nayler and his disciples are arrested, and the letters found on them were confiscated and used as evidence against them and Nayler, who is identified as 'the chief actor' in the drama. The interrogation focuses on the representation of Nayler in a letter sent to him by Hannah Stranger, which Deacon considers 'not impertient to deliver' by inserting it in his text (6–9). Nayler's responses to the authorities thereafter focus on his identification with Christ whose own evasive responses he echoes throughout. The final question deals with his authorship of his writings, which he affirms (24; misnumbered 42). Then, after recording the individual testimonies of Martha Simmonds, Hannah Stranger, Thomas Stranger, Timothy Wedlock, and Dorcus Erbury, Deacon cites further correspondence to reinforce Nayler's guilt.[63]

Among John Milton's papers is a letter, '*Mr* William Malyn *to the Lord Protector,*' which focuses not on Nayler's ceremonial entry into Bristol, the subject of most of the histories of Nayler, but on a visit to Nayler in Bridewell. William Malyn presents his reactions to Nayler's confinement in the form of an official government report describing the Quaker's physical condition, his refusal to cooperate with the authorities who command him to work for his keep, and his interactions with his visitors. Casting himself in the role of a witness and reporter, he becomes the Nuntius in this account who conveys his impressions of Nayler in the aftermath of his catastrophe. Unlike the other commentators on Nayler, this one neither defends nor denigrates the Quaker, but inquires into the motives of this mysterious person whose silence only adds to his appeal. Malyn does acknowledge the influence of others on Nayler, suggesting that his visitors 'nourish his temptation' by their admiration;[64] but he does not, as so many others do, inveigh against female waywardness and dwell on the alleged cause of his demise, Martha Simmonds. The letter describes Malyn's attempt to delve into Nayler's mind and reproduce the interior drama. A.R. Barclay in *Letters of Early Friends* notes that Malyn 'seems not a little mistaken in his opinion of J.N.'s state.'[65] Yet the fascination and frustrations with the prisoner's motives, which become as much the focus of Malyn's report as Nayler himself, enter the received tradition of Nayler's history, a history that also serves as a preface to the tragedy of Samson – the subject of Milton's final off-stage performance.[66]

In another interior drama of dissent, the early Quaker minister Sarah Blackborow turns the justice system back on those who persecute God's chosen. As a witness to the indwelling spirit, Blackborow encourages different acts of witnessing as enacted through her writings as well as her efforts at bringing other works to light. The latter include James Nayler's 1657 *How Sin Is Strengthened, and How It Is Overcome* and an account of the death of Richard Hubberthorne, which she published. Blackborow's concern to promote the examination of interior spaces and active self-scrutiny informs her visionary treatise, *A Visit to the Spirit in Prison*. '[L]et the righteous witnesse of God in your consciences Judge you,'[67] she declares in this liberation text, which frees the oppressed from external laws while sentencing those 'Ministers and Teachers of the People' who unjustly condemn and persecute God's people. Through the publication and circulation of her theological reflections, Blackborow converts her readers – the antagonists and the sympathizers – into witnesses and judges of themselves. The self-policing conscience displaces the church and state authorities as the judge of the individual.

Blackborow's *A Visit to the Spirit in Prison* prophesies the renewed persecution of Nonconformist sects in the changed social and political climate of the 1660s. Sir Philip Musgrave, a governmental official who was especially active in the suppression of recusants and nonconformists, reported in 1663: 'Those in authority can hardly bear the insolence of the Quakers who meet every week; they keep copies of proceedings against them by justices of peace, to be ready against a time when they shall call the justices to account; stricter course should be taken with them, and a few horse kept in constant pay at Carlisle.'[68] Accounts of the authorities' discomfort with Quaker meetings are hardly scarce. *A Relation of the Imprisonment of Mr. John Bunyan*, for example, presents a dialogue between Bunyan and the justices, among them Mr Foster of Bedford, who confronts John Bunyan about the communal gatherings encouraged by his preaching: 'if you will say you will call the people no more together, you may have your liberty; if not, you must be sent away to prison' (12). In an explanation addressed directly to his reader, Bunyan states: 'to have any such meetings was against the law; and therefore he would have me leave off, and say, I would call the people no more together' (13). The meetings were held to build community, to enable the confirmation and communication of the word, and to offer support to individual Quakers. They also had an additional public function and were intended to attract potential converts.[69] But the justices' reactions confirm that such meetings posed the same 'security' threat that necessitated the theatre closures.

Considerable evidence of the continuation of Quaker meetings exists in the letters, documents, autobiographical testimonies, and trial accounts of Quakers. Of particular interest for this study is the record of the courtroom dramas involving Margaret Fell and George Fox. In 1663 the magistrates at Ulverston summoned Margaret Fell for permitting illegal meetings at Swarthmore Hall. Her refusal to take the oath of allegiance resulted in a prison sentence, after which she was brought before Justice Twisden in Lancaster. *The Examination and Tryall of* Margaret Fell *and* George Fox (1664) consists of transcriptions of the two Quakers' arraignments, and ends with a sermon, titled 'Something in Answer to Bishop Lancelot Andrews Sermon concerning Swearing ...' Like the 'acts' in the *Examination*, the sermon is presented in dialogue form, each statement countered by a response challenging Bishop Andrews's defence of oath-swearing as a biblically sanctioned practice. The first trial account or 'act' in the *Examination*, 'The Examination of M.F. before Judge Twisden at the Assizes holden at Lancaster Castle the 14 day of the first month about the 9th hour in the morning 1663/4,' records Fell's arraignment for keeping 'multitudes of People at [her] house in a pretence of worshipping God.'[70] As in Bunyan's case, the magistrates demand her assurance that she will stop organizing meetings: 'put in security that you many have no more meetings at your house' (7), an order with which Fell refuses to comply. Fell's second courtroom appearance follows George Fox's interrogation by Twisden (8ff), in which the former, like his future spouse, refuses to take the oath that is read aloud to him. Fox dominates and directs the exchange. 'The appearance of M.F. The second time being the 16th day of the aforementioned moneth 1663/4' (10–12) precedes Fox's arraignment on the same day (12). Fell's following trial (12–17) consists of long speeches in which she responds to the accusations about her transgressions, insists on her liberty of conscience, and accuses the judges of treating Quakers as Catholic recusants. As a whole, *The Examination and Tryall of Margaret Fell and George Fox*, then, performs the work of the Quaker meetings in generating a readership that becomes complicit in the defence of religious toleration.

The final 'act,' 'The last Assizes holden at Lancaster the 29th of the 6th Moneth 1664' (17–24), is produced by George Fox and also printed in the *Journal of George Fox*. The familiar, oft-repeated, account of Fox's refusal to take the oath – a speech act he judges blasphemous – includes Fox's critiques of the legal procedures. Witty, learned retorts constitute an integral part of his exploitation of the theatrical potential of public confrontations, in which Lilburne had also indulged.[71] In response to the court's laughter about a humorous remark he made, Fox identifies the court with the theatre: 'I asked them if this Court was a Play-house, where is Gravity, and Sobriety, for that did not become them.'[72] The jury, he reports, becomes unsettled by the disturbance, 'And there began to be a murmuring against the Clerks' (18–19).

Fox's subsequent dismissal of the indictment against him, which was read aloud, was judged as a sign of his guilt. Yet the accused could traverse, that is, challenge the charges,[73] as Twisden had earlier advised Fell. Fox responds by identifying the numerous clerical errors in the prosecution's document (*Examination* 21; *Journal* 72, 76, 80, 86–8). The act of critical reading is complemented by verbal performances through which Fox controls the reactions of the people in attendance, including the jury members. The observers are 'struck and astonisht' by his words and 'the Jury would fain have been dismist' (22), he reports. The Justice who was himself self-judged – 'I lookt him in the face, and he was judged in himself, for he saw that I saw him' (22) – summons the jury again and repeats the order about oath-swearing. In the end, the jury members render a guilty verdict, despite contradicting their own indictment, as Fox notes in his *Journal* (19). The private *Journal* serves a public function of overriding the court's decision by vindicating Fox and setting the record straight for the jury outside the courtroom.

This chapter has examined the rescripted theatricalized performances of seventeenth-century dissenters and visionaries through print and in the 'social drama' of the trial. The courtroom dramas offer sites for the convergence of speaking and writing and for the staging of judicial speech acts, as well as for dramatic performances, interspersed with scenes of public reading. The declarative function of legal discourse – oral and written – in the trial accounts of the Levellers, the Fifth Monarchists, and Quakers enables a renegotiation of power relations, constructions of selfhood and authority, and the creation of alternative juries and arenas for judgment. In each case, the arraigned radicals act out their resistance in dramatic productions for popular audiences and readers, who were given active parts to perform. As we observe in the epilogue, interpretive communities of writers and their audiences and readers again dominate the stage in the trial accounts that take us 'beyond the fifth Act.'

'Beyond the fifth Act': Milton and Dryden on the Restoration Stage

In each of the five chapters of this book we have witnessed how the managers of the political stage and of the (ideological) power of representation are outmanoeuvred, if not outperformed, by writers, alternative dramatic productions, and by the *'guiltles press'* that *'acts'* in the place of the theatre. In chapter 1, monopolizers are forced to share the stage with pro-parliamentary writers and printers who created a culture of debate, a court of public opinion, and 'a state of intellectual free trade.'[1] In chapter 2, the tables are turned as the managers of Strafford's trial fail to anticipate the royalist actor's powerful self-defence and his refusal to deliver the required contrite, last dying speech occasioned by the scaffold performance. As recognized by his supporters and opponents alike, Laud's dignified, defiant self-authored defence at his March 1644 trial also undermined Parliament's 'show trial.' The final acts of the tragedies of Strafford and Laud set the stage for Charles's counterperformances on the scaffold and in the pages of *Eikon Basilike*, whose mesmerizing, theatrical effects not even Parliament's champion writer could diffuse. In the meantime, theatres that defied the ban on stage productions, including The Fortune, The Bull, The Cockpit, and the theatre at Salisbury Court, offered a venue for cultural and political critique. The issuing of additional ordinances following the 1642 theatre closures is evidence of the playwrights' resistance, the actors' determination, and the demands of the audiences, as well as of the threat that stage productions posed for the governing regime.[2]

More relevant for this study has been the strategic use of textual machinery, dramatic genres, and theatrical discourses to involve readers in extrajudicial and often unauthorized practices. By encouraging playreading, closet dramatists, pamphleteers, and journalists reconstituted the sites of judgment and justice. Considered in these terms, the motives for the House of Commons' printing of governmental speeches or of *Tyrannicall-Government Anatomized* are exposed. But royalist writers also developed their own common language, staged debates, and brought to print culture a space for dramas in which readers and auditors played their parts. Thus the new playtexts of the new seventeenth century became implicated in the critical and political work of writers at both ends of the political spectrum.

Dissenters likewise engaged in alternative stage acts and printed performances, particularly in response to censorship or persecution. The confrontation of radicals with the authorities is staged in the 'social drama' of the trial, which serves as a forum for speech acts, the public reading of writings judged 'incriminating,' the enactment of social conflicts generally, and the construction of interpretive communities. Like his Quaker successor George Fox, the Leveller John Lilburne became a lead actor in the courtroom dramas of the time, in which he was called to answer for his 'seditious' writings. The testimony presented as *Truths Victory over Tyrants and Tyranny*, a partisan account of Lilburne's 1649 trial, acts as a suitable prologue for the final off-stage performance examined in this book. *Truths Victory* reports that the accused requested two days to prepare a response to the charges brought before him. The officials deny Lilburne's wish, insisting that he perform now 'or for ever hold [his] tongue.'[3] Lilburne then asks for two hours, but is again refused: 'the *States* three *Beagles* yelped out with full mouth, No, no, no, not an inch of Time.' The courtroom scenario gives way to what can be nothing less than a providential act of judgment and justice that brings down the Rump's (play)house: 'So soon as they had said this, a Scaffold in the Hall fell down, some (being hurt) crying out, which so amazed, and terrifyed the unjust Judges, that for almost the space of an houre, they did nothing but stare one upon another, in which time Mr. Lilburne did so prepare himself for them that when he came to speake, he did confute them with good *Law*, and honest Reason.'[4] The stunned judges then leave the verdict to the jury, which declares Lilburne's innocence, to the elation of the crowds in attendance.

The final theatre of judgment in this book is John Milton's *Samson Agonistes*, a political closet drama designed in opposition to the interpretive communities generated by the royalist-sponsored Restoration stage and literary marketplace, communities that, however, ultimately frustrated Milton's efforts at controlling the reception of his dramatic poem. As I demonstrate, a study of the received tradition of *Samson Agonistes* that takes us 'beyond the fifth Act'[5] effectively illustrates once again the ways in which the actual uses of texts and the contexts in which they are generated defy the intentions and desires of their authors and of those 'who produced the discourses and fashioned the norms.'[6] Moreover, this epilogue is designed to identify the results of subjecting Milton's dramatic poem to paper-contestations and theatre audiences in a new area of performance which it nervously invokes in the preface, but for 'which this [canonical] work never was intended' (*SA*, Preface p. 550).

I

By the time that Parliament released *Tyrannicall-Government Anatomized*, Milton had already made his debut as a polemicist, one whose larger program of civic and political reform depended on the vital role he ascribed to aestheticism. Milton's early position on stage plays in particular is represented in a familiar passage from the 1641 *Reason of Church Government*, in which he proposes 'the managing of our publick sports, and festival pastimes, [so] that they might ... civilize, adorn and make discreet our minds by the learned and affable meetings of frequent Academies, and the procurement of wise and artfull recitations sweetned with eloquent and gracefull enticements to the love and practice of justice, temperance and fortitude.'[7] Several years later, *Areopagitica*, Milton's 1643 attack on Parliament's renewal of licensing orders included a defence of plays and specifically of play-reading as a profitable activity that should not be censored. There is no record, he explains, that 'the writings of those old Comedians were supprest, though the acting of them were forbid'; he states, moreover, that '*Plato* commended the reading *Aristophanes* the loosest of them all, to his royall scholler *Dionysius* is commonly known, and may be excus'd, if holy *Chrysostome*, as is reported, nightly studied so much the same Author' (*CPW*, 2:495–6).

Milton's use of dramatic literary modes is evident in a variety of his works, including *Comus* and *Paradise Lost*, but *Samson Agonistes* is of course most reliant on the strategic use of dramatic conventions as an expression of cultural and political resistance. An examination of early Restoration theatre culture and the various contesting interpretive communities of England in the 1660s offers an illuminating context for rereading Milton's last work. Likely a product of the Restoration,[8] *Samson Agonistes* is composed by a poet who repudiates Restoration literary culture and theatre culture. *Samson Agonistes* negotiates between print and performance: it advertises itself both as a readerly text and a drama; yet as a tragedy it imitates Greek rather than newly restored Roman models and denies its performability. While appealing to an elite, republican readership, the text registers its discomfort with popular tastes, especially those cultivated by stage plays, whose final performance Milton fantasizes when Samson in the supreme act of iconoclasm and judgment brings down the theatre on his idolatrous Philistine audience.

An exploration of the literary and political culture in which Restoration drama was generated and to which *Samson Agonistes* responds reveals the fault lines in the critical tradition of the poem and in the Miltonic oeuvre, which have commonly been buffered from 'infamy' and problems of textual variability.[9] To reread *Samson Agonistes* as a text that responds to popular influences is to oppose the strong tendency in Milton studies to enshrine the poem as a sacred text, a practice recently criticized by Leah Marcus, John Rumrich, Stephen Dobranski, and Joseph Wittreich, who have exposed its indeterminacy and internal difference. With the exception of Jackson Cope and, more recently, Steven Zwicker, Peggy Samuels, and Nancy Klein Maguire, scholars have not examined Milton's volume in relation to early modern drama, and none of these critics has conducted an extensive study of *Samson Agonistes* as a readerly text subject to practices of cultural consumption in Milton's day.[10]

The preface of *Samson Agonistes* designates the poem as part of a vertical genealogy extending from classical tragedy. Milton's intended audience of republican, Christian readers would see itself as performing the cultural and political work of carrying on that tradition. Another interpretive community invoked by the text is the encroaching, antagonistic world of Restoration drama, which Milton rebukes in his preface in remarking on the 'infamy, which ... [tragedy] undergoes at this day' (Preface, p. 550). Milton is uncomfortably aware that certain readers will bring their expectations of heroic drama to their experience of the poem. 'How else could Milton have responded but with intense curiosity and competitiveness when a form suddenly appeared in the mid-1660s that claimed to do exactly what had preoccupied him in the 1640s and toward which he had made his own notes and plans?' Zwicker asks in his study of *Paradise Regained* as a poem that interrogates the themes of Restoration heroic drama: love, empire, and glory.[11] *Samson Agonistes*, which was published together with *Paradise Regained*, is in fact in commercial competition with a culture Milton cannot effectively resist. Both the royalist-sponsored theatre – dominated by John Dryden – and the bookstore community impede Milton's efforts at controlling the reception of his closet drama, a genre that is itself on trial. A study of the received tradition of *Samson Agonistes* effectively demonstrates at the same time how the actual uses of texts defy the intentions of their authors.

The interpretive communities of relevance to this discussion develop in response to Carolean theatre culture and the marketplace, both of which were used to secure the recently restored monarchical control. The new regime at this time was responsible for a 'sharp contraction' of the public sphere as it exerted its influence over the press and modes of cultural production. Playwrights sympathetic to royalism closed off their texts from dissent by addressing a like-minded clientele captivated by spectacle. Milton responds by establishing an antagonistic relationship with the theatre and marketplace, which provide the immediate contexts and material communities for his 1671 volume. As a closet drama indebted to the classical tragedy, *Samson Agonistes* appeals to an imagined community of partisan readers – 'an invisible public of like-minded readers' – whose critical interpretation of the text becomes an 'internalised, read-only, version' of the collective experience that theatres in the ancient republics had enabled.[12] The text, then, takes on the form of an oppositional drama, produced in a climate where court sponsorship of the theatre otherwise precluded the production of such writings.[13] This reading of *Samson Agonistes* and its indebtedness to Greek and biblical models rather than heroic drama, tragicomedy, and sentimental plays concludes with competing accounts of Samson's act of (self-)destruction and sets the stage for the poem's controversial reception history.

Both as a dramatic poem and a cultural and commercial object, *Samson Agonistes* repudiates Restoration plays – on the stage and in the marketplace. Practices of collective identification and consumption include for the purposes of this epilogue the reading and purchasing of texts as well as theatre attendance. A description of the cultural and political world of the theatre Milton occupies and struggles to renounce follows, with reference to some of the more popular dramas of the day.

In England heroic sentiment developed during the reign of Charles I in the court of Henrietta Maria. The heroic emphasis in literature, notably the enthusiastic response to idealized notions of love and honour – conventionally identified with the epic and romance – found its way into the theatre. The heroic tradition lay dormant during the 1640s and 1650s, awaiting the revival that accompanied the Restoration. Charles II, who was expected to usher in the heroic age, influenced literary taste in helping to establish the rhymed heroic drama – an expression perhaps of his desire for absolute power, like that enjoyed by the French monarch across the Channel. Heroic dramas featured excessive spectacles; epic plots; love-and-honour themes; bombastic, hyperbolic speeches; stock heroes and villains; and grand and violent action. The genre developed from the plays of Beaumont and Fletcher, English opera, and French court romances, and defended the spirit of the Restoration through the use of exalted verse, imperial overtones, and historical plots highlighting the restoration of monarchy or of law and order. The anonymous *Unfortunate Usurper* draws attention to the political work of the genre: 'True Monarchy's supported by our play.' *The Generall* by Roger Boyle, the earl of Orrery, was the first rhymed heroic play in English, of which the popular *The Siege of Rhodes* was a prototype. Taking his lead from Ariosto and from his contemporary William Davenant, John Dryden declares in *Of Heroique Playes. An Essay* (Preface to *The Conquest of Granada, Part I*) that 'an Heroick Play ought to be an imitation, in little of an Heroick Poem: and consequently ... Love and Valour ought to be the Subject of it.'[14] Dryden's *Conquest of Granada*, which appeared on the stage at the same time that *Samson Agonistes* was published (1671), is generally regarded as the culmination of this form.

The fissures separating seventeenth-century and Restoration scholarship, as well as high and popular culture, have prevented Milton and Samuel Pepys from sharing the stage or from even being studied comparatively. However, Milton has avid play-goers like Pepys in mind when he composes his scornful prefatory remarks about contemporary theatre culture. Much of our information about the colourful theatre scene and the growing appeal of tragicomedy in particular is in fact derived from Pepys's *Diary*.[15] As a frequenter of the theatres, a book collector, and as a consumer and reader of printed plays, Pepys offers a significant point of entry into the world of the theatre, including the public reception to drama off the stage against which the production of *Samson Agonistes* is set and Milton's own response must ultimately be judged.

Pepys's accounts of his theatre-going are interspersed with references to purchasing or reading books, since Restoration drama made its way not only into the theatre but also into the literary marketplace. After seeing Philip Massinger's *The Bondman* performed for the third time, Pepys buys a copy of the tragicomedy at St Paul's Churchyard (25 May 1661; *Diary*, 2:106). Over the next years he attends several more productions of the play which, as he states in an entry for 2 November 1666, he read multiple times (*Diary*, 7:352). In his entries for 23 September 1664, 1 October 1665, 5 August 1666, and 19 December 1668, he mentions reading Davenant's *Siege of Rhodes* and having it read to him (*Diary*,

5:278, 6:247, 7:235, 9:352). He also makes note of his and Mrs Elizabeth Pepys's efforts at memorizing Hamlet's soliloquy 'without book' (13 November 1664; *Diary*, 5:320). Elizabeth's readings of *Mustapha* are cited in entries for 15 and 16 June 1668, that being the year in which the first printed edition of the 1665 play appeared (*Diary*, 9:241, 242).[16] Reading a play (or hearing it read) is quite different from attending a performance, and yet with few exceptions Pepys regards such experiences as complementary and continuous, though always as supplementary exercises. After a performance of Boyle's *The Black Prince* – a rhymed heroic tragedy with a happy ending – Pepys, for example, retires to his chamber to read 'the true story' on which the play was based in John Speed's *Historie of Great Britaine* (23 October 1667; *Diary*, 8:498).

For histories, volumes of poetry, romances, and plays, as well as for news and rendezvous of all kinds, Pepys frequently visited the shop of Henry Herringman, the famous bookseller of the New Exchange (10, 12 August 1667; *Diary*, 8:380, 383). A comparison of the kinds of texts printed for or sold by Herringman with those in John Starkey's shop enables a broader examination of popular tastes and reading habits during this period. Along with the volume containing *Samson Agonistes*, political histories and religious writings, including collections of sermons and works about heresy like Gerard Roberts's *Impudency and Ranterism rebuked*, were printed for Starkey in 1671. Herringman sought to appease rather different tastes: plays – mainly comedies – by William Cartwright, John Caryll, John Dryden, George Etherege, Edward Howard, Robert Howard, William Joyner, Thomas Shadwell, and Sir Samuel Tuke were available in Herringman's shop in 1671, and would have contributed to Milton's anxiety over the encroaching world of the drama, this time as commercial objects.

Since Pepys was an informed critic, it may be surprising that he reserves no place in the *Diary* for Milton. Moreover, Milton is virtually unrepresented in his library. While minor works of Milton and a biography of him appear in the catalogue, *Paradise Lost*, like John Bunyan's *Pilgrim's Progress*, is conspicuously absent. Literary taste was partly determined by political allegiances; as an employee in the court of Charles II, Pepys would in fact have judged Milton's writings as 'pernicious and subversive.'[17]

II

Pepys discontinued his *Diary* in the spring of 1669. The 1669–70 season is, therefore, different for us from the previous in that we know much less about it. On 20 June 1670 the duchess of Orleans, sister of the king, died and the theatres were closed for about six weeks while the court mourned. During this period, the volume containing *Samson Agonistes* was licensed for publication (2 July). The antiheroic brief epic *Paradise Regained* and its companion piece – unintended for the stage – were authorized in the (official) silence of the stage, whose final destruction Milton prophesies in *Samson Agonistes*.[18]

Anticipating the unpopularity of his poem from the start, Milton delays Samson's entry in *Samson Agonistes* by supplying a preface, which is sometimes used 'in case of self defence, or explanation' (550) in classical tragedies. Though Milton distinguishes his preface – presented as an epistle to the reader – from the kind of verse prologues prefixed to plays by Dryden, it resembles the prefaces and prologues used by Restoration playwrights in justifying their undertakings or publishing their anxieties. 'There is nothing more difficult; or which requires a more elevated wit, richer fancy, or subtiler judgement' than playwriting, William Joyner lamented in the preface to *The Roman Empress* (sig. A1v). In his *Defence of the Epilogue. Or, An Essay on the Dramatique Poetry of the last Age*, which serves as a postscript for *The Conquest of Granada, Part II*, Dryden fights back, declaring that the language, wit, and conversation of the present day are superior to literary expression of the '*Golden Age of Poetry*' (*Works*, 11:207) when Shakespeare, Fletcher, and Jonson ruled the stage. Even the work of great Jonson, 'the most judicious of Poets' (*Works*, 11:213), is now judged as replete with errors. The 'gallantry and civility' of the age (*Works*, 11:218) have raised the standards, making it impossible for any playwright to remain unscathed. Like Samson before the Philistine spectators, Dryden casts himself in the epilogue to *Aureng-Zebe* as a fool who performs for fools (*Works*, 12:249–50). However, in the dedication to John, Lord Haughton in *The Spanish Fryar* (1681), Dryden resolves to 'settle [him]self no reputation by the applause of fools' (*Works*, 14:101). While such commentaries do not necessarily reflect the state of theatre or even the concerns of the dramatists precisely, the brief life span of the heroic drama does lend some credibility to the repeated charges of infamy and harassment recorded in plays and dramatic criticism of this period.

In the preface to *Samson Agonistes*, Milton defends tragedy against 'the small esteem, or rather infamy, which in the account of many it undergoes at this day with other common Interludes.' The interludes to which he refers would include the kind of dramatic pieces identified in 'A True, perfect, and exact Catalogue of all the Comedies, Tragedies,

Tragi-Comedies, Pastorals, Masques, and Interludes ...,' which was added to Francis Kirkman's 1671 *Nicomede. A tragi-comedy*. The attention devoted in the preface to the genre of *Samson Agonistes* reveals the poet's efforts at locking the text in particular interpretive traditions. Michael R.G. Spiller in 'Directing the Audience in *Samson Agonistes*' judges that the preface to *Samson Agonistes* 'certainly ... reveals nothing of Milton's intentions.'[19] But the designation of a particular genre is itself a political act. Thomas Healy contends that genre is a more powerful agent of expression than critics often assume by enabling the writer 'to be more than just a force of social and cultural agency which originates the text. Exploitation of generic conventions enables the structures which allow a re-figuring of accepted representations.'[20] Milton's preface performs the political work of establishing the genre of the text and appealing to a readership removed from popular culture. Renaissance theories of tragicomedy are specifically invoked in Milton's repudiation of the 'Intermixing Comic stuff with Tragic sadness and gravity' and of the inclusion of 'trivial and vulgar persons' in works of tragedy. Through his identification with the traditions, conventions, and writings of antiquity and of scripture, he situates *Samson Agonistes* in a canon of his making, a canon separate from the works that dominated the Restoration literary scene.

The alternative readership 'hypothesized' by Milton or 'postulated' by *Samson Agonistes* consists of imitators or defenders of the ancients. His fit readers, for example, will be familiar with the Aristotelian theory of catharsis; the philosophy of Cicero and Plutarch; the works of Seneca and Martial; and the Renaissance tragedies of Italian playwrights who follow the ancients. The best judges of *Samson Agonistes* will, moreover, not be unacquainted with the greatest Greek playwrights, Aeschylus, Sophocles, and Euripides – 'the three Tragic poets unequall'd yet by any' (*SA* p. 550) who offer models for the design of the plot.

Milton nevertheless directs his poem at a readerly rather than a theatre audience, meaning that his imagined community – a *communitas* comprised of individual readers – is even more narrowly defined. He stands up against the theatre-goers and consumers of mass culture, a Restoration version of 'Image-doting rabble' (*CPW*, 3:601), which had been seduced by *Eikon Basilike* and Charles's tragic performance on the scaffold.[21] Developing an alternative notion of political action as critical engagement with a dramatic poem, Milton casts the republican-minded reader as the poem's final authority. In the end, however, he is no more able to compete successfully with the heroic drama and tragicomedy, which Charles I's 'Stage-work' imaginatively conditioned, than he could with the numerous editions of the widely circulated *Eikon Basilike*.

In his *Essay of Dramatick Poesie*, Dryden, the main apologist and practitioner of heroic drama in his day, uses the character of Neander in his defence of tragicomedy as a 'more pleasant way of writing for the Stage then was ever known to the Ancients or Moderns of any Nation'; he adds that tragicomedy is in fact produced 'in the honour of our Nation' (*Works*, 17:46). If Milton read the *Essay*, he disregarded first of all Neander's views on rhyme, as the 1667 edition of *Paradise Lost* – which 'must have come upon [Dryden] like a revelation or a thunderbolt'[22] – abundantly illustrates. And certainly Milton would have disagreed with the *Essay*'s valourizing of tragicomedy when he cites in *Samson Agonistes* 'the poet's error of intermixing Comic stuff with Tragic sadness and gravity.' Further, Milton, of course, envisioned a different kind of nation; there is a political subtext to his comments on genre, decorum, and aesthetics, as there is for Dryden/Neander. Both Milton and Dryden were (re-) imagining the nation by using their readings of the stage to advance their respective cultural and political programs.

Neander connects the revival of the theatre with recent events on England's political stage: 'with the restoration of our happiness, we see reviv'd Poesie lifting up its head, & already shaking off the rubbish which lay so heavy on it' (*Works*, 17:63). In *Samson Agonistes*, Milton's earlier prophecy of the 'noble and puissant Nation rousing herself like a strong man after sleep, and shaking her invincible locks' (*Areopagitica*, *CPW*, 2:558) is fulfilled when Israel's deliverer destroys the Philistine theatre. In Milton's mind's eye, the colourful 1660s theatre culture mirrored a nation thrown into confusion and mesmerized by spectacles that bolstered royalist power. 'Heroique Poesie has alwayes been sacred to Princes and to Heroes,' Dryden stated in his dedication to the future James II in *The Conquest of Granada, Part I* (1672) (*Works*, 11:3). Milton's dramatic poem in contrast sets the stage for the last act of royalist theatre history while attempting to reclaim the heroic for the republican and providential cause.

The largely overlooked encounter between Milton and Restoration drama is played out not only in Milton's meditations on genre but also in his choice of subject matter for *Samson Agonistes*. Milton's Samson exhibits a form of heroism that is at odds with the Restoration 'ideal,' on which characters like Dryden's Almanzor and Aureng-Zebe are modeled. 'Who would not be the Hero of an Age?' Arimant asks the Emperor in an exchange about Aureng-Zebe (*Works*, 12:1.1.222). It is true that by the time *Samson Agonistes* appeared, the heyday of Restoration heroic drama had already passed. Protagonists of heroic dramas in the later 1660s and 1670s become caught, like the playwrights themselves, in the rift between romantic idealizations and actual experience. Yet despite his delusions of grandeur and his frustrated aspirations, a character like Almanzor still manages in an act of self-exaltation to restore two thrones, as well as the freedom of a king's brother and wife.[23] In contrast, Samson's heroic actions involve a series of dramatic self-confrontations and counterperformances, represented in his exchanges with the Philistines, Dalila, and Harapha, ultimately necessitating the destruction of the self and of the theatre.

From the start, Milton's dramatic poem stubbornly resists supplying the visual effects that audiences expected from stage plays. 'A little onward lend thy guiding hand / To these dark steps, a little further on / For yonder bank hath choice of Sun or shade, / There I am wont to sit, when any chance / Relieves me from my task of servile toil,' the blind Samson utters in the opening verses (*SA* ll. 1–5). Besides the fact that the reader is left to imagine Samson's experience of restlessness and physical imprisonment, the identity of his addressee at this point in the poem also remains a mystery. In line 20 when Samson describes himself as being 'alone,' we realize that the 'guiding hand' to which he initially refers (*SA* l. 1) represents an absent physical (rather than spiritual) presence. By comparing this soliloquy (or dramatic monologue) to Tiresias's appeal to Manto in Dryden and Nathaniel Lee's adaptation of *Oedipus* (performed 1678), we recognize the differences between *Samson Agonistes* and *Oedipus* in terms of the texts' engagement with their readers or audience. Stage directions in *Oedipus* enable us to visualize the scene:

> *Enter* Tiresias, *leaning on a staff, and led by his Daughter* Manto;
>   *Tiresias.* A little farther; yet a little farther,
> Thou wretched Daughter of a dark old man,
> Conduct my weary steps: and thou, who seest
> For me and for thy self, beware thou tread not
> With impious steps, upon dead corps. – Now stay:
> Methinks I draw more open, vital air,
> Where are we?
>
>   (*Works*, 13:1.1.192–8)

Manto sees for her father while directing the audience's gaze to various parts of the stage. Milton's Samson, however, misjudges his situation and his sense of hearing does not compensate for his lack of vision; in fact sounds mislead him further about the identity of his first visitors: 'But who are these? for with joint pace I hear / The tread of many feet steering this way; / Perhaps my enemies who come to stare / At my affliction' (*SA* ll. 110–13). The reader has of course already learned that the approaching figures are the members of the Chorus, 'friends and equals of his tribe' (*SA* p. 551).

Imagery of vision and of light and darkness is endemic to heroic drama. Plays ranging from *The Siege of Rhodes* to *The Indian Emperor* customarily compared the hero to the sun to distinguish him from other characters and highlight his luminary presence and dominion. And of course the sun was frequently employed as an emblem for the king. The epilogue to the *Unfortunate Usurper* thus exalts the king over his enemies: '*Those Meteors* [Nevill, Lambert, Vane] *must* vanish, Charles *our Sun / Having* in Englands *zodiack begun / His course*' (sig. K4r). For Samson, the sun has set, giving way to darkness 'amid the blaze of noon, / Irrecoverably dark, total eclipse / Without all hope of day' (*SA* ll. 80–2) – a reflection of his inner condition. The extinction of Samson's hopes and his loss of physical sight complement his diminished heroic status. Imagery of eclipses in *Samson Agonistes* is also noteworthy because Milton invokes the meaning of the Hebrew name *Shimshon*, which is *shemesh*, 'sun,' thus heightening the irony and tragic nature of the opening scene.

At the same time, however, blindness renders Samson immune to spectacle and theatrical illusion. Theatricality is represented in a variety of forms, though most obviously in the character of Dalila. The extravagantly dressed temptress, described as 'bedeckt, ornate, and gay' (*SA* l. 712), becomes a cipher for a wide range of historical, mythological, and topical figures – all associated with opulence and exploitation. Her identity takes on new significance when *Samson Agonistes* is situated in relation to seventeenth-century theatre culture. Dalila might, for example, be identified with the daughter of Ben Jonson's Pecunia, Infanta of the Mines, in *The Staple of News*, whose array is as costly 'as furnishing a fleet' and who appears 'like a galley, / Gilt i'the prow' (2.5.42–4). The stately ship of Tarsus to which Dalila is compared in *Samson Agonistes* (*SA* ll. 714–15) recalls Old Testament symbols of pride (Psalm 48:7), as well as the city on the River Cydnus where Cleopatra, 'O'erpicturing' Venus, meets Antony in Shakespeare's play and in Dryden's adaptation thereof, *All for Love: or, The World Well Lost. A Tragedy* (1678).[24] For the fallen and now blind Samson, Dalila is a reminder of his fatal attraction to dramaturgy, sensuality, and allure: 'Then swoll'n with pride into the snare I fell / Of fair fallacious looks, venereal trains, / Softn'd with pleasure and voluptuous life' (*SA* ll. 532–4).

Dalila has sisters on the Restoration stage whose performances are as powerfully captivating as they are suspect. In Dryden's *Conquest of Granada* – the first productions of which (December 1670 and January 1671) were concurrent with the printing of *Samson Agonistes* – Lyndaraxa is featured as Dalila's counterpart. As the *femme fatale*, Lyndaraxa marches to the beat of the war drums, while strategizing about her next conquest:

Beat faster, Drums, and mingle Deaths more thick.
I'le to the Turrets of the Palace goe,
And add new fire to those that fight below.
Thence, *Hero*-like, with Torches by my side,
(Farr be the Omen, though,) my Love I'le guide.
No; like his better Fortune I'le appear:
With open Arms, loose Vayl, and flowing Hair,
Just flying forward from my rowling Sphere.
My smiles shall make *Abdalla* more then Man;
Let him look up and perish if he can.

(*Works*, vol. 11, Part 1, 3.1.260–9)

This battle cry in the *Conquest* may have provoked Richard Leigh's critique of the play's bombast and ostentation: 'An Heroick Poem never sounded so nobly, as when it was heightned with Shouts, and Clashing of Swords; and that Drums and Trumpets gain'd an absolute Dominion over the minds of the Audience ... Here an Acquaintance of the Authors interpos'd, and assur'd the Company ... that if there was any thing unintelligible in his rants, t'was the effect of that horrour those Instruments of War with their astonishing noise had precipitated him into, which had so transported him, that he writ beyond himself.'[25] Though perhaps excessive, the grandiose speeches and lavish spectacles contributed to the play's success. As the above-mentioned speech indicates, Dryden's Lyndaraxa is the best representative of opulence and indulgence in the *Conquest*. Lyndaraxa's unquenchable lust for power ignites the love of both Abdalla and Abdelmelech; ultimately only Almanzor – who is nevertheless also tempted by her dramaturgy – can rival her display of passionate grandeur. In her final moments, Lyndaraxa repeats Almanzor's boast, 'Stand off; I have not leisure yet to dye' (*Works*, vol. 11, Part 1, 1.1.233) when she declares to Abdelmelech: 'Dye for us both; I have not leysure now'; 'Tell her I am a Queen' (Part 2, 5.3.254, 261a). Indeed she sustains her performance until the end of the play when she savours the glory for which she longed: 'I'me pleas'd to taste an Empyre 'ere I goe' (Part 2, 5.3.265). Ferdinand announces that Lyndaraxa will be rewarded for her role in the conquest of Granada: 'Fair *Lyndaraxa*, for the help she lent / Shall, under Tribute, have this Government' (Part 2, 5.3.234–35).

Similarly, Milton's Dalila, who is herself double-formed like Dagon, the Philistine god, desires 'double-fac't' or 'double-mouth'd' fame (*SA* l. 971) in recognition of her part in securing the Philistines' victory over Samson. Dalila's duplicity characterizes the corrupt regime of which she is a product and of which Samson is now a prisoner. Parodoxically, Samson only manages to divorce himself from her and dismiss her from the stage when he becomes immune to her performances in his blind and weakened condition.

In the encounter between Samson and Harapha – Samson's other chief Philistine visitor – Milton further dissociates his protagonist from the heroes of Restoration drama, as well as from those on the political stage. Unlike his Restoration counterparts, Samson will earn his title as champion (/agonistes) by acknowledging that his strength is not his own: 'My trust is in the living God who gave me / At my Nativity this strength' (*SA* ll. 1140–1). Assigned his part from Heaven (*SA* l. 1217), Samson, as God's champion, 'defies [Harapha] thrice to single fight' (*SA* l. 1222); the scene recalls Samson's success at thrice resisting Dalila's efforts to extort his 'capital secret' from him (*SA* ll. 392–4) by turning her 'importunity' 'to sport' (*SA* ll. 396–7). The triple challenge also evokes (in a medieval and early modern context) the custom of challenging three times in judicial combats. This ritual was performed in coronation ceremonies, including that of Charles II, as Pepys remembers: 'And three times the King-at-armes [Sir Edward Walker] went to the three open places on the scaffold and proclaimed that if any one could show any reason why Ch. Steward should not be King of England, that now he should come and speak.' As the regal ceremony proceeds, the King's armoured champion appears on the stage, 'flings down his gauntlet; and all this he doth three times in his going up towards the king's table' (Pepys, *Diary*, 23 April 1661; 2:84, 85). In challenging Harapha, Samson proposes to confront his foe 'single and unarmed' (*SA* l. 1111); he will sport only 'an Oak'n staff' (*SA* l. 1122), thus appropriating a symbol of kingship.[26] Samson thereby aims to expose the emptiness of the pompous Harapha, the 'Tongue-doughty Giant' (*SA* l. 1181) and 'vain Boaster' (*SA* l. 1227), and undermine a performance tainted with monarchical pride. Paradoxically, humility and self-abnegation constitute heroism in *Samson Agonistes*, as suggested by the Chorus's remarks on Samson's encounter with Harapha as a display of 'plain Heroic magnitude of mind / And celestial vigor arm'd' and of patience – 'the exercise / Of Saints, the trial of thir fortitude,' (*SA* ll. 1279–80, 1287–8).

Significantly, Samson's final restoration in the poem is an act of (self-)destruction, and not enthronement. The final episode is thus not shown but rather related by a Messenger, who nevertheless invokes the language of theatrical performance and staging. The account of the 'horrid spectacle' (*SA* l. 1542) requires 'No Preface' (*SA* l. 1554), the impatient Manoa decides. The Messenger's script sets the stage inside 'a spacious Theater' (*SA* l. 1605). Milton reconstructs this classical amphitheatre from the house in Judges 16:26–7. Nicholas Jose attributes a contemporary significance to the spectacle when he identifies the theatre with Christopher Wren's Sheldonian Theatre, which was built from 1664 to 1669 and was designed to represent the glory of the Augustan Roman empire.[27] In this theatre, Samson is forced to take centre stage amidst the clamour and confusion of Philistine festivities (*SA* ll. 1616–22). Samson's sports are featured in the first act, which is followed by an intermission (*SA* l. 1629). Cast as a jester or fool in the tragedy, Samson manages, nevertheless, to rewrite his enemies' script in the second act and steal the show. The last dying speech is designed to convince the audience of Samson's full participation and cooperation in the spectacle of punishment:

> 'Hitherto, Lords, what your commands impos'd
> I have perform'd, as reason was, obeying,
> Not without wonder or delight beheld.
> Now of my own accord such other trial
> I mean to show you of my strength, yet greater;
> As with amaze shall strike all who behold.' (ll. 1640–5)

Samson's stage productions, which initially provoked the wonder and delight of the stage-managers and viewers, are contained here in a speech that serves as a prologue and epilogue for his final performance – and Milton's. The final words are then converted into a show of strength that amazes and strikes all spectators, and brings the house down. And here one cannot help but note that the court of Charles II made up much of the theatre audience of 1660–72.

Samson's trials of conscience throughout the poem are reminiscent of the illegally printed testimonies and trial accounts of the regicides – the royalist's political prisoners – in the early Restoration.[28] At the same time, Milton's representation of the final act remains a site of competing interpretations about the motivation for Samson's self-sacrifice, as the tragic hero and the poem resist judgment.[29] Manoa first raises the issue of 'Self-violence' (*SA* l. 1584) in his inquiry about the events leading to the deaths of the Philistines and Samson. Though the Messenger declares that Samson committed the slaughter with his own hands, he responds to Manoa by identifying the cause 'At once to destroy and be destroy'd' (*SA* l. 1588) as 'Inevitable' (*SA* l. 1586). Thereafter, however, the Nuntius complicates matters when he recreates the interior drama and attempts to decipher Samson's motives; he was 'as one who pray'd, / Or some great matter in his mind revolv'd' (*SA* ll. 1637–8). Nevertheless, Manoa insists in the end that retribution and redemption are of Samson's own doing in accordance with divine will: '*Samson* hath quit himself / Like *Samson*, and heroicly hath finish'd / A life Heroic' (*SA* ll. 1709–11). From a regenerationist perspective, Samson, in anticipation of Christ, has pulled down the Philistine structure and raised the temple of his body, phoenixlike.

The interpretive process does not conclude with Manoa's observation, even though the Danites seize upon this response in hailing the martyr as God's 'faithful Champion' (*SA* l. 1751). The poem raises the possibility that both the Chorus and Manoa 'contradict Samson into a heroism he is perhaps not meant to enjoy.'[30] As demonstrated most recently by Dennis Kezar, *Samson Agonistes* resists the pull either towards a regenerationist Samson or towards a singularly sceptical or indeterminate reading of the hero's art of dying. Moreover, the poem frustrates its readers' efforts at interpreting Samson's final performance, the meaning of which is reserved for a place and time much beyond the final act and beyond the conventions of heroic drama and even dramatic poetry.

Committed to a coherent idea of Milton's literary career and poetic identity, Miltonists have conventionally mapped out the poet's oeuvre in terms of his progress towards *Samson Agonistes*.[31] This practice, coupled with the insistence on separating Milton from contemporary Restoration writers, has discouraged investigations of *Samson Agonistes* that venture 'beyond [its] fifth Act.' The final years of Milton and Dryden were played out in their different though intersecting struggles with the politics of print and performance. Both authors eventually and publicly renounced theatrical productions. Dryden repudiated 'all those *Dalilahs* of the Theatre' in his 'Dedication of the *Spanish Fryar*,' and directed his attention instead to his readers: 'But, as 'tis my Interest to please my Audience, so 'tis my Ambition to be read; that I am sure is the more lasting and the nobler Design: for the propriety of thoughts and words, which are the hidden beauties of a Play, are but confus'dly judg'd in the vehemence of Action: All things are there beheld, as in a hasty motion, where the objects onely glide before the Eye and disappear' (*Works*, 14:102). Later, in the 'Preface of the Translator, with a Parallel, of Poetry and Painting' in *De Arte Graphica* (1695), Dryden rehearsed Lisideius's (and Milton's) earlier charges against tragicomedy: 'our *English* Tragicomedy must be confess'd to be wholly *Gothique*, notwithstanding the Success which it has found upon our Theatre ... Mirth and Gravity destroy each other, and are no more to be allow'd for decent, than a gay Widow laughing in a mourning Habit' (*Works*, 20:70–1). Milton's criticism in the preface to *Samson Agonistes* of the multigenre drama that combines 'Comic stuff with Tragic sadness and gravity' echoes in Dryden's lines, though Dryden's response to theatre culture is not, like Milton's, motivated by political opposition. Here we are reminded, nevertheless, of the curious meeting of minds of writers occupying otherwise discrete cultural and political positions.

To put *Samson Agonistes* and Restoration drama on the stage together is ultimately to expose and redefine the ruptures in literary history. But more than that, it is to confront the conflicting and colliding ideologies, the various interpretive communities, and the fault lines that unsettle the fixed nature of any text and its received tradition. Finally, it means that readings of canonical works like *Samson Agonistes* will be dramatically unsettled when the practices of consumption that govern the reception of texts and inform their meaning are investigated.

My concluding study of the cultural and political climate to which Milton responded and which in turn affected the reception of his dramatic, antitheatrical poem underscores the interaction of competing textual communities in this era. The composition of *Samson Agonistes* caps a period that witnessed the interplay and permeation of print culture and theatrical culture in an unprecedented manner. Writing, reading, and the transmission of texts, as we have seen, became at this time alternative practices of collective identification and of resistance, as well as of performance, counterperformance, and political action. Through communicative acts, shared discourses, and engagements with sympathetic and antagonistic readerships (implied and actual), writers invested the reconstituted dramatic form with a new affective power to participate in judicial debates, but also to generate communities. A study of press acts, print wars, interpretive practices, and the reception histories and judicial functions of theatricalized works is thus essential for understanding this revolutionary era. This study, then, challenges us to change the way we think, first about the dynamics of political, cultural, and literary history, second about drama and its transgression of boundaries, and finally about how analyses of the politics of consensus and contestation that animated seventeenth-century culture expose 'the many groups and texts, ideas and beliefs that made up the commonwealth which authority endeavoured to construct as a unified whole.'[32]

Notes

Prologue

1 The formation of readerships and interpretive communities, a subject of much recent critical inquiry, is a particularly vexed one. See Zwicker, 'Reading the Margins.'

2 See, for example, Zaret, *Origins of Democratic Culture*; Norbrook, *Writing the English Republic*; Wiseman, *Drama and Politics in the English Civil War*; Halasz, *The Marketplace of Print*; Randall, *Winter Fruit*; Achinstein, *Milton and the Revolutionary Reader*; Smith, *Literature and Revolution in England, 1640–1660*; Zwicker, *Lines of Authority*; Potter, *Secret Rites and Secret Writing.*

3 Kastan, 'Performances and Playbooks,' 171.

4 See, for example, *Books and Readers in Early Modern England*; Zaret, *Origins of Democratic Culture*; Ezell, *Social Authorship and the Advent of Print*; Freist, *Governed by Opinion*; Sherman, *John Dee*; Marotti, *Manuscript, Print, and the English Renaissance Lyric*; Love, *The Culture and Commerce of Texts*; and Watt, *Cheap Print and Popular Pamphlets.*

Readers' responses must in turn be located in relation to what Pierre Bourdieu has defined as a *habitus* – a class-related predilection to engage in particular social practices (see 'Structure, Habitus, Practices'). 'The *habitus* of becoming well-informed about what's going on' was an impetus for the production of technologies and for advances in communication (Marotti and Bristol, Introduction to *Print, Manuscript, Performance*, 24).

5 Building on the definitions of subjectivity proposed by Anthony Giddens, Pierre Bourdieu, and Louis Montrose, Eve Rachele Sanders argues that the 'possibilities for action available to individuals, to differing degrees depending on their gender, class, ethnicity, and circumstances, include appropriating self-fashioning techniques for ends for which they were not originally

intended' (*Gender and Literacy on Stage in Early Modern England*, 3). In reference to Civil War history, see David Norbrook who critiques the application of Foucauldian notions of power which interpret the transition from the Stuart monarchy to the republic not as the consequence of popular political agency but as being determined from above ('*Areopagitica*, Censorship, and the Early Modern Public Sphere').

6 Sharpe, *Reading Revolutions*, 60. Reception theory, reader response criticism, and the formation of interpretive communities have all been subjects of considerable interest and debate since the 1970s. See, for example, Iser, *The Act of Reading*; Fish, *Is There a Text in This Class?*; Jauss, *Toward an Aesthetic of Reception*. Fish's scholarly contributions on this topic have of course proven highly influential, certainly among literary critics but also among historians. However, the authoritarian interpretive community Fish posits has repeatedly been subject to interrogation. In developing his theories on the interpretive community, M.M. Bakhtin foregrounds the critic's dialogic role and the concrete social and historical milieu in which the readers or critics are situated (Shepherd, 'Bakhtin and the Reader,' *Bakhtin and Cultural Theory*, 96–7). Bakhtin's model thus differs radically from that of Fish, who characterizes intercommunal relations as devoid of conflict. Roger Chartier identifies the construction of 'communities of readers as "interpretative communities" (Stanley Fish's expression)' as one of the avenues available to those who wish to understand the nature of reading practices as historians. However, he also judges Fish's models as wanting insofar as they simplify and dehistoricize the relationship between reader and text; see Chartier, *The Order of Books*, 23, and 'Texts, Printing, Readings,' 157–8.

7 On the revisionists, see Morrill, *The Revolt of the Provinces*; Sharpe, *Faction and Parliament*; Fletcher, *The Outbreak of the English Civil War*, and Russell, *Parliaments and English Politics, 1621–1629*, and *Unrevolutionary England, 1603–1642*. On Kevin Sharpe's revised reading of history, see *Remapping Early Modern England*; esp. 3–27, and *Reading Revolutions*, 3–11. See also Norbrook, 'The English Revolution and English Historiography'; Lake, 'Retrospective: Wentworth's Political World in Revisionist and Post-Revisionist Perspective'; Zaret, *Origins of Democratic Culture*, esp. 35–9; and Susan Wiseman, *Drama and Politics*, esp. 7–10. The postrevisionist challenge of explaining how early modern England 'escaped conflict for so long' (Sharpe, *Reading Revolutions*, 9) is best addressed in a study of the conjunctures between political and religious strife and the unprecedented explosion of print in the early 1640s.

8 Butler, *Theatre and Crisis*; Maguire, *Regicide and Restoration*, 107.

9 [Ford], *The Queen, or the Excellency of Her Sex*, A3r.

10 Treadwell, 'The Stationers and the Printing Acts at the End of the Seventeenth Century,' 755–6.

11 *The Actors Remonstrance*, 6, 7.

12 Like Heinemann's *Puritanism and Theatre*, Butler's *Theatre and Crisis*, and *The Theatrical City*, which investigate the integral connection between drama and politics, I use the words 'acting,' 'performance,' and 'theatre' as 'plastic' terms. However, I begin where these studies left off by concentrating on the post-1640 period, and by expanding the definition of the words. The 'acting' press refers in this book first to transference of power invested in the theatre to the printed text, and second to the activities of writers and printers who use the press to perform the social, cultural, and political work – of criticism, correction, and community building – identified with the theatre. Acting and performance, then, are associated with, but not restricted to, legislative acts, stage productions, or even the concept of the world as stage – *theatrum mundi*. See also Lake and Questier, *The Anti-Christ's Lewd Hat*, in which theatrical language is identified as a significant discourse for understanding such genres as prison literature, murder pamphlets, and gallows speeches in Elizabethan and Jacobean England.

13 Walter Raleigh recognized the dichotomy between the divine potential of the human being as a rational creature and the actuality of humanity's frailty when he spoke of the temptation by 'the false and durelesse pleasures of this stage-play world' (*The History of the World*, 125).

14 Ann Hughes, 'Approaches to Presbyterian Print Culture.'

15 Zaret, 'Religion, Science, and Printing in the Public Spheres of England,' 216.

16 Nigel Smith, *Literature and Revolution*, 1; *Scutum Regale, The Royal Buckler*, A3v.

17 *Mercurius Britanicus*, no. 49, 26 August–2 September 1644, 386, 387. Steven N. Zwicker comments on the combative nature of books in 'Habits of Reading and Early Modern Literary Culture,' 189–94.

18 *The Fallacies of Mr. William Prynne*, 33, 1.

19 May, *The History of the Parliament of England*, Bk. 2, 20, 96.

20 Part of the work performed by texts involves the migration of generic modes and conventions into other texts. For that reason, this study is not limited to one particular genre. My concern to analyse the textual apparatus of printed works, particularly the front matter, is appropriate in light of the fact that it performs the most important work in prompting engagement by readers. Roger Chartier stresses the importance of considering how texts and the printed works that convey them organize prescribed reading – through textual machinery like prefaces, prologues, commentaries, notes ('Texts, Printing, Readings,' 157–8).

21 Neither the monolithic concept of the public sphere nor the notion of thick description does justice to the concept of the community. In Renaissance new historicist studies thick description has come under attack as being fragmentary, as it fails to characterize the activities of an entire culture. In fact the emergence of a number of many bodies of public opinion unsettles the assumption of a unified public sphere and of a continuum of history. See Lake, 'Retrospective: Wentworth's Political World,' 277–8; Lake, 'Puritans, Popularity and Petitions'; and Cressy, 'Conflict, Consensus, and the Willingness to Wink,' 132. For a critique of the continuum of history, see Fumerton, *Cultural Aesthetics,* 11. For Edward Pechter, the missing organizing principle of the method is community, 'community' being among the many terms, including 'radical,' 'citizen,' 'court,' 'country,' 'nation,' 'religion,' and 'politics,' that have resonances for us that inevitably permeate our use of them ('The New Historicism and Its Discontents,' 301). See also Condren, *The Language of Politics in Seventeenth-Century England.*

22 Aers and Kress, 'Historical Process, Individuals and Communities in Milton's *Areopagitica*,' 175.

23 The engagement with books generated the *communitas,* which Victor Turner defined as 'a bond uniting ... people over and above any formal social bonds' (*Dramas, Fields, and Metaphors,* 45). On books as objects implicated in the material processes of textual production and transmission, see Chartier, *The Order of Books,* 9; Bell, 'Introduction: The Material Text,' and the new series by the University of Pennsylvania Press, 'Material Studies,' that includes *Books and Readers in Early Modern England* (2002).

24 Jagodzinski, *Privacy and Print,* 12. Steven N. Zwicker reminds us that while reading is a solitary experience, it is also 'situated within a community of interpretive and hence political practices' ('Reading the Margins,' 106).

25 See Stock, 'Textual Communities,' in *The Implications of Literacy.*

26 Cressy, *Literacy and the Social Order,* tables 6.1–6.5. Thomas, 'The Meaning of Literacy in Early Modern England'; see 102 for Thomas's response to Cressy's statistics. Ferguson, 'A Room Not Their Own'; Sanders, *Gender and Literacy*; and Barry, 'Literacy and Literature in Popular Culture'; on the interaction of oral, visual, and textual expression, see Fox, *Oral and Literate Culture in England*; Eisenstein, *The Printing Press as an Agent of Change.*

27 Nigel Smith, *Literature and Revolution*; Mendle, *Henry Parker and the English Civil War*; Achinstein, *Milton and the Revolutionary Reader*; Raymond, *The Invention of the Newspaper*; Wiseman, *Drama and Politics*; and Halasz, *The Marketplace of Print.*

28 Lake, 'Agency and Appropriation at the Foot of the Gallows: Catholics (and Puritans) Confront (and Constitute) the English State,' *The Anti-Christ's Lewd*

Hat, Lake and Questier, 262. The bibliography on news and public opinion in early modern England is large and burgeoning. The following try to adapt Habermas's public sphere to early modern English circumstances: Lake and Questier, 'Puritans, Papists, and the "Public Sphere" in Early Modern England'; Zaret, 'Religion, Science, and Printing,' and *Origins of Democratic Culture*; Achinstein, *Milton and the Revolutionary Reader*; Norbrook, '*Areopagitica*, Censorship, and the Early Modern Public Sphere'; Raymond, 'The Newspaper, Public Opinion, and the Public Sphere in the Seventeenth Century'; Cust, 'News and Politics in Early Seventeenth-Century England'; Raymond, *Making the News*; and Friedman, *The Battle of the Frogs and Fairford's Flies*.

29 Kilburn and Milton, 'The Public Context of the Trial and Execution of Strafford,' 231. As print culture spread and literacy increased, modes of reading became more various and distinct: 'Once the book became a more common object and less distinctive by its being merely possessed, the manners of reading took over the task of showing the variations, of making manifest differences in the social hierarchy' (Chartier, 'Texts, Printing, Readings,' 174).

30 Milton, *Areopagitica*, in *Complete Prose Works of John Milton*, 2:555. Hereafter cited *CPW*.

31 Aers and Kress, 'Historical Process, Individuals and Communities in Milton's *Areopagitica*, 179.

32 Achinstein, *Milton and the Revolutionary Reader*, 65, 66–7. Internal quotation is from Corns, 'Freedom of Reader-Response,' 95. On the identity of the people, see Hill, 'Parliament and the People in Seventeenth-Century England'; and *The Middling Sort of People*. On Milton's position as a licenser in the Cromwellian government, see Sabrina A. Baron, who maintains that 'Milton is better understood not as the enemy of licensing, but rather as the proponent of the freedom to read' ('Licensing Readers, Licensing Authorities in Seventeenth-Century England,' 237). See also Dobranski, 'Licensing Milton's Heresy,' and *Milton, Authorship, and the Book Trade*.

33 Chartier, *The Culture of Print, Power and the Uses of Print in Early Modern Europe*, 4; Watt, *Cheap Print*, 3.

34 An example of a writer transgressing political boundaries is Marchamont Nedham, the most prominent journalist of the period, who changed his allegiance from royalist to republican; Joseph Frank adds that while working under different pen names, Mercurius, 'Britanicus-Pragmaticus-Politicus Nedham wrote well enough for some of his prose to be attributed to Milton.' (*The Beginnings of the English Newspaper*, 272). Nedham had a monopoly of the newsbook industry between October 1655 and April 1659.

35 Raymond, *Invention of the Newspaper*, 243; Morrill, *The Revolt of the Provinces*, 35.

36 4 February 1648/9, *The Diary of Ralph Josselin*. See chapter 3 of this book.

37 Hirst, 'Samuel Parker, Andrew Marvell, and Political Culture, 1667–73,' 145.

38 On appropriation, see Chartier, 'Texts, Printing, Readings,' 171.

39 Victor Turner, who applied the discourse and perspective of drama to anthropology, maintained that social dramas achieve their fullest elaboration in the political forum (*The Anthropology of Performance*, 33). Politics, James E. Combs argues, 'more than any other area of social life, is a dramatic magnification of the human condition. Politics is the most theatrical of social arenas.' And if this is the case, he continues, then trials may well be the most theatrical of political dramas (*Dimensions of Political Drama*, 16, 59).

40 Hyde, *The History of the Rebellion*, 3:56, 263–4; Cromartie, 'The Printing of Parliamentary Speeches,' 40.

41 Kilburn and Milton, 'The Public Context of the Trial and Execution of Strafford,' 251; see also James Sharpe, 'The People and the Law.'

42 Turner, *Anthropology*, 34.

43 Foucault, *Discipline and Punish*, 47.

44 Recently, more nuanced readings of censorship have resisted the oppositional and insufficiently historicized model of absolute censorship, particularly that attributed to monolithic – and most often monarchical – governments. Kevin Sharpe, Anthony Milton, and Cyndia Susan Clegg thus complicate the earlier historical models of censorship practices offered by Patterson in *Censorship and Interpretation*, and Hill in 'Censorship and English Literature.' See Sharpe, *Reading Revolutions*, 43–4; Milton, 'Licensing, Censorship, and Religious Orthodoxy in Early Stuart England'; and Clegg, *Press Censorship in Jacobean England*, 6–8, 201–2.

45 The notion of 'community' is central for the radical sects, with which the concept is most frequently associated in this period. Margaret Benefiel has argued that the term 'community' had a specific meaning for early Friends, who shared a 'strong sense of corporate identity with other Friends. For them, coming to the Light meant not only a personal transformation, it also meant initiation into a group of believers. In fact the personal transformation could only happen, in their view, in the context of such a group. This group was referred to by them as the body of Christ or Christian community'; see '"Weaving the Web of Community,"' 443–4. Also see Spufford, *Contrasting Communities*. Robert Coster identified the community with 'a common Treasury of Livelihood for all ... [where] none should Lord over his own kind' (*A Mite Cast into the Common Treasury* [1649], 285); Gerrard Winstanley and his coauthors in *The True Levellers Standard Advanced* [1649], likewise use 'community' and 'common treasury' interchangeably throughout this treatise, which condemns the Protectorate for failing to fulfil its

promise to liberate the English people. Critics, however, characterized such communities as licentious and incestuous, as illustrated by Richard Brathwaite's remark: 'But if *Community* their Title prove, / 'Tis all in all with Family of love. / Where like our wandring *Gipsies* in mixt seedes / Without distinction One with other breedes' ('The Quaker' [1658], ll. 7–10). James Ussher referred to the Anabaptists' practice of holding a 'community of goods' as a 'gross errour' and as a violation of the eighth commandment (*A Body of Divinitie* [1647], 2). See also Gary S. De Krey's discussion of the dissenters' 'community of discourse,' whose origins lay in the 1640s and 50s (De Krey, 'Radicals, Reformers, and Republicans,' esp. 94–9).

46 See Fish, *Is There a Text*; Ormsby-Lennon, '"The Dialect of Those Fanatick Times"'; and Habermas, *The Structural Transformation of the Public Sphere.*

47 See, for example, Knott, 'Joseph Besse and the Quaker Culture of Suffering,' 126–41.

48 See Bauman, *Let Your Words Be Few,* 103–4.

49 Norbrook, *Writing,* 11.

50 Bauman, *Let Your Words,* 104.

51 Gregerson, 'Milton's Post-Modernity,' 23.

52 Marcus, *Unediting the Renaissance,* 211.

53 Chartier, *Order,* ix.

54 Dryden, *The Spanish Fryar, The Works of John Dryden,* 14:101.

55 S.H., 'To the Reader,' in *Rectifying Principles.*

56 Weimann, 'Towards a Literary Theory of Ideology,' 269. As Kevin Sharpe recognized, 'The history of reading belongs in the master narrative of the history of politics' (*Reading Revolutions,* 342).

Chapter 1

1 Sharon Achinstein observes that the courtroom in particular 'provided a kind of entertainment sorely lacking after the closing of the theaters' (*Milton and the Revolutionary Reader,* 43). In ceremonies of public execution that followed, 'the main character was the people,' Michel Foucault has shown (*Discipline and Punish,* 57).

2 See Green, *Verdict, According to Conscience,* 119.

3 Boerner, 'The Trial Convention in English Renaissance Drama,' 226.

4 James Sharpe, 'The People and the Law,' 256.

5 Cogswell, 'Underground Verse and the Transformation of Early Stuart Political Culture,' 278, 295.

6 Pocock, 'Thomas May and the Narrative of Civil War,' 124.

7 *A Presse full of Pamphlets,* [5].

8 See Pocock, 'Texts as Events.'

9 [Bond], *The Poets Knavery Discovered,* A2, A2–A2v. See chapter 2 for Bond's indictment by Parliament.

10 D'Ewes, *The Journals of all the Parliaments During the Reign of Queen Elizabeth,* 644.

11 Bacon, *Historie of the Raigne of King Henry the Seventh,* 163.

12 Edward Misselden, *Free Trade,* 55. Later he states that a 'Monopoly is a kinde of Commerce, in buying, selling, changing or bartering, usurped by a few, and sometimes but by one person, and fore-stalled from all others, to the Gaine of the Monopolist, and to the Detriment of other men' (57).

13 Coke, *Institutes of the Laws of England,* 181.

14 Lilburne et al., *The Soap-makers Complaint,* 4.

15 See Sacks, 'Parliament, Liberty, and the Commonweath,' esp. 94–5.

16 Heywood, *Reader, Here you'l plainly see Judgement Perverted,* 5. Lilburne, *Soap-makers,* title page.

17 Nigel Smith, '*Areopagitica*: Voicing Contexts, 1643–5'; Achinstein, *Milton and the Revolutionary Reader;* Norbook, '*Areopagitica,* Censorship, and the Early Modern Public Sphere'; Blum, 'The Author's Authority'; Dobranski, 'Licensing Milton's Heresy,' and *Milton, Authorship, and the Book Trade*; and Baron, 'Licensing Readers, Licensing Authorities in Seventeenth-Century England.'

18 Dunn, 'Milton among the Monopolists,' esp. 186–9; and Hoxby, *Mammon's Music.* Aee also Kendrick, *Milton: A Study in Ideology and Form,* 40–2, and Wilding, 'Milton's *Areopagitica,* 7–38.

19 Hoxby, *Mammon's Music,* 25, 47.

20 Fuller quoted in Sacks, 'Parliament, Liberty, and the Commonwealth,' 98. Manley, *Literature and Culture in Early Modern London,* 553 (emphasis mine).

21 The first patent was issued in 1552 to Henry Smyth for the privilege of making glass and was followed by patents to search for and work metals. See Thirsk, *Economic Policy and Projects,* 34.

22 Price, *English Patents of Monopoly,* 156.

23 Ibid., 42.

24 Ibid., 45.

25 Quoted in Sacks, 'Parliament, Liberty, and the Commonwealth,' 98.

26 Coke, *Institutes of the Laws of England,* 181.

27 Ibid.

28 *The Judges Judgement ... against the Judges,* A3r.

29 Heywood, *Reader, Here you'l plainly see,* 4.

30 Ibid., 5.

31 Price, *The English Patents of Monopoly,* 126–8.

32 *A Short and True Relation concerning the Soap-busines*, 4.

33 *A Pack of Patentees*, 4.

34 *A Short and True Relation concerning the Soap-business*, 6

35 *The Copie of a Letter sent from the Roaring Boyes in Elizium; To the two arrant Kings of the Grape, in Limbo*, A4v.

36 *A Dialogue or accidental discourse Betwixt Mr. Alderman Abell, and Richard Kilvert*, 3.

37 Ibid., 5.

38 'Concerning the Prices of Wine, &c.,' 350.

39 *A Dialogue or accidental discourse*, 8.

40 *The last Discourse Betwixt Master Abel and Master Richard Kilvert, interrupted at the first by an ancient and angry Gentlewoman*, 3.

41 Ibid., 3, 6.

42 *A Description of the Passage of Thomas late Earle of Strafford, over the River of Styx*, A3v. Although forbidden by the Petition of Right in 1628, the ship-money tax for naval defence was levied by Charles I between 1634 and 1638 without the consent of Parliament. It was a source of great discontent in the pre–Civil War period and was abolished in 1641 by the Long Parliament.

43 *Englants ende Irlands drees schaw tooneel oft Willem Lauds gewessene Bischop van Cantelberg Droomgesicht. England and Irelands sad Theater* ([Netherlands], 1645). See chapter 2.

44 Calendar of State Papers, Domestic Series, Charles II, 3:496.

45 *Boston Gazette* 2 June 1755, quoted in Jeffery A. Smith, *Printers and Press Freedom*, 21.

46 Milton, *Areopagitica*, *CPW*, 2:548.

47 Baron, 'Licensing Readers, Licensing Authorities in Seventeenth-Century England,' 223.

48 Dobranski, *Milton, Authorship, and the Book Trade*, 111.

49 Critics are divided about the boldness of the statement that the title page makes; cf. Blum, 'The Author's Authority,' 76–82, and Dobranski, *Milton*, 108–13. On the typographical resemblance of the title page to that of plays or closet dramas of the period, see chapter 4.

50 'Protestation,' a word Milton invokes as 'Protestations,' has a topical referent as a Parliamentary defence produced in May 1641 to resist monarchical absolutism and to support religion, the Crown, Parliament, and the rights of the people (*CPW*, 2:540).

51 Hoxby, *Mammon's Music*, 45, 47.

52 Foxe, *Acts and Monuments*, 3:718, 721.

53 Henry Burton, *Truth's Triumph over Trent*, 231.

Chapter 2

1 On Strafford as the first royalist tragic hero on the eve of the Civil War, see John H. Timmis III, *Thine Is the Kingdom*, 1.

2 *Proceedings between the Lady Frances Howard ... and Robert Earl of Essex* (1613), in *Cobbett's Complete Collection of State Trials* (hereafer *ST*), 2:786–861; *The Trial of Robert Carr, Earl of Somerset, for the Murder of Sir Thomas Overbury* (1616), *ST*, 2:966–1021; *The Trial of Mervin Lord Audley, Earl of Castlehaven, for a Rape and Sodomy* (1631), *ST*, 3:402–26.

3 On the Essex affair, see Lindley, *The Trials of Frances Howard*. On the Overbury affair, see Bellany, *The Politics of Court Scandal in Early Modern England*. Bellany's archival research reveals that only 17 printed sources appeared on the Overbury case (282–3). On the richly documented case of Castlehaven, see Herrup, *A House in Gross Disorder*. Printed sources consulted by Herrup again postdate the trial. Andrew McRae identifies a 'cultural gulf' between the late 1630s and early 1640s which he attributes to the increasingly public and prevalent nature of satire, whose production signals a breakdown between authorized and unauthorized discourse (*Literature, Satire and the Early Stuart State*, 208).

4 *The Trial of Thomas Earl of Strafford* (1640), *ST*, 3:1385–1536; *The Trial of Dr. William Laud* (1640–4), *ST*, 4:315–626. See also *A Collection of Scarce and Valuable Tracts*.

5 Kilburn and Milton, 'The Public Context of the Trial and Execution of Strafford'; Wedgwood, *Thomas Wentworth First Earl of Strafford*; Timmis III, *Thine Is the Kingdom*; Russell, *The Fall of the British Monarchies 1637–1642*; Heinemann, *Puritanism and Theatre*; Butler, *Theatre and Crisis 1632–1642*; and Wilcher, *The Writing of Royalism, 1628–1660*.

6 May, *The History of the Parliament of England*, Bk. 1, 87, 88.

7 Kilburn and Milton, 'The Public Context of the Trial and Execution of Strafford,' 230.

8 Herbert, *An Answer to the most Envious ... Pamphlet*, 2.

9 Carlton, *Archbishop William Laud*, 214.

10 May, *The History of the Parliament of England*, Bk. 1, 91; Evelyn, *The Diary of John Evelyn*, 17.

11 The verb 'manage' is used in a legal context throughout the narrative of Strafford's and Laud's trials to describe the strategic assembly of evidence. See Rushworth, Preface to *The Tryall of Thomas Earl of Strafford*, Cv; *The Trial of Dr. William Laud*, *ST*, 4:346.

12 May, *The History of the Parliament of England*, Bk. 1, 92. May's account influenced the great champion of the parliamentary cause, John Milton, who

would soon be commissioned to produce *Eikonoklastes* to counteract the effects of the king's memorable performance in *Eikon Basilike.* 'None were [Strafford's] Friends but Courtiers, and Clergimen,' Milton taunts; 'the worst at that time, and most corrupted sort of men; and Court Ladies, not the best of Women; who when they grow to that insolence as to appeare active in State affaires, are the certain sign of a dissolute, degenerat, and pusillanimous Common-wealth' (*Eikonoklastes, CPW,* 3:370).

13 Zaret, *Origins of Democratic Culture,* 205.

14 *Mr. Maynards Speech Before Both Houses in Parliament,* A3r.

15 May, *The History of the Parliament of England,* Bk. 1, 93.

16 See *Speeches and Passages of this Great and Happy Parliament,* 348–9. Glyn's speech was printed in *The Replication of Mr Glyn ... to the generall answer ... of Strafford* (13 April 1641).

17 Timmis, III, *Thine Is the Kingdom,* 119.

18 Fletcher, *The Outbreak of the English Civil War,* 9.

19 May, *The History of the Parliament of England,* Bk. 1, 92.

20 *The Conclusion of the Earle of Straffords Defence,* 3.

21 Ibid., 4.

22 *In Answer to the Earle of Straffords Conclusion,* 4.

23 Heylyn, *Cyprianus Anglicus,* 478.

24 *Speeches and Passages of this Great and Happy Parliament,* 303.

25 Fletcher, *The Outbreak of the English Civil War,* 16; Cromartie, 'The Printing of Parliamentary Speeches, 29–30.

26 *The Lord Digby His last Speech Against the Earle of Strafford* (1641). The printer omitted (anon) his name from the text, which was burnt by the common hangman. See Kilburn and Milton, 'The Public Context of the Trial and Execution of Strafford,' 243; May, *The History of the Parliament of England,* Bk. 1, 96.

27 *An Aproved Answer,* 1.

28 Quoted in Fletcher, *The Outbreak of the Civil War,* 14.

29 Heylyn, *Cyprianus Anglicus,* 479; see also Hyde, *History of the Rebellion,* 3:141, 307; Rushworth, Preface, 59.

30 Hyde, *History of the Rebellion,* 3:196–7, 337–8; Manning, *The English People and the English Revolution,* 10–18.

31 May, *The History of the Parliament of England,* Bk. 1, 93.

32 Heylyn, *Cyrianus Anglicus,* 479; Timmis III, *Thine Is the Kingdom,* 170.

33 King, 'An Elegy Upon the most Incomparable K. Charles,' 7.

34 '*The Earl of Strafford's Letter,*' in *A Collection of Scarce and Valuable Tracts,* 4:247. Also found in *Cobbett's State Trials,* 3:1516–17.

35 The marginal note is in Fanshawe, 'On the Earle of Straffords Tryall,' in *Shorter Poems and Translations,* 68; the quotations are ll. 20, 34.

36 Thomas, 'Cases of Conscience in Seventeenth-Century England,' 33.

37 *Eikon Basilike*, 7.

38 Stanley, 'Upon the Earl of Strafford's Death,' A2r–A2v, ll. 1–4.

39 Milton, *Eikonoklastes*, *CPW*, 3:373.

40 Ibid., 3:376. See also Collop, 'On *Lord Wentworth Earl of Strafford*.'

41 Kilburn and Milton, 'The Public Context of the Trial and Execution of Strafford,' 230.

42 Trevelyan, *A Shortened History of England*, 298.

43 J.A. Sharpe, '"Last Dying Speeches."'

44 *Great Satisfaction concerning the Death of the Earle of Strafford* (1641), quoted in *A Collection of Science and Valuable Tracts*, 4:278.

45 *The Earle of Strafford, his speech in the Tower* (1641), in Kilburn and Milton, 'The Public Context of the Trial and Execution of Strafford,' 247.

46 *Calendar of State Papers, Domestic Series*, Charles I, 7 June 1641, 18:4.

47 B[ond], *The Poets Knavery Discovered*, A2–A2v.

48 Noy died in 9 August 1634, a loss lamented by Laud (*Diary*, 3:221). *A Description of the Passage of Thomas late Earle of Strafford*, A4r–v.

49 *The Great Eclipse of the Sun*, A3r.

50 The images in this tract and those from its source are reproduced in *Wonderfull Predictions* (29 December 1647) and *Strange Predictions* (25 May 1648), which both portend the fall of the monarchy.

51 *The Earle of Straffords Ghost*, 2, 5, 6.

52 Denham 'On the Earl of Strafford's Tryal and Death' (BL, Egerton MS 2421, ll. 9–10), in *The Poetical Works of Sir John Denham*, 19–20.

53 Marvell, 'An Horatian Ode,' *The Complete Poems*, l. 54; Potter, '"True Tagicomedies" of the Civil War and Commonwealth,' 205.

54 *The Fallacies of Mr. William Prynne*, 33. See also Lamont, *Marginal Prynne 1600–1669*, 47.

55 See Laud in *The Earl of Strafforde's Letters and Dispatches*, 2:101.

56 Laud, *Diary*, 3:228.

57 See Heylyn, *Cyprianus Anglicus*, 359; see Prynne's *Breviate*, 21, on the 1637 libels, which Prynne notes in the margin. The title page of Prynne's *A Breviate of the Life, of William Laud* indicates that the printing of the work was ordered by the House of Commons on 16 August.

58 Heylyn, *Cyprianus Anglicus*, 359.

59 Ibid.

60 'The Archbishop ... to the Lord Deputy: 28 Aug. 1637,' in *Earl of Strafforde's Letters and Dispatches*, 2:99.

61 Ibid.

62 Since the early reign of Charles I, the court deemed the composition of a

libel as an offence that would justify the punishment of the author (Adam Fox, *Oral and Literate Culture in England*, 308–9).

63 Heylyn, *Cyprianus Anglicus*, 453.

64 See also Laud, *The History of the Troubles and Tryal*, 3:391.

65 This is a statement Prynne notes in the margins of *A Breviate*, 21.

66 The Lord Mayor sent Laud a statement which described Laud's speech on the pillory. The caption of the speech read: '"The man that put the saints of God into a pillory of wood, stands here in a pillory of ink"' (Laud, *Works*, 7:371).

67 McRae, *Literature, Satire and the Early Stuart State*, 205.

68 Laud, *Diary* 3:235–6; see Cogswell, 'Underground Verse.'

69 Overton, *New Lambeth-Fayre*, B4v.

70 Overton, *A new Play called Canterburie His Change of Diot*, A4v.

71 Heinemann, *Puritanism and Theatre*, 245.

72 *Archy's Dreame*, A3r. On 9 March 1638 Archie Armstrong was heard denouncing Laud, saying 'Who's the fool now? Did you not hear the news from Stirling about the liturgy?' (Oxford, Bodleian Library, Bankes MSS, 18/24 and 42/30, and 20/3/36).

73 Heinemann, *Puritanism and Theatre*, 247; also see Butler, *Theatre and Crisis*, 240–1.

74 Laud, *Works* 6:597. The editor questions the attribution of this ca.1642 letter to Laud, though he claims that it would have served 'party purposes' to identify these views with the archbishop (596ns).

75 Ibid., 3:444; *The Discontented Conference* was seen by Laud in the Tower ([May] 1641).

76 Carlton, *Archbishop William Laud*, 203; see Heylyn, *Cyprianus Anglicus*, 480.

77 See Siebert, *Freedom of the Press in England, 1476–1776*, chapter 8, 165–78.

78 Hall, *An humble remonstrance to the High Court of Parliament*, 6–7.

79 Carlton, *Archbishop William Laud*, 222.

80 Cleveland, 'On the Archbishop of Canterbury,' in *The Poems of John Cleveland*, ll. 23–4.

81 Heylyn, *Cyprianus Anglicus*, 536.

82 *The Archbishop of Canterbury's Speech*, 18. See also *Cobbett's State Trials*, 4:623.

83 Heylyn, *Cyprianus Anglicus*, 529, 536.

84 Prynne, *Canterburies Doome*, C2.

85 *Mercurius Aulicus*, 5–12 January, 1644/5, p. 1340; *A Perfect Diurnall of Some Passages in Parliament no. 76* January 6–13 1644/5; see Raymond, *Making the News*, 304–5. Hinde's version of the speech is included in *Cobbett's State Trials*, 4:618–22.

86 *England and Irelands Sad Theater*, in *Catalogue of Political and Personal Satires*, 1:295.

Chapter 3

1 *Mercurius Pragmaticus*, no. 42, 16–30 January 1649, Hhh1v–Hhh2.

2 Marvell, 'An Horatian Ode,' in *The Complete Poems*, ll. 53, 58.

3 Milton, *Eikonoklastes*, in *Complete Prose Works of John Milton* (*CPW*), 3:342–43. Citations from *Eikonoklastes* are marked 'E.'

4 Compare Ong who observes that even a room full of readers does not build communities in a way that people sharing in an oral/aural presentation does ('Reading, Technology, and the Nature of Man,' 140).

5 Gauden, 21 Jan. 1660/61; Wordsworth, Documentary Supplement to '*Who Wrote Eikon Basilike?*' 16. My epigraph is also taken from this letter.

6 Randall refers to the spectators of executions as characters (*Winter Fruit*, 98).

7 Muir, *Ritual in Early Modern Europe*, 262.

8 *Perfect Occurrences of Every Daie journall*, no. 107, 12–19 January 1649.

9 *A perfect Narrative of the whole Proceedings ... in the Trial of the King ... Published by Authority, to prevent false and impertinent Relations*, in *Cobbett's State Trials*, 4:993, 994. Citations from *A perfect Narrative* are abbreviated *ST* (*State Trials*). [Henry Robinson], *A Short Discourse Between Monarchical and Aristocratical Government* (1649) maintained that the activities of the 'Publique State' were 'more open to the view of the world' than those of the monarchy (12).

10 See Achinstein, *Milton and the Revolutionary Reader*, 27–30.

11 Quoted in Wedgwood, *The Trial of Charles I*, 122; Rowse, *The Regicides and the Puritan Revolution*, 98.

12 Walker, *Anarchia Anglicana*, 98.

13 Leslie, *The Martyrdome of King Charles*, 27.

14 Charles challenged the arbitrary jurisdiction (ST 4:998, 999, 1000); see *His Majesties Reasons against the Pretended Jurisdiction of the High Court of Justice* (1648/9), in Muddiman, *The Trial of King Charles the First*, 231–2.

15 The loss of the stutter – 'so often the symptom of some intense inner psychological conflict' – was one indication that the final performance had made him whole again. See Carlton, *Charles I*, 359.

16 *A Perfect Diurnall of Some Passages in Parliament*, no. 288, 29 January–5 February 1649, 2315. Anyone 'on the point of making an exit, as from a kind of stage' would be inclined to act and speak accordingly, Milton notes, dismissing the speech as a mock performance (*Second Defence*, *CPW*, 4:646). See also J.A. Sharpe, '"Last Dying Speeches,"' 144–67.

17 Henry describes the postexecution scene: 'There was according to Order one Troop immediately marching from-wards charing-cross to Westm[inster] & another from-wards Westm[inster] to charing cross purposely to masker the people, & to disperse & scatter them, so that I had much adoe

amongst the rest to escape home without hurt' (*Diaries and Letters of Philip Henry*, 12).

18 J.A. Sharpe, '"Last Dying Speeches,"' 161.

19 Fumerton, *Cultural Aesthetics*, 14. Fumerton analyses the dramaturgy of the execution in chapter 1 of her book.

20 Fumerton, *Cultural Aesthetics*, 14.

21 *The Great Eclipse of the Sun*, A3r. See chapter 2 of this book.

22 *Eikon Basilike*, ed. Knachel. Citations from the text are marked EB. The authorship has been contested since the publication of *Eikon Alethine*; see publishing history in Milton, *CPW*, 3:147–50; and Madan, *A New Bibliography of the Eikon Basilike of King Charles I*, 126ff. A recent statement about the authorship of *Eikon Basilike* was made by Marshall Grossman who cites the opinion of J.P. Kenyon: 'On balance [Kenyon] inclines to the view that roughly the first two-thirds of EB (up to 1646) *was* written by the king' ('The Dissemination of the King,' 265n14).

23 Turner, *The Anthropology of Performance*, 34.

24 Lois Potter argued that tragicomedy influenced political events. '"True Tragicomedies" of the Civil War and Commonwealth,' 214; see also Maguire, *Regicide and Restoration*.

25 [Robert Brown], *The Subject's Sorrow*, 45. Bishop Juxon is another possible author of the sermon. The first pamphlet to draw parallels between Christ and Charles after the execution was *The Life and Death of King Charles the Martyr, Paralleled with Our Saviour* (London, 1649).

26 Helgerson, 'Milton Reads the King's Book,' 14. On the language of the theatre in the treatise, see Maguire, 'The Theatrical Mask/Masque of Politics.'

27 There were guides to consult to ensure that the writing of the self was properly conducted. King James I's *A Paterne for a Kings Inauguration*, which was intended for Charles, identified Christ as the pattern for every Christian but especially for a Christian king whose life experience is destined to recall Christ's passion. George Herbert's *The Temple*, which invites the Christian to interpret the Crucifixion as the event that characterizes the present life, was a favourite of the king, who used the collection as a model for his own monument.

28 James I and VI, *The Basilicon Doron of King James VI*, 15.

29 See Wall, 'Disclosures in Print'; and Maus, *Inwardness and the Theater*.

30 *The Princely Pellican*, 4.

31 See Briggs, *This Stage-Play World*, 5. See also Hibbard, 'The Early Seventeenth Century and the Tragic View of Life,' and Sandler, 'Icon and Iconoclast,' 172.

32 [Brown], The Subject's Sorrow,' 23.

33 Madan, *A New Bibliography of the Eikon Basilike of Charles I*, 4n10.

34 Joselin, *Diary*, 4 February 1648/9, 155.

35 In 'Texts as Events,' 29, Pocock characterizes texts as 'actions performed in language contexts that make them possible.'

36 *An Elegie upon the Death of Our Dread Sovereign*, ll. 15–18.

37 See also Patterson, *Censorship and Interpretation*; and Potter, *Secret Rites and Secret Writing*.

38 See Kevin Sharpe, '"An Image Doting Rabble,"' 37.

39 [Parker], *The King's Cabinet Opened*, A4v.

40 This is cited in *Perfect Diurnall*, no. 294, 12–19 March 1648/49, 2375. The page adjacent to the title page of *A Declaration* contains the 17 March 1648/49 order that the document 'be forthwith printed and published.'

41 Leslie, *The Martyrdom of King Charles*, 28.

42 *Mercurius Pragmaticus* no. 44, 27 February–5 March 1649, Hhh2.

43 *Eikon alethine*, a1r–a1v, A1v.

44 *Eikon e piste … Basilike*, 4.

45 John Selden was first asked 'to unsheathe his pen against the book *Eikon Basilike*,' but he refused, as J. Milton French reports in explaining how Milton acquired the job (*Life Records of John Milton*, 2:237).

46 Cook, *King Charles his Case*, 13. Cook referred to the trial as 'the most Comprehensive, Impartial, and Glorious piece of Justice, that was ever Acted and Executed upon the Theatre of *England*' (5).

47 *Mercurius Britanicus*, no. 49, 26 August–2 September 1644, 386.

48 Dobranski, *Milton, Authorship, and the Book Trade*, 151.

49 Norbrook, *Writing the Republic*, 205.

50 Jane, *Eikon Aklastos*, 3.

51 Ibid., 4.

52 Marcus, *Unediting the Renaissance*, 221.

53 [John Crouch], *New-Market-Fayre* (1649), A2v, in '*New-Market-Fayre*,' 85.

54 See Jagodzinski, *Privacy and Print*, 16–17.

55 Wright, *Parnassus Biceps*, 1.

56 Ibid., 54.

57 Nigel Smith, *Literature and Revolution*, 289.

58 Carlton, *Archbishop William Laud*, 152–3.

59 The prayers were first printed by William Dugard with his edition of the *Eikon Basilike* on 15 March 1648/9.

60 A note on the flyleaf of a copy of this 1636 edition of the *Book of Common Prayer* (*STC* 16403) indicates that the book was owned by John Boyle, 5th earl of Cork, who inherited it from Roger Boyle, 1st earl of Cork. *Booke of common prayer and administration of the sacraments … London, Robert Barker and the*

Assignes of John Bill, 1636. The book is housed in the Bindings Collection of the Pierpont Morgan Library, shelf number 5482.

61 See Knoppers, *Historicizing Milton*, 44–7. On the fate of Charles I in the Restoration, Potter, 'The Royal Martyr in the Restoration.'

62 *The Royal Martyr*, 7.

63 *Virtus Redeviva*, 18.

64 Grossman, 'The Dissemination of the King,' 263.

Chapter 4

1 See Barish, *The Antitheatrical Prejudice*.

2 Prynne, *Histrio-Mastix*, 832, 834.

3 Jordan, 'The Players Petition to the Long Parliament,' 79–80.

4 *Rombus the Moderator*, 13.

5 Lois Potter observes that the question '"Was it acted?" fails to account for the numerous works that appeared in dramatic form in the mid-century ('Closet Drama and Royalist Politics,' 264).

6 Heinemann, *Puritanism and Theatre*, 239; see also Wright, 'The Reading of Plays during the English Revolution,' 75. David Scott Kastan makes this point in 'Performances and Playbooks,' 171, by arguing that the injunction was 'a pragmatic response to the spreading public discontent and disorder in the summer of 1642.'

7 *A Declaration of the Lords and Commons*, A2v.

8 *Tyrannicall-Government Anatomized: Or, A Discourse Concerning Evil-Councellors* (London: Printed for John Field, 1642/3). See also *Tyrannicall-Government Anatomized*, in *A Critical Edition of George Buchanan's Baptistes*, ed. Berkowitz. In the citations throughout this essay, the first numbers refer to verses in Berkowitz's edition; the second numbers in square brackets refer to page numbers in the original 9 Feb 1642/3 prose version. For a fuller discussion of this work, see Sauer, 'Closet Drama and the Case of *Tyrannicall-Government Anatomized*.'

9 Straznicky, 'Closet Drama,' 417. Straznicky's rich history of closet drama focuses on the late sixteenth and early seventeenth centuries.

10 Francis Peck first made this attribution in *New Memoirs of the Life and Poetical Works of Mr. John Milton*, 278.

11 Nigel Smith, *Literature and Revolution*, 92.

12 Stephen Gosson, among the more famous readers of the play, observed that the moralizing and didactic effects of *Baptistes* depended upon its being read and not performed (Kinney, *Markets of Bawdrie: The Dramatic Criticism of Stephen Gosson*, 177–8).

13 See Phillips, 'George Buchanan and the Sidney Circle'; Kerman, 'George Buchanan and the Genre of *Samson Agonistes*'; Samuels, '*Samson Agonistes* and Renaissance Drama'; and Samuels, 'Fire not Light.'

14 Aitken, *The Trial of George Buchanan*, 24, 25. On the sources for *Baptistes*, see McFarlane, *Buchanan*, 381–5, and Buchanan, *Baptistes*, ed. Berkowitz, 105–59.

15 See Buchanan, *Baptistes*, ed. Berkowitz, 113–17.

16 Kevin Sharpe, *Reading Revolutions*, 335.

17 W. Ames, *Conscience with the Power and Cases thereof* (n.p., 1639), ii. 1, quoted in Keith Thomas, 'Cases of Conscience in Seventeenth-Century England,' 34.

18 Randall, *Winter Fruit*, 103. Susan Wiseman reads the poem as a contemporary political allegory and in terms of its 'alliance with a Protestant tradition of tyrannicide found in the writings of Buchanan and others' (*Drama and Politics*, 70). As a topical political allegory, Parliament might have considered the play remarkably apt, according to Harbage, *Cavalier Drama*, 178.

19 Peck, *New Memoirs of the Life of ... John Milton*, 271.

20 See Wiseman, *Drama and Politics*, 79; on the play generally, see ibid., 70–80 and Randall, *Winter Fruits*, 266–73.

21 Sharpe, *Reading Revolutions*, 291.

22 Straznicky, 'Closet Drama,' 427.

23 Milton, *Samson Agonistes*, in *Poems*, ll. 24–5, p. 550.

24 On the attribution of the translation of *Baptistes* to Milton, see Kerman, 'George Buchanan and the Genre of *Samson Agonistes*,' 23–4; Buchanan, *Baptistes*, ed. Berkowitz, 343–6; Butler, *Theatre and Crisis*, 99; Heinemann, *Puritanism and Theatre*, 234–5.

25 Kevin Sharpe, '"An Image Doting Rabble,"' 26. The term 'royalist' was not needed until the governing class polarized into parties engaged in an ideological and military struggle over the locus of supreme power in the state. The first instance of the word 'royalist' in the *OED* is in William Prynne's *Sovereign Power of Parliaments* (1643); see also Tim Harris, *Politics under the Later Stuarts*.

26 Potter, *Secret Rites and Secret Writing*, 74.

27 Literary critics and historians who have argued that the Cavaliers retreated during the period include Miner, *The Cavalier Mode from Jonson to Cotton*; Underdown, *Royalist Conspiracy in England 1649–1660*; and Hardacre, *The Royalists during the Puritan Revolution*. Those who take an opposing position include Wilcher, *The Writing of Royalism*; Susan Wiseman, *Drama and Politics*; Randall, *Winter Fruit*; Potter, *Secret Rites*; Patterson, *Censorship and Interpretation*.

28 [Ford], *The Queen, or the Excellency of her Sex*, A3v, A4r.

29 Moseley, 'The Stationer to the Reader,' in *Comedies and Tragedies Written by Francis Beaumont and John Fletcher Gentlemen*, xi.

30 Chartier, 'Texts, Printing, Readings,' 157.

31 Richard Meighen, 'Epistle Dedicatory,' in *Three Excellent Tragœdies*, by Goffe, H3v.

32 Aston Cokaine, '*A Prœludium*,' in *Five New Playes*, by Brome (1653), A2.

33 Alexander Brome, 'To the Readers,' in *Five new Playes*, by Brome (1659), A3r–v.

34 *The Second Part of the Tragi-Comedy, called New-Market Fayre* (1649), title page. On the contested authorship of the *New-Market Fayre* pamphlets, see chapter 5 of this book. Also see Wiseman, 'Pamphlet Plays in the Civil War News Market, esp. 67 on the influence of pamphlets on the marketplace.

35 Greg, *A Bibliography of the English Printed Drama to the Restoration*, 1:xiv–vx, 2.677.

36 Potter, 'Short Plays: Drolls and Pamphlets,' 4:290.

37 *An Ordinance of the Lords and Commons*, 2, 3, 4. Not until March 1649 were the ordinances against playhouses actually put into effect through the dismantling of the interiors of the Fortune, Cockpit, and Salisbury Court, though Ford's *The Queen* (cited above) suggests that performances at the Red Bull continued.

38 *Mercurius Bellicus*, no. 4, 14–20 February 1648/49, 7. *Mercurius Melancholicus*, no. 58, 25 September–2 October 1648, 6. See also Hotson, *The Commonwealth and the Restoration Stage*, 35, 36, 39.

39 *Craftie Cromwell*, A1v.

40 *The Second Part of the Tragi-Comedie called Craftie Cromwell*, A2.

41 *Rombus the Moderator*, 12.

42 Ernest Sirluck observes that there was no decline in the frequency of printed allusions to Shakespeare and Jonson, but only a change in their character from predominantly literary to the political ('Shakespeare and Jonson among the Pamphleteers of the First Civil War,' 88).

43 Wright, *Parnassus Biceps*, 89.

44 Birkenhead, 'The Assembly-man,' 18.

45 See *The Trial of Dr. John Hewet, before the High Court of Justice, for High Treason: 10 Charles II. the 1st of June, A.D. 1658*, in *Cobbett's Complete Collection of State Trials*, 5:891.

46 The biographical information about Hewit/Hewet is taken from *DNB* 9:757–8.

47 Gayton, *Pleasant Notes upon Don Quixot*, bk. 4, 270.

48 On *Panthalia*, see Sauer, 'Emasculating Romance.'

49 See Pepys, *King Charles Preserved*, 31.
50 Webster and Rowley, *The Thracian Wonder*, A2.

Chapter 5

1 Manning, 'The Levellers and Religion,' 66–7; Thomas, 'The Meaning of Literacy in Early Modern England'; Brailsford, *The Levellers*, 534; Haller and Davies, *The Leveller Tracts, 1647–1653*, 384.
2 The concept of a drama of dissent is derived from the title of Sharon Achinstein's '*Samson Agonistes* and the Drama of Dissent.'
3 Bauman, *Let Your Words Be Few*, 104, 105. See also Nigel Smith, 'Non-Conformist Voices and Books,' 426.
4 Bauman, *Let Your Words Be Few*, 104, 105. Referring to an earlier work by Bauman, Kate Peters recommends consulting other genres, including manuscript writings, letters, and printed tracts ('Patterns of Quaker Authorship, 1652–1656,' 9–10).
5 Yule, *Pragmatics*, 47, 53–4. Actions performed via utterances are called 'speech acts' (47). See also Austin, *How to Do Things with Words*.
6 The considerable importance that Quakers associated with documenting courtroom proceedings is evidenced in George Fox's appeal to Quakers in 1657 that they present their sufferings to judges of assize, and in his organization in 1658 of a system of recording sufferings, including trial accounts, which would be incorporated by Ellis Hookes into the *Great Book of Suffering*.
7 Tawney, *Religion and the Rise of Capitalism*, 212–13.
8 Whiting, *Studies in English Puritanism*, 88.
9 See Reay, 'Quakerism and Society,' 144.
10 Barbour, *The Quakers in Puritan England*, 1.
11 See, for example, Prynne, *The Quakers Unmasked*. See also chapter 1 of this book.
12 *Puritanism and Liberty*, 100.
13 Nigel Smith, *Literature and Revolution*, 131. David Loewenstein also refers to the theatrical language of the Levellers' writings (see his discussion of *The Hunting of the Foxes from New-Market* [1649] in *Representing Revolution in Milton and His Contemporaries*, 39–40; on the performances of the Ranter, Abiezer Coppe, in his theatricalized world, see chapter 3 of *Representing Revolution*, esp. 112–13).
14 Wiseman, *Drama and Politics*, 42.
15 Nigel Smith, *Literature and Revolution*, 142.
16 *Trial of Lilburne and Wharton for publishing Seditious Books*. In *Cobbett's Complete Collection of State Trials*, 3:1350.

17 Lilburne, *A Worke of the Beast*, 20.

18 Heinemann, *Puritanism and Theatre*, 237–57; Frank, *The Levellers*, 94–5; Webber, *The Eloquent 'I,'* 53–79.

19 Overton *An Alarum to the House of Lords*, 8, 9.

20 Lilburne et al., *An Agreement of the People*, 227.

21 See Brailsford, *The Levellers*, chapter 13; *The Levellers in the English Revolution*, 28–33; and especially Gentles, 'The *Agreements of the People* and Their Political Contexts.'

22 Mercurius Pragmaticus, *The Levellers levell'd. Or, The Independents Conspiracie to root out Monarchie. An Interlude*, A1r; *The Levellers Levelled*, ed. Dust, 199, ll. 19–20.

23 See Gentles, '*The Agreements of the People* and Their Political Contents,' 172–3.

24 *The Famous Tragedie of King Charles I*, C1v–2r.

25 Gerrard Winstanley et al., *The True Levellers Standard Advanced*, 9.

26 See Lilburne, Walwyn, Prince, and Overton, *An Agreement of the Free People of England*.

27 *Englands Standard Advanced*, 2.

28 Overton, *The Baiting of the Great Bull*, A1v.

29 *A New Bull-Bayting*, 5, 4.

30 As Wiseman observed in her discussion of *A New Bull-Bayting*, 'the swiftly shifting political situation generated more ambivalent and blended criticisms' (*Drama and Politics*, 48).

31 *The Triall, of Lieut. Collonell John Lilburne*, 67. Lilburne created a model of a national jury for his audience, 'a public endowed with the highest authority in the land,' Sharon Achinstein observed in *Milton and the Revolutionary Reader*, 49.

32 *Truths Victory over Tyrants and Tyranny*, 4.

33 Gregg, *Free-born John*, 295.

34 Lilburne identified the jury as judges of fact and of the law (*Cobbett's Complete Collection of State Trials*, 4:1379); see also Green, *Verdict according to Conscience*, 173.

35 *The Man in the Moon*, 233.

36 Wiseman, *Drama and Politics*, 49–50, 233n17.

37 See also Crawford, '"The Poorest She"'; Higgins, 'The Reaction of Women.'

38 Forster, *These several Papers was sent to the Parliament*; for the list of signatures, see 7–72; the final two pages are in manuscript, with a note 'copied by ... Matilda Fry 1849.'

39 Hinds, '*The Cry of a Stone*' *by Anna Trapnel*, xxxi. On female communities in particular, see Hobby, '"Come to live a preaching life"'; and Benefiel, '"Weaving the Web of Community."'

40 Kelly, 'Did Women Have a Renaissance?' and Ferguson, 'Moderation and its Discontents,' 352. Crawford, 'The Challenges to Patriarchalism,' 113. Cf. Ferguson, who questions the assumption of Elaine Hobby, Margaret L. King, Tina Krontins, and Barbara Kiefer Lewalski, whose works she reviews, that women enjoyed increased spiritual autonomy in the early modern era. See also Schwoerer, 'Women's Public Political Voice.'

41 This statistic is taken from Crawford, 'Women's Published Writings 1600–1700,' 266, and quoted in the introduction to *Women and the Literature of the Seventeenth Century*, xii. On the female radical tradition and the literature of suffering, see Sauer, 'The Experience of Defeat.' See also Ostovich and Sauer, 'Religion, Prophecy, and Persecution,' in *Reading Early Modern Women*, chapter 4.

42 Graham et al., Introduction to *Her Own Life*, 24.

43 On the bodily theatrics, malleable identity, and acts of preaching and prophesying of female Quakers, see Mack, 'Gender and Spirituality in Early English Quakerism,' and *Visionary Women*, esp. 15–211.

44 *Calendar of State Papers, Domestic Series, The Commonwealth*, 6:50–1.

45 Hinds, '*The Cry of a Stone*' by Anna Trapnel, xxxv. Hinds observes that 'the genres of prophecy and spiritual autobiography are not sharply separable: *The Cry of a Stone* is itself primarily prophetic, but also has an initial section which follows the conventions and structures of the spiritual autobiography' (xli, n80).

46 Trapnel, *The Cry of a Stone*, 2. See also Hinds, '*The Cry of a Stone*' by Anna Trapnel, xvii, 84n7.

47 Otten, *English Women's Voices*, 57.

48 Trapnel, Preface to *Anna Trapnel's Report and Plea*, A3.

49 Trapnel, *A Legacy for Saints*, 10.

50 Bell, Parfitt, and Shepherd, *A Biographical Dictionary of English Women Writers 1580–1720*, 256. In reference to Quakers, Phyllis Mack states that their collective identity mattered most (*Visionary Women*, 208), and that the development of this identity was enabled through prophetic utterances, visionary writings, dramatic posturing, and through symbolic discourses that resisted rational methods of analysis and comprehension.

51 Trapnel, *Report and Plea*, 25; Cary, *Little Horns Doom & Downfall*, 42.

52 *Severall Proceedings of State Affaires*, no. 225, 12–19 January 1653/54, 3562–3.

53 *Calendar of State Papers, Domestic Series, The Commonwealth*, 6:393.

54 *Mercurius Politicus*, no. 201, 13–20 April 1654, 3430.

55 *The Grand Politique Post*, no. 127, 10–17 January 1653/54, 1236; Channel, *A Message from God*, 7.

56 The controversy about the authorial role of Trapnel and her 'ravishings of the spirit' is not restricted to seventeenth-century writings. See Tindall, *John Bunyan*, 31, and Hinds, *God's Englishwomen*, 2.

57 McGuire, *Speechless Dialect*, 37.

58 Farmer, *Sathan Inthron'd in his Chair of Pestilence*, C1v. For books on Nayler, see Joseph Smith, *A Descriptive Catalogue of Friends' Books*, 2:232–4.

59 Brink, '*Paradise Lost* and James Nayler's Fall,' 102.

60 *Cobbett's Complete Collection of State Trials* 5:808–12. See chapters 5 and 6 of Bittle, *James Nayler 1618–1660.*

61 See *Cobbett's Complete Collection of State Trials* 5:817, 821–8; Cromwell, *The Writings and Speeches of Oliver Cromwell*, 4:358–9.

62 Deacon, *The Grand Imposter Examined*, 6–9. The publisher was Giles Calvert, the printer who acted as a link between radical groups in the 1640s and 50s. His sister Martha married Thomas Simmonds, who was possibly related to Milton's publishers Thomas, Mary, and Sarah Simmonds (Hill, *Milton and the English Revolution*, 135).

63 Correspondence about Nayler is presented in William Caton's writings, 3:100–1; Richard Hubberthorne writes to Margaret Fell about the disruptions of meetings by Nayler's deluded female followers, especially Martha, who acts out of line.

64 '*Mr* William Malyn *to the Lord Protector,*' in *Original Letters and Papers of State*, 144.

65 Barclay, *Letters of Early Friends*, 54; Thomas Burton, *Diary of Thomas Burton*, 1:33.

66 Hill alludes to the connection between Nayler and Milton's Samson (*Milton and the English Revolution*, 443).

67 Blackborow, *A Visit to the Spirit in Prison*, 4.

68 *Calendar of State Papers, Domestic Series, Charles II*, 3:251. For the importance of print to nonconformist identity see Keeble, *The Literary Culture of Nonconformity in Later Seventeenth-Century England*, Mascuch, 'A Press of Witnesses'; and O'Malley, 'The Press and Quakerism 1653–1659'; and Wright, 'Distribution of Literature.'

69 See also the epigraph on pp. 8–9 of this book.

70 *The Examination and Tryall of Margaret Fell and George Fox*, MS 1 (manuscript pages are included in the printed document).

71 The Quakers inherited both the soul of Lilburne, who converted to their cause after his acquittal, and his new concept of the right and duty of the English criminal trial jury (Green, *Verdict according to Conscience*, 198–9). In October 1655, two years before his death, he officially joined the Quakers. After his death, Lilburne's corpse was moved to London, 'to the house called the Mouth, in Aldersgate, which is the usual meeting place of the people

called the Quakers, to whom [it seems] he had lately joined in opinion.'
Quoted in Barclay, *Letters of the Early Friends*, 55n.

72 *Examination and Tryall of Margaret Fell and George Fox*, 18; *Journal of George Fox*, 73.

73 Horle, *The Quakers and the English Legal System 1660–1688*, 41.

Epilogue

1 Hoxby, *Mammon's Music*, 43.

2 See Nigel Smith, *Literature and Revolution*, 72–3; Randall, *Winter Fruit*, 44–50; and Hotson, *The Commonwealth and the Restoration Stage*, 35–47.

3 *Truths Victory over Tyrants and Tyranny*, 6.

4 Ibid.

5 Milton, Preface to *Samson Agonistes*, in *John Milton: Complete Poems and Major Prose*, 550. Henceforth referred to as *SA*.

6 Chartier, *The Cultural Uses of Print in Early Modern France*, 7.

7 Milton, *Reason of Church-Government*, in *Complete Prose Works*, 1:819. Hereafter cited *CPW*. See also Jacob and Raylor, 'Opera and Obedience,' 208.

8 On the controversy about the dating of the text which I examine as a product of the Restoration, see Low, 'Milton's *Samson* and the Stage, with Implications for Dating the Play.'

9 Marcus, Rumrich, Dobranski, and Wittreich have challenged the unifying imperative of Miltonists. See Marcus, *Unediting the Renaissance*; Rumrich, *Milton Unbound*; Dobranksi, 'Samson and the Omissa,' and *Milton, Authorship, and the Book Trade*; Wittreich, *Shifting Contexts*.

10 See Cope, '*Paradise Regained*: Inner Ritual,' 53–4. On *Paradise Regained* as a repudiation of Restoration drama, see Zwicker, 'Milton, Dryden, and the Politics of Literary Controversy.' Peggy Samuels develops a convincing reading of *Samson Agonistes*' engagement with the concerns and structures of tragicomedy, but does not examine Restoration drama specifically ('Fire not Light'). Nancy Klein Maguire's fascinating study on Carolean tragicomedy barely mentions Milton (*Regicide and Restoration*). Nicholas Jose examines Restoration drama and *Samson Agonistes* in two illuminating but separate chapters in *Ideas of the Restoration in English Literature, 1660–71*. See also Cox, 'Renaissance Power and Stuart Dramaturgy.'

11 Zwicker, 'Milton, Dryden, and the Politics of Literary Controversy,' 275.

12 Marcus, *Unediting the Renaissance*, 211; Nigel Smith, *Literature and Revolution*, 92. Also see Sauer, 'The Politics of Performance in the Inner Theatre.'

13 According to Alfred Harbage, only a few closet dramas were produced in the Restoration years, and these consisted mainly of political dialogues and Latin

plays (*Annals of English Drama 975–1700*, 154ff.). *Samson Agonistes* belongs in neither category and thus merits special consideration as an anti-theatrical and, as I argue, a politically charged text.

14 *Unfortunate Usurper* (1663), sig. K4r. Dryden, *The Conquest of Granada, Part I* (1672), in *The Works of John Dryden*, 11:10. All citations of Dryden's prose are to this edition.

15 Pepys, *The Diary of Samuel Pepys*, 9:367. For Pepys's reading of Restoration audiences, see McAfee, *Pepys on the Restoration Stage*, 277–85.

16 Chapter 2 of Roberts, *The Ladies: Female Patronage of Restoration Drama 1660–1700*, offers a useful account of Elizabeth and Samuel Pepys's theatre-going and play-reading practices.

17 Ollard, *Pepys: A Biography*, 212.

18 No copy of the volume with a date of 1670 is known, although this date is given by some early biographers and library catalogues. *A Catalogue of books printed and published at London in Michaelmass-term, 1670*, dated 22 November 1670, lists the volume, and it was also advertised in *A Catalogue of books. Printed for John Starkey*, dated, in part, in May 1670. Various other post-1670 catalogues printed for Starkey contain this entry. A second edition of *Samson Agonistes* is published in 1680 and two more issues, not surprisingly, in 1688.

19 Spiller, 'Directing the Audience in *Samson Agonistes*,' 122.

20 Healy, *New Latitudes*, 172.

21 Milton's earlier readers had been replaced by a critical, even hostile, royalist readership 'bent on revenge,' Nicholas von Maltzahn observes ('Milton's Readers,' 2nd ed. 241). His erudite essay does not, however, consider the readership/audience of *Samson Agonistes*.

22 Masson, *The Life of Milton*, 6:633. See also Freedman, 'Dryden's "Memorable Visit" to Milton.'

23 Derek Hughes suggests that Dryden's *Of Heroique Playes* (1672) characterizes Almanzor as a 'flawed and self-deluding character,' though he acknowledges that critics are divided over the character's heroism (*Dryden's Heroic Plays*, 11; see also 81). While Dryden actually invites a critical response of the hero of his play, Almanzor is in the end subsumed within the conquering family (Part 2, 5.3.272–5) and victory over the Moors is accorded to him and Spain.

24 Shakespeare, *The Tragedy of Antony and Cleopatra*, 2.2.192–3, 206; Dryden, *All for Love: or, The World Well Lost. A Tragedy*, 3.1.162.

25 Leigh, *The Censure of the Rota*, 3–4.

26 See Pepys, *King Charles Preserved*, 19.

27 Jose, *Ideas of the Restoration in English Literature*, 156.

28 Knoppers, in *Historicizing Milton*, admirably discusses Samson's trials of conscience. This book is a fine source of information on the iconography of the

spectacle of punishment in 1649 and in the Restoration. Knoppers argues that Milton's choice and treatment of a tragedy on the biblical figure of Samson has, in relation to the punishment of the regicides, more specific, extensive, and resonant political implications than have previously been recognized (55).

29 For a reading of *Samson Agonistes* that supports both regenerationist and sceptical interpretations of Samson's final act, see Dennis Kezar's prize-winning, 'Samson's Death by Theater and Milton's Art of Dying.'

30 Wittreich, *Interpreting 'Samson Agonistes,'* 121; see also Wittreich, *Shifting Contexts.*

31 As Mary Nyquist and Margaret W. Ferguson observe, Milton 'continues to enjoy the status of the most monumentally unified author in the canon' (Preface to *Re-membering Milton,* xii).

32 Sharpe, *Reading Revolutions,* 60.

Works Cited

Achinstein, Sharon. *Milton and the Revolutionary Reader.* Princeton: Princeton University Press, 1994.

– '*Samson Agonistes* and the Drama of Dissent.' *Milton Studies* 33 (1996): 133–57.

The Actors Remonstrance, or Complaint: For the Silencing of their profession. London, 1643.

Aers, David, and Gunther Kress. 'Historical Process, Individuals and Communities in Milton's *Areopagitica.*' In *Literature, Language and Society in England 1580–1680*, edited by David Aers, Bob Hodge, and Gunther Kress, 152–83. Totowa: Barnes & Noble Books, 1981.

Aitken, James M. *The Trial of George Buchanan before the Lisbon Inquisition.* London: Oliver & Boyd, 1939.

In Answer to the Earle of Straffords Conclusion. 13 April 1641.

An Answer to the Lord Digbies Speech in the House of Commons; To the Bill of Attaineder of the Earle of Strafford, the 21th. of Aprill. 1641. 1641.

An Aproved Answer to the Partiall and Unlikt of Lord Digbies Speech to the Bill of Attainder of the Earle of Strafford. 1641.

The Archbishop of Canterbury's Speech: or His Funerall Sermon. London, 1645.

Archy's Dreame, Sometimes Jester to his Majestie, But Exiled the Court by Canterburies Malice. 1641.

Austin, J.L. *How to Do Things with Words.* New York: Oxford University Press, 1962.

Bacon, Francis. *Historie of the Raigne of King Henry the Seventh.* London, 1622.

Barbour, Hugh. *The Quakers in Puritan England.* New Haven: Yale University Press, 1964.

Barclay, A.R. *Letters of Early Friends.* In *The Friends' Library*, edited by William Evans and Thomas Evans, vol. 11. Philadelphia: Joseph Rakestraw, 1847.

Barish, Jonas. *The Antitheatrical Prejudice.* Berkeley and Los Angeles: University of California Press, 1981.

Baron, Sabrina A. 'Licensing Readers, Licensing Authorities in Seventeenth-Century England.' In *Books and Readers in Early Modern England: Material Studies,* edited by Jennifer Andersen and Elizabeth Sauer, 217–42. Philadelphia: University of Pennsylvania Press, 2002.

Barry, Jonathan. 'Literacy and Literature in Popular Culture: Reading and Writing in Historical Perspective.' In *Popular Culture in England, c. 1500–1850,* edited by Tim Harris, 69–94. New York: St Martin's Press, 1995.

Bauman, Richard. *Let Your Words Be Few: Symbolism of Speaking and Silence among Seventeenth-Century Quakers.* New York: Cambridge University Press, 1983.

Beaumont, Francis, and John Fletcher. *Comedies and Tragedies Written by Francis Beaumont and John Fletcher Gentlemen. The Works of Francis Beaumont and John Fletcher,* edited by Arnold Glover. Cambridge: Cambridge University Press, 1905.

Bell, Maureen. 'Introduction: The Material Text.' In *Re-constructing the Book: Literary Texts in Transmission,* edited by Maureen Bell et al., 1–8. Aldershot: Ashgate, 2001.

Bell, Maureen, George Parfitt, and Simon Shepherd, eds. *A Biographical Dictionary of English Women Writers 1580–1720.* London: Harvester Wheatsheaf, 1990.

Bellany, Alastair. *The Politics of Court Scandal in Early Modern England: News Culture and the Overbury Affair, 1603–1660.* Cambridge: Cambridge University Press, 2002.

Benefiel, Margaret. '"Weaving the Web of Community": Letters and Epistles.' In *Hidden in Plain Sight: Quaker Women's Writings 1650–1700,* edited by Mary Garman et al., 443–52. Wallingford, PA: Pendle Hill, 1996.

Birkenhead, John. 'The Assembly-man; written in the year 1647.' London, 1663.

Bittle, William G. *James Naylor 1618–1660: The Quaker Indicted by Parliament.* Richmond, IN: Friends United Press, 1986.

Blackborow, Sarah. *A Visit to the Spirit in Prison.* London, 1658.

Blum, Abbe. 'The Author's Authority: *Areopagitica* and the Labour of Licensing.' In *Re-membering Milton: Essays on the Texts and Traditions,* edited by Mary Nyquist and Margaret W. Ferguson, 74–96. New York: Methuen, 1987.

Boerner, Dorothy Payne. 'The Trial Convention in English Renaissance Drama.' PhD diss., University of Maryland, 1980.

B[ond], J[ohn]. *The Poets Knavery Discovered, in all their lying Pamphlets ... Well worth the reading ... to distinguish betwixt the Lyes, and reall Books.* London, [Feb] 1642.

Booke of common prayer and administration of the sacraments. London: Robert Barker and the Assignes of John Bill, 1636. Pierpont Morgan Library, Shelf number 5482.

Books and Readers in Early Modern England: Material Studies. Edited by Jennifer Andersen and Elizabeth Sauer. Philadelphia: University of Pennsylvania Press, 2002.

Bourdieu, Pierre. 'Structure, Habitus, Practices.' In *Contemporary Sociological Theory,* edited by Craig Calhoun, 276–88. Oxford: Blackwell, 2002.

Brailsford, Henry Noel. *The Levellers and the English Revolution.* London: Cresset Press, 1961.

Brathwaite, Richard. 'The Quaker.' In *The Honest Ghost, or, a voice from the Vault,* 320–1. London, 1658.

– *Panthalia: or the Royal Romance. A Discourse Stored with infinite variety in relation to State-Government And Passages of matchless affection gracefully interveined, And presented on a Theatre of Tragical and Comical State, in a successive continuation to these Times. Faithfully and ingenuously rendred.* London, 1659.

Briggs, Julia. *This Stage-Play World: English Literature and its Background 1580–1625.* Oxford: Oxford University Press, 1983.

Brink, Andrew W. '*Paradise Lost* and James Nayler's Fall.' *Journal of the Friends' Historical Society* 53.2 (1973): 99–112.

Brome, Richard. *Five New Playes, viz. The Madd Couple well matcht. The Novella. The Court Begger ... By Richard Brome.* London, 1653.

– *Five new Playes, viz. The English Moor ... The Love-Sick Court ... Covent Garden ... By Richard Brome.* London, 1659.

[Brown, Robert]. *The Subject's Sorrow: Or, Lamentations upon the Death of Britaines Josiah King Charles.* N.p., 1649.

Buchanan, George. *Baptistes.* 1577. In *A Critical Edition of George Buchanan's Baptistes and of Its Anonymous Seventeenth-Century Translation Tyrannicall-Government Anatomized,* edited by Stephen Berkowitz. New York: Garland, 1992.

Burton, Henry. *Truth's Triumph over Trent.* London, 1629.

Burton, Thomas. *Diary of Thomas Burton ... from 1656 to 1659.* Edited by John Towill Rutt. London: H. Colburn, 1828.

Butler, Martin. *Theatre and Crisis 1632–1642.* Cambridge: Cambridge University Press, 1984.

Calendar of State Papers, Domestic Series, Charles I. Edited by William Douglas Hamilton. 23 vols. London: Public Record Office, 1887.

Calendar of State Papers, Domestic Series, Charles II. Edited by Mary Anne Everett Green. 28 vols. London: Public Record Office, 1860.

Calendar of State Papers, Domestic Series, The Commonwealth. Edited by Mary Anne Everett Green. 13 vols. London: Public Record Office, 1875–86.

Carlton, Charles. *Charles I: The Personal Monarch.* Boston: Routledge & Kegan Paul, 1983.

– *Archbishop William Laud.* London: Routledge, 1987.

Cary, M. *Little Horns Doom & Downfall ... A New and More Exact Mappe; or, Description of New Jerusalems Glory.* London, 1651.

A Catalogue of books printed and published at London in Michaelmass-term, 1670. No. 3. Dated 22 November 1670.

A Catalogue of books. Printed for John Starkey. Dated, in part, in May 1670.

Caton, William. *MS. Vol. S 81. Listing and Index* by Craig W. Horle. London: Friends' Library, 1975.

Channel, Elinor. *A Message from God, [By a Dumb woman].* 1654.

Charles I. *Eikon Basilike: The Portraiture of His Sacred Majesty in His Solitudes and Sufferings.* Edited by Philip A. Knachel. Ithaca: Cornell University Press, 1966.

A Charme for Canterburian Spirits, which (since the death of this Arch-Prelate) have appeared ... in the City of London. N.p., 1645.

Chartier, Roger. *The Cultural Uses of Print in Early Modern France.* Translated by Lydia G. Cochrane. Princeton: Princeton University Press, 1987.

– *The Culture of Print, Power and the Uses of Print in Early Modern Europe.* Translated by Lydia G. Cochrane. Cambridge: Polity Press, 1989.

– 'Texts, Printing, Readings.' In *The New Cultural History,* edited by Lynn Hunt, 154–75. Berkeley and Los Angeles: University of California Press, 1989.

– *The Order of Books: Readers, Authors, and Libraries in Europe Between the Fourteenth and Eighteenth Centuries.* Trans. Lydia G. Cochrane. Stanford: Stanford University Press, 1994.

Clegg, Cyndia Susan. *Press Censorship in Jacobean England.* Cambridge: Cambridge University Press, 2001.

Cleveland, John. *The Poems of John Cleveland.* Edited by Brian Morris and Eleanor Withington. Oxford: Clarendon Press, 1967.

Cobbett's Complete Collection of State Trials. Edited by Thomas Bayley Howell. 33 vols. London: R. Bagshaw, 1809–26.

Cogswell, Thomas. 'Underground Verse and the Transformation of Early Stuart Political Culture.' In *Political Culture and Cultural Politics in Early Modern England: Essays Presented to David Underdown,* edited by Susan D. Amussen and Mark A. Kishlansky, 277–300. Manchester: Manchester University Press, 1995.

Coke, Edward. *The Third Part of the Institutes of the Laws of England: Concerning high treason, and other pleas of crown, and criminall Cases.* London, 1644.

A Collection of Scarce and Valuable Tracts ... of the Late Lord Somers. 1810. Edited by Walter Scott. New York: AMS Press, 1965.

Collop, John. 'On *Lord Wentworth Earl of Strafford.*' In *Poesis Rediviva: or, Poesie Reviv'd,* 32–3. London, 1656.

Combs, James E. *Dimensions of Political Drama.* Santa Monica, CA: Goodyear, 1980.

'Concerning the Prices of Wine, &c.' In *Speeches and Passages of this Great and Happy Parliament.* London, 1641.

Condren, Conal. *The Language of Politics in Seventeenth-Century England.* Basingstoke: Macmillan, 1994.

Cook, John. *King Charles his Case, or an Appeal to all Rational Men Concerning His Trial in the High Court of Justice.* London, 1649.

Cope, Jackson. '*Paradise Regained*: Inner Ritual.' *Milton Studies* 1 (1969): 51–65.

The Conclusion of the Earle of Straffords Defence. 12 April 1641.

The Copie of a Letter sent from the Roaring Boyes in Elizium; To the two arrant Kings of the Grape, in Limbo. N.p., 1641.

Corns, Thomas N. 'The Freedom of Reader-Response: Milton's *Of Reformation* and Lilburne's *Christian Mans Triall.*' In *Freedom and the English Revolution: Essays in History and Literature,* edited by R.C. Richardson and G.M. Ridden, 93–110. Manchester: Manchester University Press, 1986.

Coster, Robert. *A Mite Cast into the Common Treasury.* 1649.

Cox, John D. 'Renaissance Power and Stuart Dramaturgy: Shakespeare, Milton, Dryden.' *Comparative Drama* 22.4 (1988–9): 323–58.

Craftie Cromwell: or: Oliver ordering our New State. A Tragi Comedie. Feb. 1648.

Crawford, Patricia. 'Women's Published Writings 1600–1700.' In *Women in English Society, 1500–1800,* edited by Mary Prior, 211–82. New York: Methuen, 1985.

– 'The Challenges to Patriarchalism: How Did the Revolution Affect Women?' In *Revolution and Restoration: England in the 1650s,* edited by John Morrill, 112–28. London: Collins and Brown, 1992.

– '"The Poorest She": Women and Citizenship in Early Modern England.' In *The Putney Debates of 1647: The Army, The Levellers, and the English State,* edited by Michael Mendle, 197–218. Cambridge: Cambridge University Press, 2001.

Cressy, David. *Literacy and the Social Order: Reading and Writing in Tudor and Stuart England.* Cambridge: Cambridge University Press, 1980.

– 'Conflict, Consensus, and the Willingness to Wink: The Erosion of Community in Charles I's England.' *Huntington Library Quarterly* 61.1 (2000): 131–49.

Cromartie, A.D.T. 'The Printing of Parliamentary Speeches, November 1640–July 1642.' *Historical Journal* 33.1 (1990): 23–44.

Cromwell, Oliver. *The Writings and Speeches of Oliver Cromwell.* Edited by W.C. Abbott. 4 vols. New York: Russell & Russell, 1970.

Cromwell's Conspiracy: A Tragy-Comedy. London, 1660.

Culture and Society in the Stuart Restoration. Edited by Gerald MacLean. Cambridge: Cambridge University Press, 1995.

Cust, Richard. 'News and Politics in Early Seventeenth-Century England.' *Past and Present* 112 (1986): 60–90.

Deacon, John. *The Grand Imposter Examined: or The Life, Tryal, and Examination of James Nayler.* London, 1656.

A Declaration of the Lords and Commons ... For the appeasing and quietting of all unlawfull Tumults and Insurrections ... Also an Ordinance of both Houses for the suppressing of Stage-Playes. London, 1642.

A Declaration of the Parliament of England, expressing the grounds of their late proceedings. London, 1649.

De Krey, Gary S. 'Radicals, Reformers, and Republicans: Academic Language and Political Discourse in Restoration London.' In *A Nation Transformed: England after the Restoration,* edited by Alan Houston and Steve Pincus, 71–99. Cambridge: Cambridge University Press, 2001.

Denham, John. *The Poetical Works of Sir John Denham,* edited by Theodore Howard Banks. New Haven: Yale University Press, 1928.

A Description of the Passage of Thomas late Earle of Strafford, over the River of Styx. 1641.

D'Ewes, Simonds. *The Journals of all the Parliaments During the Reign of Queen Elizabeth.* London, 1682.

A Dialogue or accidental discourse Betwixt Mr. Alderman Abell, *and* Richard *Kilvert.* 1641.

The Diary of Ralph Josselin, 1616–1683. Edited by Alan Macfarlane. London: Oxford University Press, 1976.

Dictionary of National Biography. Edited by Leslie Stephen [and Sidney Lee]. London: Smith, Elder, 1885–1900.

The Discontented Conference betwixt the two great Associates, William, Archbishop of Canterbury, and Thomas, late Earle of Strafford. N.p., 1641.

Dobranski, Stephen B. 'Samson and the Omissa.' *Studies in English Literature* 36 (1996): 149–69.

– 'Licensing Milton's Heresy.' In *Milton and Heresy,* edited by Dobranski and John P. Rumrich, 139–58. Cambridge: Cambridge University Press, 1998.

– *Milton, Authorship, and the Book Trade.* Cambridge: Cambridge University Press, 1999.

Dryden, John. *The Works of John Dryden.* Edited by Edward Niles Hooker and H.T. Swedenberg. 20 vols. Berkeley and Los Angeles: University of California Press, 1956–2000.

Dunn, Kevin. 'Milton among the Monopolists: *Areopagitica,* Intellectual Property, and the Harlib Circle.' In *Samuel Hartlib and Universal Reformation: Studies in Intellectual Communities,* edited by Mark Greengrass, Michael Leslie, and Timothy Raylor, 177–92. Cambridge: Cambridge University Press, 1994.

The Earl of Strafforde's Letters and Dispatches. Edited by William Knowler. Vol. 2. Dublin, 1740.

The Earle of Straffords Ghost. Complaining of the Cruelties of his Countrey-men, in Killing one another. London, 1644.

Eikon alethine, The pourtraiture of truths most sacred majesty truly suffering. London, 1649.

Eikon e piste. Or, The faithfull pourtraicture of a loyal subject, in vindication of Eikon Basilike. [London], 1649.

Eisenstein, Elizabeth L. *The Printing Press as an Agent of Change: Communication and Cultural Transformations in Early Modern Europe.* Cambridge: Cambridge University Press, 1979.

An Elegie upon the Death of Our Dread Sovereign Lord King Charles the Martyr. London, 1649.

England and Irelands Sad Theater. In *Catalogue of Political and Personal Satires Preserved in the Department of Prints and Drawings in the British Museum,* by Frederick George Stephens, 1:293–300. London: printed by order of the Trustees, 1870–1954.

Englands Standard Advanced, a Declaration from M. Will. Thompson and the oppressed People of this nation ... 6 May 1649.

Englants ende Irlands drees schaw tooneel oft Willem Lauds gewessene Bischop van Cantelberg Droomgesicht. England and Irelands sad Theater. [Amsterdam], 1645.

Evelyn, John. *The Diary of John Evelyn.* Edited by E.S. De Beer. London: Oxford University Press, 1959.

The Examination and Tryall of Margaret Fell and George Fox at the severall Assizes held at Lancaster. 1664.

Ezell, Margaret. *Social Authorship and the Advent of Print.* Baltimore: Johns Hopkins University Press, 1999.

The Fallacies of Mr. William Prynne, Discovered and Confuted: In A Short View of his late Bookes ... Oxford, 1644.

The Famous Tragedie of King Charles I. [London?], 1649.

The Famous tragedie of the life and death of Mris. Rump shewing how she was brought to bed of a monster ... as it was presented ... the 29th of May, 1660. London, 1660.

Fanshawe, Sir Richard. *Shorter Poems and Translations.* Edited by N.W. Bawcutt. Liverpool: Liverpool University Press, 1964.

Farmer, Roger. *Sathan Inthron'd in his Chair of Pestilence ... 1656.* London, 1657.

Ferguson, Margaret W. 'A Room Not Their Own: Renaissance Women as Readers and Writers.' In *The Comparative Perspective on Literature: Approaches to Theory and Practice,* edited by Clayton Koelb and Susan Noakes, 93–116. Ithaca: Cornell University Press, 1988.

– 'Moderation and its Discontents: Recent Work on Renaissance Women.' *Feminist Studies* 20.2 (1994): 349–66.

Fish, Stanley. *Is There a Text in This Class? The Authority of Interpretive Communities.* Cambridge: Harvard University Press, 1980.

Fletcher, Anthony. *The Outbreak of the English Civil War.* London: Arnold, 1981.

[Ford, John], *The Queen, or the Excellency of Her Sex: An Excellent old Play.* London, 1653.

Forster, Mary, comp. *These several Papers was sent to the Parliament … Being above Seven Thousand of the Names of the Hand-Maids and Daughters of the Lord … Who Witness Against the Oppression of Tithes and Other Things.* London, 1659.

Foucault, Michael. *Discipline and Punish: The Birth of the Prison.* New York: Pantheon Books, 1977.

Fox, Adam. *Oral and Literate Culture in England, 1500–1700.* Oxford: Oxford University Press, 2000.

Fox, George. *The Journal of George Fox.* Edited by Norman Penny. Intro. by T.E. Harvey. Cambridge: Cambridge University Press, 1911.

Foxe, John. *The Acts and Monuments of John Foxe.* Edited by George Townsend. 8 vols. New York: AMS Press, 1965.

Frank, Joseph. *The Levellers: A History of the Writings of Three Seventeenth-Century Social Democrats, John Lilburne, Richard Overton, William Walwyn.* Cambridge, MA: Harvard University Press, 1955.

– *The Beginnings of the English Newspaper 1620–1660.* Cambridge, MA: Harvard University Press, 1961.

Freedman, Morris. 'Dryden's "Memorable Visit" to Milton.' *Huntington Library Quarterly* 2 (1955): 99–108.

Freist, Dagmar. *Governed by Opinion: Politics, Religion, and the Dynamics of Communication in Stuart London, 1637–1647.* New York: St Martin's Press, 1997.

French, J. Milton. *Life Records of John Milton.* 5 vols. New York: Gordian Press, 1966.

Friedman, Jerome. *The Battle of the Frogs and Fairford's Flies: Miracles and the Pulp Press during the English Revolution.* New York: St Martin's Press, 1993.

Fumerton, Patricia. *Cultural Aesthetics: Renaissance Literature and the Practice of Social Ornament.* Chicago: University of Chicago Press, 1991.

Gayton, Edmund. *Pleasant Notes upon Don Quixot.* London, 1654.

Gentles, Ian. 'The *Agreements of the People* and their Political Contexts, 1647–1649.' In *The Putney Debates of 1647: The Army, The Levellers, and the English State,* edited by Michael Mendle, 148–74. Cambridge: Cambridge University Press, 2001.

Goffe, Thomas. *Three Excellent Tragœdies.* London, 1656.

Graham, Elspeth, et al. *Her Own Life: Autobiographical Writings by Seventeenth-Century Englishwomen.* New York: Routledge, 1989.

The Grand Politique Post. No. 127. 10–17 January 1653/54.

The Great Eclipse of the Sun, or, Charles his Waine Over-clouded By the evill Influences of the Moon ... Eclipsed by the destructive perswasions of His Queen, by the pernicious aspects of his Cabbinet Counsell ... London: printed by G.B. [Bishop], 1644.

Green, Thomas Andrew. *Verdict according to Conscience: Perspectives on the English Criminal Trial Jury 1200–1800.* Chicago: University of Chicago Press, 1985.

Greg, W.W. *A Bibliography of the English Printed Drama to the Restoration.* 4 vols. London: Bibliographical Society, 1962.

Gregerson, Linda. 'Milton's Post-Modernity: Community after the Commonwealth.' Paper given at Newberry Milton Seminar, Newberry Library, Chicago, May 9, 1998.

Gregg, Pauline. *Free-Born John: A Biography of John Lilburne.* London: Harrap, 1961.

Grossman, Marshall. 'The Dissemination of the King.' In *The Theatrical City: Culture, Theatre and Politics in London, 1576–1649*, edited by David L. Smith, Richard Strier, and David Bevington, 260–81. Cambridge: Cambridge University Press, 1995.

H.S. *Rectifying Principles. About the Power and Soveraignty of Kingdoms.* London, 1648/9.

Habermas, Jürgen *The Structural Transformation of the Public Sphere: An Inquiry into a Category of Bourgeois Society.* Translated by T. Burger. Cambridge, MA: MIT Press, 1989.

Halasz, Alexandra. *The Marketplace of Print: Pamphlets and the Public Sphere in Early Modern England.* Cambridge: Cambridge University Press, 1997.

Hall, Joseph. *An humble remonstrance to the High Court of Parliament.* London, 1641.

Haller, William, and Godfrey Davies. *The Leveller Tracts, 1647–1653.* Gloucester, MA: P. Smith, 1964.

Harbage, A.L. (Alfred). *Cavalier Drama: An Historical and Critical Supplement to the Study of the Elizabethan and Restoration Stage.* New York: Russell & Russell, 1936. Reprinted 1964.

– *Annals of English Drama 975–1700.* Revised by S. Schoenbaum, 2nd ed. London: Methuen, 1964.

Hardacre, Paul Hoswell. *The Royalists during the Puritan Revolution.* The Hague: Nijhoff, 1956.

Harris, Tim. *Politics under the Later Stuarts: Party Conflict in a Divided Society, 1660–1715.* London: Longman, 1993.

Healy, Thomas. *New Latitudes: Theory and English Renaissance Literature.* London: Edward Arnold, 1992.

Heinemann, Margot. *Puritanism and Theatre: Thomas Middleton and Opposition Drama under the Early Stuarts.* Cambridge: Cambridge University Press, 1980.

Helgerson, Richard. 'Milton Reads the King's Book: Print, Performance, and the Making of a Bourgeois Idol.' *Criticism* 29 (1987): 1–25.

Henry, Philip. *Diaries and Letters of Philip Henry.* Edited by Matthew Henry Lee. London: Kegan, Paul, and Trench, 1882.

Herbert, Thomas. *An Answer to the most Envious ... Pamphlet, entitled Mercuries Message.* London, [May] 1641.

Herrup, Cynthia B. *A House in Gross Disorder: Sex, Law, and the 2nd Earl of Castlehaven.* New York: Oxford University Press, 1999.

Heylyn, Peter. *A Briefe Relation of the Death and Sufferings of The Most Reverend and Renowned Prelate the L. Archbishop of Canterbury.* Oxford, 1645.

– *Cyprianus Anglicus.* London, 1668.

Heywood, Thomas. *Reader, Here you'l plainly see Judgement Perverted By these three; A Priest, A Judge, A Patentee.* N.p., 1641.

Hibbard, George R. 'The Early Seventeenth Century and the Tragic View of Life.' *Renaissance and Modern Studies* 5 (1961): 5–28.

Higgins, Patricia. 'The Reaction of Women, with Special Reference to Women Petitioners.' In *Politics, Religion & the English Civil War,* edited by Brian Manning, 179–222. London: Edward Arnold, 1973.

Hill, Christopher. *Milton and the English Revolution.* New York: Viking, 1977.

– 'Parliament and the People in Seventeenth-Century England.' *Past and Present* 92 (1981): 100–24.

– 'Censorship and English Literature.' In *Writing and Revolution in 17th-Century England.* Vol. 1 of *The Collected Essays of Christopher Hill,* 32–72. Brighton, Sussex: Harvester Press, 1985.

Hinds, Hilary. *God's Englishwomen: Seventeenth-Century Radical Sectarian Writing and Feminist Criticism.* Manchester: Manchester University Press, 1996.

Hinds, Hilary, ed. *'The Cry of a Stone' by Anna Trapnel.* Tempe: Arizona Center for Medieval and Renaissance Studies, 2000.

Hirst, Derek. 'Samuel Parker, Andrew Marvell, and Political Culture, 1667–73.' In *Writing and Political Engagement in Seventeenth-Century England,* edited by Derek Hirst and Richard Strier, 145–64. Cambridge: Cambridge University Press, 1999.

Hobby, Elaine. '"Come to live a preaching life": Female Community in Seventeenth-Century Radical Sects.' In *Female Communities 1600–1800: Literary Visions and Cultural Realities,* edited by Rebecca D'Monté and Nicole Pohl, 76–92. London: Macmillan; New York: St Martin's Press, 2000.

Horle, Craig W. *The Quakers and the English Legal System 1660–1688.* Philadelphia: University of Pennsylvania Press, 1988.

Hotson, Leslie. *The Commonwealth and the Restoration Stage.* Cambridge, MA: Harvard University Press, 1928.

Hoxby, Blair. *Mammon's Music: Literature and Economics in the Age of Milton.* New Haven: Yale University Press, 2002.

Hughes, Ann. 'Approaches to Presbyterian Print Culture: Thomas Edwards's *Gangraena* as Source and Text.' In *Books and Readers in Early Modern England: Material Studies,* edited by Jennifer Andersen and Elizabeth Sauer, 97–116. Philadelphia: University of Pennsylvania Press, 2002.

Hughes, Derek. *Dryden's Heroic Plays.* London: Macmillan, 1981.

Hyde, Edward, Earl of Clarendon. *The History of the Rebellion.* Edited by W. Dunn Macray. 6 vols. Oxford: Clarendon, 1958.

Iser, W. *The act of Reading: A Theory of Aesthetic Response.* Baltimore: Johns Hopkins University Press, 1978.

Jacob, James R., and Timothy Raylor, 'Opera and Obedience: Thomas Hobbes and *A Proposition for Advancement of Moralitie* by Sir William Davenant.' *The Seventeenth Century* 6.2 (1991): 205–50.

Jagodzinski, Cecile M. *Privacy and Print: Reading and Writing in Seventeenth-Century England.* Charlottesville: University Press of Virginia, 1999.

James I and VI. *The Basilicon Doron of King James VI.* Edited by James Craigie. Edinburgh: Scottish Text Society, 1944.

Jane, Joseph. *Eikon Aklastos: The Image Unbroken. A Perspective of the Imprudence ... in ... Eikonoklastes.* N.p., 1651.

Jauss, H.R. *The Authority of Interpretive Communities.* Cambridge, MA: Harvard University Press, 1980.

– *Toward an Aesthetic of Reception.* Trans. T. Bahti. Minneapolis: University of Minneapolis Press, 1982.

Jonson, Ben. *The Staple of News.* Edited by Devra Rowland Kifer. Lincoln: University of Nebraska Press, 1975.

Jordan, Thomas. 'The Players Petition to the Long Parliament, after being long silenc'd, that they might Play again, 1642.' In *A nursery of novelties in Variety of Poetry. Planted for the delightful leisures of Nobility and Ingenuity.* Composed by Thomas Jordan, 78–80. London: printed for the author [1665?].

Jose, Nicholas. *Ideas of the Restoration in English Literature, 1660–71.* Cambridge, MA: Harvard University Press, 1984.

Josselin, Ralph. *The Diary of Ralph Josselin, 1616–1683.* Edited by Alan Macfarlane. London: Oxford University Press, 1976.

Journal of George Fox. Edited by Norman Penney. Introduction by T.E. Harvey. Cambridge: Cambridge University Press, 1911.

The Judges Judgement ... against the Judges. [Dec] 1641.

Kastan, David Scott. 'Performances and Playbooks: The Closing of the Theatres and the Politics of Drama.' In *Reading, Society, and Politics in Early Modern England*, edited by Kevin Sharpe and Steven N. Zwicker, 167–84. Cambridge: Cambridge University Press, 2003.

Keeble, N.H. *The Literary Culture of Nonconformity in Later Seventeenth-Century England.* Leicester: Leicester University Press, 1987.

Kelly, Joan. 'Did Women Have a Renaissance?' In *Women, History and Theory: The Essays of Joan Kelly*, 19–50. Chicago: University of Chicago Press, 1984.

Kendrick, Christopher. *Milton: A Study in Ideology and Form.* New York: Methuen, 1986.

Kerman, Sandra. 'George Buchanan and the Genre of *Samson Agonistes.' Language and Style* 19.1 (1986): 21–5.

Kezar, Dennis. 'Samson's Death by Theater and Milton's Art of Dying.' *English Literary History* 66 (1999): 295–336.

Kilburn, Terrence, and Anthony Milton. 'The Public Context of the Trial and Execution of Strafford.' In *The Political World of Thomas Wentworth, Earl of Strafford, 1621–1641*, edited by J.F. Merritt, 230–51. Cambridge: Cambridge University Press, 1996.

King Charles, His Farewell. Left as a Legacy to his deare Children. London, 1649.

King, Henry. 'An Elegy Upon the most Incomparable K. Charles.' London, 1648.

Kinney, Arthur F. *Markets of Bawdrie: The Dramatic Criticism of Stephen Gosson.* Salzburg: University of Salzburg Press, 1974.

Knoppers, Laura Lunger. *Historicizing Milton: Spectacle, Power, and Poetry in Restoration England.* Athens: University of Georgia Press, 1994.

Knott, John R. 'Joseph Besse and the Quaker Culture of Suffering.' In *The Emergence of Quaker Writing: Dissenting Literature in Seventeeth-Century England*, edited by Thomas N. Corns and David Loewenstein, 126–41. London: Frank Cass, 1996.

Lake, Peter. 'Retrospective: Wentworth's Political World in Revisionist and Post-Revisionist Perspective.' In *The Political World of Thomas Wentworth, Earl of Strafford, 1621–1641*, edited by J.F. Merritt, 252–83. Cambridge: Cambridge University Press, 1996.

– 'Puritans, Papists, and the "Public Sphere" in Early Modern England: The Edmund Campion Affair in Context.' *Journal of Modern History* 72 (2000): 587–627.

– 'Puritans, Popularity and Petitions: Local Politics in National Context, Cheshire, 1641.' In *Politics, Religion and Popularity in Early Stuart Britain*, edited by Thomas Cogswell, Richard Cust, and Peter Lake, 259–89. Cambridge: Cambridge University Press, 2002.

Lake, Peter, and Michael Questier. *The Anti-Christ's Lewd Hat: Protestants, Papists and Players in Post-Reformation England.* New Haven: Yale University Press, 2002.

Lambeth Faire. N.p., 1641.

Lamont, William M. *Marginal Prynne 1600–1669.* London: Routledge; Toronto: University of Toronto Press, 1963.

The last Discourse Betwixt Master Abel *and Master* Richard *Kilvert, interrupted at the first by an ancient and angry Gentlewoman.* 1641.

Laud, William, Archbishop of Canterbury. *Diary.* In *The Works of ... William Laud.* Vol. 3, edited by James Bliss, 129–255. Oxford: Parker, 1853.

– *The History of the Troubles and Tryal of ... William Laud ... Wrote by Himself, during his Imprisonment in the Tower.* Edited by Henry Wharton. London, 1694/5. In *The Works of ... William Laud.* Vol. 3, edited by James Bliss, 273–463. Oxford: Parker, 1853.

– *The Works of ... William Laud.* Edited by W. Scott and J. Bliss. 7 vols. Oxford: Parker, 1847–60.

Leigh, Richard. *The Censure of the Rota.* Oxford, 1673.

Leslie, Henry. *The Martyrdome of King Charles, Or his conformity with Christ in his sufferings.* London, 1649.

The Levellers in the English Revolution. Edited by G.E. Aylmer. Ithaca: Cornell University Press, 1975.

The Levellers levell'd. Or, The Independents Conspiracie to root out Monarchie. An Interlude. [London], 1647.

The Levellers Levelled. Edited by Philip C. Dust. *Analytical and Enumerative Bibliography* 4 (1980): 182–240.

The Life and Death of King Charles the Martyr, Paralleled with Our Saviour. London, 1649.

The life and death of Mris Rump. And the fatal end of her base-born brat. London, 1660.

Lilburne, John. *A Worke of the Beast.* 1638.

Lilburne, John, et al., *The Soap-makers Complaint.* London, 1650.

– *An Agreement of the People for a firme and present Peace ...* 1647. In *Leveller Manifestoes,* edited by Don M. Wolfe, 223–34. New York: Humanities Press, 1967.

Lilburne, John, William Walwyn, Thomas Prince, and Richard Overton. *An Agreement of the Free People of England. Tendered as a Peace-Offering to this distressed Nation.* 1 May 1649. In *Leveller Manifestoes,* edited by Don M. Wolfe, 397–410. New York: Humanities Press, 1967.

Lindley, David. *The Trials of Frances Howard: Fact and Fiction at the Court of King James.* London: Routledge,1993.

Loewenstein, David. *Representing Revolution in Milton and His Contemporaries: Religion, Politics, and Polemics in Radical Puritanism.* Cambridge: Cambridge University Press, 2001.

The Lord Digby His last Speech Against the Earle of Strafford. 1641.

Love, Harold. *The Culture and Commerce of Texts: Scribal Publication in Seventeenth-Century England.* Amherst: University of Massachusetts Press, 1993.

Low, Anthony. 'Milton's *Samson* and the Stage, with Implications for Dating the Play.' *Huntington Library Quarterly* 40 (1977): 313–24.

Mack, Phyllis. 'Gender and Spirituality in Early English Quakerism, 1650–1665.' In *Witnesses for Change: Quaker Women over Three Centuries,* edited by Elisabeth Potts Brown and Susan Mosher Stuard, 31–63. New Brunswick, NJ: Rutgers University Press, 1989.

Mack, Phyllis. *Visionary Women: Ecstatic Prophecy in Seventeenth-Century England.* Berkeley and Los Angeles: University of California Press, 1992.

Madan, Francis F. *A New Bibliography of the Eikon Basilike of King Charles I.* Oxford: Oxford Bibliographical Society Publications, n.s. 3, 1949.

Maguire, Nancy Klein. 'The Theatrical Mask/Masque of Politics: The Case of Charles I.' *Journal of British Studies* 28 (1989): 1–22.

– *Regicide and Restoration: English Tragicomedy, 1660–1671.* Cambridge: Cambridge University Press, 1992.

The Man in the Moon. Discovering a World of Knavery under the Sunne. No. 29, 7–14 November 1649.

Manley, Lawrence. *Literature and Culture in Early Modern London.* Cambridge: Cambridge University Press, 1995.

Manning, Brian. *The English People and the English Revolution, 1640–1649.* London: Heinemann, 1976.

– 'The Levellers and Religion.' In *Radical Religion in the English Revolution,* edited by J.F. McGregor and B. Reay, 65–90. Oxford: Oxford University Press, 1984.

Marcus, Leah S. *Unediting the Renaissance: Shakespeare, Marlowe, Milton.* New York: Routledge, 1996.

Marotti, Arthur. *Manuscript, Print, and the English Renaissance Lyric.* Ithaca: Cornell University Press, 1995.

Marotti, Arthur F., and Michael D. Bristol, eds. *Print, Manuscript, Performance: The Changing Relations of the Media in Early Modern England.* Columbus: Ohio State University Press, 2000.

Marvell, Marvell. *The Complete Poems.* Edited by Elizabeth Story Donno. Harmondsworth: Penguin, 1972. Reprinted 1985.

Mascuch, Michael. 'A Press of Witnesses: The Impact of Print.' In *Origins of the Individualist Self,* 97–131. Oxford: Polity Press, 1997.

Masson, David. *The Life of John Milton: Narrated in Connexion with the ... History of his Time.* Vol. 6. London: Macmillan, 1880.

Maus, Katharine Eisaman. *Inwardness and the Theater in the English Renaissance.* Chicago: University of Chicago Press, 1995.

May, Thomas. *The History of the Parliament of England which began November the third, MDCXL. With a short and necessary view of some precedent yeares. Written by Thomas May, Esquire, Secretary for the Parliament, Published by Authority.* London, 1647.

McAfee, Helen. *Pepys on the Restoration Stage.* New York: Benjamin Blom, 1916.

McFarlane, Ian D. *Buchanan.* London: Duckworth, 1981.

McGuire, Philip C. *Speechless Dialect: Shakespeare's Open Silences.* Berkeley and Los Angeles: University of California Press, 1985.

McRae, Andrew. *Literature, Satire and the Early Stuart State.* Cambridge: Cambridge University Press, 2004.

Mendle, Michael. *Henry Parker and the English Civil War.* Cambridge: Cambridge University Press, 1995.

Mercurius Aulicus. 16–30 January 1645.

Mercurius Bellicus, or, an Allarum to all Rebels. No. 4. 14–20 February 1648/49.

Mercurius Britanicus. No. 49. 26 August–2 September 1644.

Mercurius Melancholicus. Or, News from Westerminster. No. 58. 25 September– 2 October 1648.

Mercurius Politicus. No. 201. 13–20 April 1654.

Mercurius Pragmaticus. 1649. No. 42. 16–30 January 1649.

– No. 44. 27 February–5 March 1649.

The Middling Sort of People: Culture, Society and Politics in England, 1550–1800. Edited by Jonathan Barray and Christopher Brooks. London: Macmillan, 1994.

Milton, Anthony. 'Licensing, Censorship, and Religious Orthodoxy in Early Stuart England.' *The Historical Journal* 41 (1998): 625–51.

Milton, John. *Complete Prose Works of John Milton.* Edited by Don Wolfe et al. 8 vols. New Haven: Yale University Press, 1953–82.

– *John Milton: Complete Poems and Major Prose.* Edited by Merritt Hughes. New York: Odyssey, 1957.

Miner, Earl. *The Cavalier Mode from Jonson to Cotton.* Princeton: Princeton University Press, 1971.

Misselden, Edward. *Free Trade. Or, The Meanes to Make Trade Florish.* London, 1622.

Mistress Parliament Presented in her Bed. Edited by Lois Potter. *Analytical and Enumerative Bibliography* ns 1.3 (1987): 130–43.

Mistris Parliament Brought to Bed of a Monstrous Childe of Reformation. Edited by Lois Potter. *Analytical and Enumerative Bibliography* ns 1.3 (1987): 111–29.

Mr. Maynards Speech Before Both Houses in Parliament, upon … Straffords Answer to his Articles at the Barre. N.p., 1641.

Mris. Rump brought to bed of a monster … and the great misery she endured by this … monster of reformation. [London], 1660.

Morrill, J.S. *The Revolt of the Provinces: Conservatives and Radicals in the English Civil War, 1630–1650.* London: Allen and Unwin, 1976.

Muddiman, J.G. *The Trial of King Charles the First.* London, W. Hodge, 1928.

Muir, Edward. *Ritual in Early Modern Europe.* Cambridge: Cambridge University Press, 1997.

A New Bull-Bayting: Or, A Match Play'd at the Town-Bull of Ely. London, 1649.

New-Market-Fayre. 1649. '*New-Market-Fayre.*' Edited by Paul Werstine. *Analytical and Enumerative Bibliography* 6.2 (1982): 71–103.

Norbrook, David. '*Areopagitica,* Censorship, and the Early Modern Public Sphere.' In *The Administration of Aesthetics: Censorship, Political Criticism, and the Public Sphere,* edited by Richard Burt, 3–33. Minneapolis: University of Minnesota Press, 1994.

– *Writing the English Republic: Poetry, Rhetoric and Politics 1627–1660.* Cambridge: Cambridge University Press, 1999.

– 'The English Revolution and English Historiography.' *The Cambridge Companion to Writing of the English Revolution,* edited by N.H. Keeble, 233–50. Cambridge: Cambridge University Press, 2001.

Nyquist, Mary, and Margaret W. Ferguson, eds. *Re-membering Milton: Essays on the Texts and Traditions.* New York: Methuen, 1987.

Ollard, Richard. *Pepys: A Biography.* London: Hodder & Stoughton, 1974.

O'Malley, Thomas P. 'The Press and Quakerism 1653–1659.' *Journal of the Friends' Historical Society* 54 (1979): 167–84.

Ong, Walter J. 'Reading, Technology, and the Nature of Man: An Interpretation.' *Yearbook of English Studies* 10 (1980): 132–49.

An Ordinance of the Lords and Commons ... for The Utter Suppression and Abolishing of all Stage-Playes and Interludes. London, [11 Feb.] 1647/8.

Original Letters and Papers of State, addressed to Oliver Cromwell. Edited by John Nicholls, Jr. London, 1743.

Ormsby-Lennon, Hugh. '"The Dialect of those Fanatick Times": Language Communities and English Poetry from 1580–1660.' PhD diss. University of Pennsylvania, 1977.

Ostovich, Helen, and Elizabeth Sauer, eds. *Reading Early Modern Women: An Anthology of Manuscripts and Texts in Print, 1550–1700.* New York and London: Routledge, 2004.

Otten, Charlotte F., ed. *English Women's Voices.* Miami: Florida International University Press, 1992.

Overton, Richard. *A new Play called Canterburie His Change of Diot.* London, 1641.

– *New Lambeth-Fayre.* 1642.

– *Araignement of Mr. Persecution.* 1645.

– *An Alarum to the House of Lords.* [London], 1646.

- *The Baiting of the Great Bull of Bashan Unfolded, and Presented to the Affecters and approvers of the Petition of the 11 Sept. 1648.* London, 16 July 1649.

A Pack of Patentees. London, 1641.

[Parker, Henry]. *The King's Cabinet Opened: or, Certain Packets of Secret Letters & Papers, written with the King's own hand, and taken in his Cabinet at Naseby-Field June 14 1645.* London, 1645.

Patterson, Annabel. *Censorship and Interpretation: The Conditions of Writing and Reading in Early Modern England.* Madison: University of Wisconsin Press, 1984.

Pechter, Edward. 'The New Historicism and Its Discontents: Politicizing Renaissance Drama.' *PMLA* 102.3 (1987): 292–303.

Peck, Francis. *New Memoirs of the Life and Poetical Works of Mr. John Milton.* London, 1740.

Pepys, Samuel. *King Charles Preserved: An Account of his Escape after the Battle of Worcester dictated by the King himself to Samuel Pepys.* Illus. by Maurice Bartlett. London: Rodale Press, 1956.

- *The Diary of Samuel Pepys.* Edited by Robert Lathan and William Matthews. 11 vols. Berkeley and Los Angeles: University of California Press, 1970.

A Perfect Diurnall of Some Passages in Parliament. No. 76. 6–13 January 1645.

- No. 288. 29 January–5 February 1648/49.

- No. 294. 12–19 March 1648/49.

Perfect Occurrences of Every Daie journall. No. 107. 12–19 January 1648/49.

Peters, Kate. 'Patterns of Quaker Authorship, 1652–1656.' In *The Emergence of Quaker Writing: Dissenting Literature in Seventeenth-Century England,* edited by Thomas N. Corns and David Loewenstein, 6–24. London: Frank Cass, 1996.

Phillips, James Emerson. 'George Buchanan and the Sidney Circle.' *Huntington Library Quarterly* 12 (1948–9): 23–55.

Pocock, J.G.A. 'Texts as Events: Reflections on the History of Political Thought.' In *Politics of Discourse: The Literature and History of Seventeenth-Century England,* edited by Kevin Sharpe and Steven N. Zwicker, 21–34. Berkeley and Los Angeles: University of California Press, 1987.

- 'Thomas May and the Narrative of Civil War.' In *Writing and Political Engagement in Seventeenth-Century England,* edited by Derek Hirst and Richard Strier, 112–44. Cambridge: Cambridge University Press, 1999.

Potter, Lois. 'Closet Drama and Royalist Politics.' In *The Revels History of English Drama,* edited by Philip Edwards, Gerald Eades Bentley, Kathleen McLuskie, and Lois Potter, 263–79. London: Methuen, 1981.

- 'Short Plays: Drolls and Pamphlets.' In *The Revels History of English Drama,* vol. 4, edited by Philip Edwards et al., 280–93. London: Methuen, 1981.

- '"True Tragicomedies" of the Civil War and Commonwealth.' In *Renaissance*

Tragicomedy: Explorations in Genre and Politics, edited by Nancy Klein Maguire, 196–217. New York: AMS, 1987.

– *Secret Rites and Secret Writing: Royalist Literature, 1641–1660*. Cambridge: Cambridge University Press, 1989.

– 'The Royal Martyr in the Restoration.' In *The Royal Image: Representations of Charles I*, edited by Thomas N. Corns, 240–62. Cambridge: Cambridge University Press, 1999.

A Presse full of Pamphlets: Wherein, Are set Diversity of Prints ... Composed into Books fraught with Libellous and Scandalous Sentences. London: printed for R.W., 1642.

Price, William Hyde. *English Patents of Monopoly*. Cambridge, MA: Harvard University Press, 1913.

The Princely Pellican. Royall Resolves ... Extracted from His Majesties Divine Meditations. N.p., 1649.

Prynne, William. *Histrio-Mastix. The Players Scourge, or, Actors Tragædie*. London, 1633.

– *A Breviate of the Life, of William Laud ... Collected and published ... as a necessary Prologue to the History of His Tryall*. London, 1644.

– *Canterburies Doome. or The First Part of a Compleat History of The Commitment, Charge, Tryall, Condemnation, Execution of WILLIAM LAUD Late Arch-Bishop of Canterbury*. London, 1646.

– *The Quakers Unmasked, and clearly detected to be but the Spawn of Romish Frogs, Jesuites, and Franciscan Freers, sent from Rome ...* London, 1654.

Puritanism and Liberty: Being the Army Debates (1647–9) from the Clarke Manuscripts with Supplementary Documents. Edited and introduced by A.S.P. Woodhouse. London: Dent, 1938.

Raleigh, Walter. *The History of the World*. Edited by C.A. Patrides. New York: Macmillan, 1971.

Randall, Dale B.J. *Winter Fruit: English Drama, 1642–1660*. Lexington: University Press of Kentucky, 1995.

Raymond, Joad. *The Invention of the Newspaper: English Newsbooks, 1641–1649*. Oxford: Clarendon Press, 1996.

– 'The Newspaper, Public Opinion, and the Public Sphere in the Seventeenth Century.' In *News, Newspapers, and Society in Early Modern Britain*, edited by Joad Raymond, 109–40. London: Frank Cass, 1999.

Raymond, Joad, ed. *Making the News: An Anthology of the Newsbooks of Revolutionary England, 1641–1660*. Gloucester: Windrush Press, 1993.

Reay, B. 'Quakerism and Society.' In *Radical Religion in the English Revolution*, edited by J.F. McGregor and B. Reay, 141–64. Oxford: Oxford University Press, 1984.

A Relation of the Imprisonment of Mr. John Bunyan ... 1660. London, 1765.

The Replication of Mr Glyn ... to the generall answer ... of Strafford. 13 April 1641.

Roberts, David. *The Ladies: Female Patronage of Restoration Drama 1660–1700.* Oxford: Clarendon Press, 1989.

[Robinson, Henry]. *A Short Discourse Between Monarchical and Aristocratical Government.* 1649.

Rombus the Moderator: or, The King Restored. 1648.

Rowse, A.L. *The Regicides and the Puritan Revolution.* London: Duckworth, 1994.

The Royal Martyr: or, Fanatick Piety. 2nd ed. London, 1719.

Rumrich, John P. *Milton Unbound: Controversy and Reinterpretation.* Cambridge: Cambridge University Press, 1996.

Rushworth, John. Preface to *The Tryall of Thomas Earl of Strafford.* London, 1680.

– *Historical collections of private passages of state ... 1618 ... 1648.* London: D. Browne, 1721–2.

Russell, Conrad. *Parliaments and English Politics, 1621–1629.* Oxford: Clarendon Press, 1979.

– *Unrevolutionary England, 1603–1642.* London: Hambledon Press, 1990.

– *The Fall of the British Monarchies 1637–1642.* Oxford: Clarendon, 1991.

Sacks, David Harris. 'Parliament, Liberty, and the Commonweath.' In *Parliament and Liberty from the Reign of Elizabeth to the English Civil War,* edited by J.H. Hexter, 85–121. Stanford: Stanford University Press, 1992.

Samuels, Peggy Anne. 'Fire not Light: Milton's Simulacrum of Tragicomedy.' *Milton Quarterly* 30 (1996): 1–15.

– '*Samson Agonistes* and Renaissance Drama,' PhD diss., City University of New York, 1993.

Sanders, Eve Rachele. *Gender and Literacy on Stage in Early Modern England.* Cambridge: Cambridge University Press, 1998.

Sandler, Florence. 'Icon and Iconoclast.' In *Achievements of the Left Hand: Essays on the Prose of John Milton,* edited by Michael Lieb and John T. Shawcross, 160–84. Amherst: University of Massachusetts Press, 1974.

Sauer, Elizabeth. 'The Politics of Performance in the Inner Theatre: *Samson Agonistes* as Closet Drama.' In *Milton and Heresy,* edited by Stephen B. Dobranski and John P. Rumrich, 199–215. Cambridge: Cambridge University Press, 1998.

– 'Emasculating Romance: Historical Fiction in the Protectorate.' In *Prose Fiction and Early Modern Sexualities in England, 1570–1640,* edited by Constance Relihan and Goran Stanivukovic, 195–213. New York: Palgrave Macmillan, 2003.

– 'The Experience of Defeat: Milton and Some Female Contemporaries.' In *Milton and Gender,* edited by Catherine Gimelli Martin, 133–52. Cambridge: Cambridge University Press, 2004.

- 'Closet Drama and the Case of *Tyrannicall-Government Anatomized.*' In *The 'Booke' of the Play in Early Modern England: Stationers, Censors, and 'Curteous' Readers*, edited by Marta Straznicky. Amherst: University of Massachusetts Press, forthcoming.

Schwoerer, Lois G. 'Women's Public Political Voice in England: 1640–1740.' In *Women Writers and the Early Modern British Political Tradition*, edited by Hilda L. Smith, 56–74. Cambridge: Cambridge University Press, 1998.

Scutum Regale, The Royal Buckler; or Vox Legis, A Lecture to Traytors: Who most wickedly murthered Charles the I. 1660.

The Second Part of the Tragi-Comedie called Craftie Cromwell. 1648.

The Second Part of the Tragi-Comedy, called New-Market Fayre. 1649.

Shakespeare, William. *The Tragedy of Antony and Cleopatra.* Edited by Barbara Everett. New York: Penguin, 1998.

Sharpe, J.A. '"Last Dying Speeches": Religion, Ideology and Public Execution in Seventeenth-Century England.' *Past and Present* 107 (1985): 144–67.

- 'The People and the Law.' In *Popular Culture in Seventeenth-Century England*, edited by Barry Reay, 244–70. London: Crom Helm, 1985.

Sharpe, Kevin. '"An Image Doting Rabble": The Failure of Republican Culture in Seventeenth-Century England.' In *Refiguring Revolutions: Aesthetics and Politics from the English Revolution to the Romantic Revolution*, edited by Kevin Sharpe and Steven N. Zwicker, 25–56. Berkeley and Los Angeles: University of California Press, 1998.

- *Reading Revolutions: The Politics of Reading in Early Modern England.* New Haven: Yale University Press, 2000.

- *Remapping Early Modern England: The Culture of Seventeenth-Century Politics.* Cambridge: Cambridge University Press, 2000.

Sharpe, Kevin, ed. *Faction and Parliament: Essays on Early Stuart History.* Oxford: Clarendon Press, 1978.

Shepherd, David. 'Bakhtin and the Reader.' In *Bakhtin and Cultural Theory*, edited by Ken Hirschkop and David Shepherd, 91–108. Manchester: Manchester University Press, 1989.

Sherman, William H. *John Dee: The Politics of Reading and Writing in the English Renaissance.* Amherst: University of Massachusetts Press, 1995.

A Short and True Relation concerning the Soap-busines. London, 1641.

Siebert, Fredrick S. *Freedom of the Press in England, 1476–1776: The Rise and Decline of Government Controls.* Urbana: University of Illinois Press, 1965.

Sirluck, Ernest. 'Shakespeare and Jonson among the Pamphleteers of the First Civil War: Some Unreported Seventeenth-Century Allusions.' *Modern Philology* 53.2 (1955): 88–99.

Smith, Jeffery A. *Printers and Press Freedom: The Ideology of Early American Journalism*. New York: Oxford University Press, 1988.

Smith, Joseph. *A Descriptive Catalogue of Friends' Books*. London: Library of Friends House, 1867.

Smith, Nigel. '*Areopagitica*: Voicing Contexts, 1643–5.' In *Politics, Poetics and Hermeneutics in Milton's Prose*, edited by David Lowenstein and James Grantham Turner, 103–22. Cambridge: Cambridge University Press, 1990.

– *Literature and Revolution in England, 1640–1660*. New Haven: Yale University Press, 1994.

– 'Non-Conformist Voices and Books.' In *The Cambridge History of the Book in Britain*, edited by John Barnard and D.F. McKenzie, with the assistance of Maureen Bell, 4:410–30. Cambridge: Cambridge University Press, 2002.

Speeches and Passages of this Great and Happy Parliament. London, 1641.

The Speech suggested to bee the late Earl of Straffords ... scandalously imputed to him. 1641.

Spiller, Michael R.G. 'Directing the Audience in *Samson Agonistes*.' In *Of Poetry and Politics: New Essays on Milton and His World*, edited by P.G. Stanwood, 121–9. Binghamton, NY: Medieval & Renaissance Texts & Studies, 1995.

Spufford, Margaret. *Contrasting Communities: English Villagers in the Sixteenth and Seventeenth Centuries*. Cambridge: Cambridge University Press, 1974.

Stanley, Thomas. 'Upon the Earl of Strafford's Death.' In *Psalterium Carolinum. The Devotions of his Sacred Majesty Charles the First in his Solitudes and Sufferings, Rendred in Verse by T.S. Esq., And set to Musick for three voices*, A2v–B1v. London, 1660.

Stock, Brian. *The Implications of Literacy: Written Langauge and Models of Interpretation in the Eleventh and Twelfth Centuries*. Princeton: Princeton University Press, 1983.

Strange Predictions. 25 May 1648.

Straznicky, Marta. 'Closet Drama.' In *Blackwell Companion to Renaissance Drama*, edited by Arthur F. Kinney, 416–30. Oxford: Blackwell, 2002.

Tawney, R.H. *Religion and the Rise of Capitalism: A Historical Study*. London: Murray, 1929.

The Theatrical City: Culture, Theatre and Politics in London, 1576–1649. Edited by David L. Smith, Richard Strier, and David Bevington. Cambridge: Cambridge University Press, 1995.

Thirsk, Joan. *Economic Policy and Projects: The Development of a Consumer Society in Early Modern England*. Oxford: Clarendon Press, 1978.

Thomas, Keith. 'The Meaning of Literacy in Early Modern England.' In *The Written Word: Literacy in Transition*, edited by Gerd Baumann, 97–131. Oxford: Clarendon Press, 1986.

– 'Cases of Conscience in Seventeenth-Century England.' In *Public Duty and Private Conscience in Seventeenth-Century England*, edited by John Morrill, Paul Slack, and Daniel Woolf, 29–56. Oxford: Clarendon Press, 1993.

Timmis III, John H. *Thine Is the Kingdom: The Trial for Treason of Thomas Wentworth, Earl of Strafford, First Minister to King Charles I, and Last Hope of the English Crown.* Alabama: University of Alabama Press, 1974.

Tindall, William York. *John Bunyan: Mechanick Preacher.* New York: Russell & Russell, 1964.

The Tragedy of That Famous Roman Oratour Marcus Tullius Cicero. London, 1651.

Trapnel, Anna. *Anna Trapnel's Report and Plea, or a Narrative of her Journey from London into Cornwal.* London, 1654.

– *The Cry of a Stone: Or a Relation of Something Spoken in Whitehall.* London, 1654.

– *A Legacy for Saints, Being Several Experiences of the Dealings of God with Anna Trapnel.* London, 1654.

Treadwell, Michael. 'The Stationers and the Printing Acts at the End of the Seventeenth Century.' In *The Cambridge History of the Book in Britain*, edited by John Barnard and D.F. McKenzie, with the assistance of Maureen Bell, 4:755–76. Cambridge: Cambridge University Press, 2002.

Trevelyan, G.M. *A Shortened History of England.* 1942. Reprinted, Harmondsworth: Penguin, 1976.

The Triall, of Lieut. Collonell John Lilburne ... Being as exactly pen'd and taken in short hand, as it was possible to be done in such a croud and noyes ... that so matter of Fact, as it was there declared, might truly come to publick view. London, 1649.

A True Narrative of the Examination, Tryall, and Suffering of James Nayler. 1656.

Truths Victory over Tyrants and Tyranny. Being the Tryall of ... John Lilburne. 1649.

Turner, Victor. *Dramas, Fields, and Metaphors: Symbolic Action in Human Society.* Ithaca: Cornell University Press, 1974.

– *The Anthropology of Performance.* Preface by Richard Schechner. New York: Performing Arts Journal Publications, 1986.

The two last Speeches of Thomas Wentworth, late Earle of Strafford. 12 May 1641.

Two Ordinances of the Lords and Commons ... to suppresse Stage-playes, Interludes, and common Playes ... The other For setling of the Mayor, and Sheriffes ... of Chester. London, 1647.

Tyrannicall-Government Anatomized: Or, A Discourse Concerning Evil-Councellors. London: printed for John Field, 9 February 1642/3.

Underdown, David. *Royalist Conspiracy in England 1649–1660.* New Haven: Yale University Press, 1960.

Unfortunate Usurper. 1663.

Ussher, James. *A Body of Divinitie.* 2nd ed. London, 1647.

Virtus Rediviva: A Panegyrick on Our Late King Charles I. London, 1660.

Von Maltzahn, Nicholas. 'Milton's Readers.' In *The Cambridge Companion to Milton*, edited by Dennis Danielson, 236–52. 2nd ed. Cambridge: Cambridge University Press, 1999.

Walker, Clement. *Anarchia Anglicana: or The History of Independency. The Second Part.* London, Royston, 1661.

Walker, Henry. *Severall Proceedings of State Affaires.* No. 225. 12–19 January 1653/54.

Wall, Wendy. 'Disclosures in Print: The "Violent Enlargement" of the Renaissance Voyeuristic Text.' *Studies in English Literature* 29 (1989): 35–59.

Watt, Tessa. *Cheap Print and Popular Pamphlets, 1550–1640.* Cambridge: Cambridge University Press, 1991.

Webber, Joan. *The Eloquent 'I': Style and Self in Seventeenth-Century Prose.* Madison: University of Wisconsin Press, 1968.

Webster, John, and William Rowley, *The Thracian Wonder. A comical History ...* London: printed by Tho. Johnson, and ... sold by Francis Kirkman, 1661.

Wedgwood, C.V. *Thomas Wentworth First Earl of Strafford 1593–1641: A Revaluation.* London: Jonathan Cape, 1961.

– *The Trial of Charles I.* London: Collins, 1964.

Weimann, Robert. 'Towards a Literary Theory of Ideology: Mimesis, Representation, Authority.' In *Shakespeare Reproduced: The Text in History and Ideology*, edited by Jean E. Howard and Marion F. O'Connor, 265–72. London: Methuen, 1987.

Whiting, Charles Edwin. *Studies in English Puritanism: From the Restoration to the Revolution, 1660–1688.* London: SPCK, 1931.

Wilcher, Robert. *The Writing of Royalism: 1628–1660.* Cambridge: Cambridge Unviersity Press, 2001.

Wilding, Michael. 'Milton's *Areopagitica*: Liberty for the Sects.' In *The Literature of Controversy: Polemical Strategy from Milton to Junius*, edited by Thomas N. Corns, 7–38. London: Frank Cass, 1987.

Winstanley, Gerrard, et al. *The True Levellers Standard Advanced: The State of Community opened, and Presented to the Sons of Men.* London, 1649.

Wiseman, Susan. *Drama and Politics in the English Civil War.* Cambridge: Cambridge University Press, 1998.

– 'Pamphlet Plays in the Civil War News Market: Genre, Politics, and "Context."' In *News, Newspapers, and Society in Early Modern Britian*, edited by Joad Raymond, 66–83. London: Frank Cass, 1999.

Wittreich, Joseph A. *Interpreting 'Samson Agonistes.'* Princeton: Princeton University Press, 1986.

– *Shifting Contexts: Reinterpreting Samson Agonistes.* Pittsburgh: Duquesne University Press, 2002.

Women and the Literature of the Seventeenth Century: An Annotated Bibliography Based on Wing's Short-Title Catalogue. Compiled by Hilda L. Smith and Susan Cardinal. New York: Greenwood Press, 1990.

Wonderfull Predictions. 29 December 1647.

Wordsworth, Christopher. Documentary Supplement to '*Who Wrote Eikon Basilike?' Considered and Answered.* London: John Murray, 1824.

Wright, Abraham. *Parnassus biceps. Or several choice pieces of poetry.* London, 1656.

Wright, Louis. 'The Reading of Plays during the English Revolution.' *Huntington Library Bulletin* 6 (1934): 73–108.

Wright, Luella Margaret. 'Distribution of Literature.' In *The Literary Life of the Early Friends, 1650–1725,* introduction by Rufus M. Jones, 74–86. New York: Columbia University Press, 1932.

Yule, George. *Pragmatics.* Oxford: Oxford University Press, 1996.

Zaret, David. 'Religion, Science, and Printing in the Public Spheres of England.' In *Habermas and the Public Sphere,* edited by Craig Calhoun, 212–35. Cambridge: MIT Press, 1992.

– *Origins of Democratic Culture: Printing, Petitions and the Public Sphere in Early Modern England.* Princeton: Princeton University Press, 2000.

Zwicker, Steven N. *Lines of Authority: Politics and English Literary Culture, 1649–1689.* Ithaca: Cornell University Press, 1993.

– 'Milton, Dryden, and the Politics of Literary Controversy.' In *Heirs of Fame: Milton and Writers of the English Renaissance,* edited by Margo Swiss and David A. Kent, 270–89. Lewisburg, NY: Bucknell University Press, 1995.

– 'Reading the Margins: Politics and the Habits of Appropriation.' In *Refiguring Revolutions: Aesthetics and Politics from the English Revolution to the Romantic Revolution,* edited by Kevin Sharpe and Steven N. Zwicker, 101–15. Berkeley and Los Angeles: University of California Press, 1998.

– 'Habits of Reading and Early Modern Literary Culture.' In *The Cambridge History of Early Modern Literature,* edited by David Loewenstein and Janel Mueller, 170–98. Cambridge: Cambridge University Press, 2002.

Index

STUDIES IN BOOK AND PRINT CULTURE

General editor: Leslie Howsam

Lightning Source UK Ltd.
Milton Keynes UK
UKHW010635230222
399111UK00001B/82